# MOZART'S OPERAS

# Mozart's Operas

## A Critical Study

# EDWARD J. DENT

**Second Edition**

CLARENDON PRESS · OXFORD

Oxford University Press, Walton Street, Oxford OX2 6DP

Oxford New York Toronto
Delhi Bombay Calcutta Madras Karachi
Petaling Jaya Singapore Hong Kong Tokyo
Nairobi Dar es Salaam Cape Town
Melbourne Auckland

and associated companies in
Berlin Ibadan

Oxford is a trade mark of Oxford University Press

Published in the United States
by Oxford University Press, New York

First published 1913 by Chatto and Windus
Second Edition published 1947 by Oxford University Press

ISBN 0 19 816264 2

Printed in Great Britain by
St Edmundsbury Press Ltd.
Bury St Edmunds, Suffolk

# CONTENTS

# INTRODUCTION

MOZART's operas today rank beyond dispute, along with those of Wagner and Verdi, as one of the supreme peaks of the musical theatre; not surprisingly they continue to inspire new books and new interpretations almost every year. It was not always so. At the beginning of this century, apart from *The Marriage of Figaro* and *Don Giovanni*, they were seldom performed and generally misunderstood, and had never been the subject of serious scholarly study. Much of the subsequent rise in their reputation has been due to Edward Dent. He first made his mark as moving spirit and translator in a production of *The Magic Flute* at Cambridge in 1911, which was acclaimed as a revelation, and followed it up with this book, first published in 1913 and extensively revised and rewritten in 1947.

The book threw fresh light on almost every aspect of the subject and was soon accepted as a classic, a status it has never lost. Dent was the first to place Mozart's operas in their historical and social context, to make a close study of their librettos, and to consider them as mature and complex works of musico-dramatic art. To an extensive knowledge of the musical background—he quotes from no fewer than eight of Mozart's lesser contemporaries—he added wide reading, which enabled him to draw illuminating parallels from the other arts, a practical knowledge of the theatre, and a felicitous and witty style. Not all his judgements command universal assent. Some will jib at his dismissal of *Die Entführung*, for all its mixed style, as 'a thoroughly unsatisfactory work', and the Requiem as 'the product of a morbid and diseased imagination'; and recent experience has proved that *La Clemenza di Tito* is no mere museum piece. But his singling out of *Idomeneo* in 1911, when it was virtually unknown and long before its first production in Britain, as an indispensable key to the understanding of Mozart's genius for the theatre ('There is a monumental strength and a white heat of passion that we find in this early work of Mozart's and shall never find again') is only one example of his exceptional insight.

Dent says in his 1947 Preface that he intended the book for the general reader rather than the musicologist. Perhaps for that reason he does not always give full references, and some of his citations are so recondite that they are difficult to check. But he wears his learning lightly. Discussion of solemn matters is always liable to punctuation by shafts of sly humour: see the footnotes on pages 92 and 161 and the reference to Mozart's *Musical Joke* on page 145. The book is full of fruitful digressions, or apparent digressions, for example on national variations in recitative and musical nationalism in general, on the ramifications of the *Don Giovanni* story and the links between *The Magic Flute*, *Fidelio*, and the opera of the nineteenth century; there is even a learned historical note on the *jus primae noctis*. Dent cannot always resist a shy at a favourite Aunt Sally. He tells us that 'priests in opera are always odious', and that the High Priest in *Idomeneo* no doubt stage-managed the oracle; but he treats Sarastro with all reverence. When he is provocative, his object is usually to provoke the reader into thinking for himself.

Such errors of fact as I have discovered (with help from Professor Peter Branscombe) are for the most part relatively unimportant. Many of them occur in the chapters on *The Magic Flute* and the last year of Mozart's life, which have been the subject of much recent research. The dates given for the commissioning of *The Magic Flute*, the Requiem and *La Clemenza di Tito* are more precise than the known facts allow; and Alan Tyson's paper studies have modified the chronology of Mozart's work on these projects. Both *La Clemenza di Tito* and *The Magic Flute* enjoyed more immediate success than Dent suggests. Schikaneder's Theater auf der Wieden was no 'flimsy erection' (see Dent's Note to the Second Impression); he was not the author of the words of the Masonic cantata (K. 623), first performed on 18 November 1791. There are even minor mistakes in the plot of *The Magic Flute*: the Orator (Der Sprecher) does not appear until Act II, Monostatos's sentence to the bastinado is commuted by Sarastro, and the Queen of Night orders Pamina to obtain from Sarastro a circle or orb, not the sevenfold shield of the sun.

More misleading is the untenable supposition that the plot was radically changed after the libretto was complete and some of the music written. Dent's hostility to Schikaneder—there is no evidence that he led Mozart into a riotous and profligate life, or that he was critical of the music—caused him to promote Gieseke (*sic*), a literary nonentity whose *Oberon* libretto for Wranitzky is a

crass plagiarization of the work of the North German actress–
writer Sophie Seyler, into part-authorship of the *Magic Flute*
libretto.

It would no doubt be possible to introduce corrections and
qualifications into the text, but that would impair the flavour of
the book, and incidentally deprive us of Dent's very entertaining
account of Gieseke's activities in Greenland and Ireland. (The
only changes to the text are the correction of some half dozen
misprints.) While Dent was sometimes careless over detail or
even occasionally wrong-headed, he had a firm grasp of essentials
and a deep understanding of Mozart's character as a creative
artist. The book has lost very little of its value and is a pleasure to
read. The sentence with which Dent ended his 1947 edition, on a
troubled world's need of 'the profound and noble sincerity of
*Idomeneo* and the serene spirituality of *The Magic Flute*' conveys
a truth without temporal limitation.

WINTON DEAN

*October* 1990

# PREFACE TO THE SECOND EDITION

WHEN the first edition of this book was published in 1913 most of Mozart's operas were almost completely unknown in this country. Of those which I have discussed, *Idomeneo* had never been performed here at all; *Die Entführung* had been revived by Sir Thomas Beecham for a few performances in 1910, but before that had not been seen since 1881; *Figaro* and *Don Giovanni* were, of course, items of the regular repertory, at any rate of the Carl Rosa and Moody-Manners companies, though from the time of the Wagnerian invasion they were not so often given at Covent Garden. *Così fan Tutte*, after long years of oblivion, had been revived for one English performance under Stanford in 1890, sung by students of the Royal College of Music, and twenty years later it was revived by Beecham; *La Clemenza di Tito*, the first Mozart opera to be seen in London (1811), had been given again in German in 1840 and after that forgotten altogether. *Die Zauberflöte*, during the first half of the nineteenth century, had been performed in Italian, German and English at various dates; after that it had a fair number of performances in Italian, whenever star singers of the requisite calibre were available. The last Italian performance took place under Lago in 1892. The Cambridge performance in English (December 1911) was what originally led me to write this book. In those days people all talked of the opera as *Il Flauto Magico* and few even among musicians seemed to be aware that it had been composed to German words; the usual verdict on it was that it contained Mozart's divinest music set to the most ridiculous and unintelligible libretto.

The new outlook on Mozart dates back to the Mozart festivals which began at Munich about 1896 under the stage direction of Ernst von Possart and the conductorship of Hermann Levi. As they were organized as a sort of appendix to the Wagner festivals at Bayreuth, they were attended by a good many English visitors, and through them English people gradually began to realize that *Figaro* and *Don Giovanni* were both operas for a small and intimate theatre, that *Così fan Tutte* was an exquisite artificial comedy, and *Die Zauberflöte* a profoundly moving allegory. I have no intention, in this new edition, of reviewing all the subsequent revivals of Mozart's operas; it would be a task beyond my knowledge to survey even those which have taken place in this country. There is no need to criticize the experiments of the past; we must concentrate our energies on the future. It is characteristic of our musical life that the most interesting Mozart revivals in recent years have been the productions of amateurs. *Idomeneo* was staged for the very first time in this country by an amateur society at Glasgow in 1934, and in English too; further performances were given elsewhere under the direction of the Misses Radford, the authors of the translation. The opera has also been performed by amateurs at Cambridge and Haslemere. To the initiative of the Misses Radford we also owe the revival of *La Clemenza di Tito*, first at Falmouth and then in London. *The Magic Flute*, neglected altogether since the 1890's, was staged at Cambridge in 1911, and this performance led eventually to the Mozart revivals in English that took place at the Old Vic soon after the end of the last war. And Sir Thomas Beecham will forgive me, I hope, if I class him amongst the amateurs in so far as he has organized performances of Mozart purely for love of the works without the least hope of professional profit thereon. Nor would I omit the extraordinary achievement of a pioneer in education, Mr. C. T. Smith, who in 1919 staged an astonishingly convincing performance of *The Magic Flute* performed by the boys of an elementary school in the Isle of Dogs, followed up by another at a similar school in Whitechapel. A German professor, who did not see the performance, asked me if it was not a shocking desecration of a masterpiece; a distinguished singer who did come to see it said to me, 'I have sung in this opera dozens of times in Germany; I now understand it for the first time.'

In revising this book for a second edition I have felt happily compelled to consider an entirely new class of readers, a younger generation which, thanks mainly to the Old Vic and Sadler's Wells, has learned to enjoy Mozart's operas in the English language. We stand, I hope, on the threshold of a new era in the history of English opera and opera in English, and we seem to have accepted Mozart as the foundation of our foreign repertory, and to be gradually learning to think of Purcell as that of our native musical drama. If any reader takes the trouble to compare this edition with the first, he will find that I have cut out large quantities of dead wood; it may have been desirable to say certain things in 1913, but it would be superfluous to reprint them now.

I have done my best to bring the book up to date in accordance with modern historical research, but I have rewritten it for the general reader rather than for the musicologist. Finally, I am glad to have revised many of my own critical judgements; I do not repent of my errors in this respect, for they were natural to the period at which they were set down. But thirty years and more of operatic study, including a good deal of practical work for the stage and the unique experience which one derives from making operatic translations, have given me, I hope, a wider view of opera in general and of Mozart in particular.

My thanks are due to my original publishers, Messrs. Chatto and Windus, for facilitating the production of this edition, although they were not inclined to undertake it themselves. They treated me very generously in 1913, and, considering the number of years it required to put that small edition out of print, I cannot blame them. For kind help in various matters I must thank Dr. Alfred Loewenberg, whose *Annals of Opera* has been my daily reading ever since it was published (and indeed for some time before that); Miss Barbara Banner, librarian of the Royal College of Music; Professor J. B. Trend, who has been my director of studies in Spanish; and, once more, Mr. Lawrence Haward, who gave me useful criticism on my first edition, and has supplied me with much valuable information for this one.

LONDON
*January* 1946


## NOTE TO THE SECOND IMPRESSION

THE description of Schikaneder's theatre as 'little more than a wooden barn' (p. 211) is not strictly accurate. From the summer of 1786 there had been some sort of theatrical booth in a courtyard of the Starhembergisches Freihaus, and in January 1787 Christian Rossbach applied for permission to erect 'a wooden hut' there, but this permission was not granted. In March, however, Rossbach was given leave to erect a theatre with walls of masonry and a tiled roof, provided that adequate precautions were taken for safety and comfort. The interior was of wood, and there were two galleries. The total area was about 100 feet by 50, and the stage was about 40 feet deep; the pit was not more than a few feet longer. The building was approached by a longish covered way in wood across the garden. Various alterations and improvements were made during the next few years, but even as late as 1794 Schikaneder himself described it as 'a deficient and irregular building'. It was first opened for performances on Sunday, 14 October 1787, but there is no record of what works were performed there. Rossbach's management lasted barely six months, and the theatre was taken over by Johann Friedel, an actor who had been for some years in Schikaneder's travelling company and had run off with Schikaneder's wife. He died in March 1789 and left everything to Frau Schikaneder. Her husband rejoined her, and having found a financial backer (a fellow freemason), Josef von Bauernfeld, took over the management in the summer. Friedel had produced only plays there; Schikaneder started off with an operetta, *Der Dumme Gärtner*, words by himself, music by Schack and Gerl. Various plays and comic operas followed, some of which were seen by Mozart.

An exhaustive history of the theatre and its complete repertory, as far as recorded, from 1787 to 1801, when the theatre was closed and Schikaneder migrated to the newly built Theater an der Wien, has been written by Dr. Otto Erich Deutsch.[1]

1948

---

[1] O. E. Deutsch, *Das Freihaus-Theater auf der Wieden*. Mitteilungen des Vereines für Geschichte der Stadt Wien, Band XVI. 1937.

# MOZART AS A CLASSIC

TO the historian of the future the first forty years of the present century may well appear to be the age of archaeology. Not only in the musical world, but in every department of culture and for the general reader as well as the specialist, there seems to have been prevalent an extraordinary interest in every possible kind of antiquarian study. It has been to some extent interrupted by the periods of war, but it existed before 1914, it was universally conspicuous during the period 1918–39 and there is every probability that it may continue, at least for some time, after the world returns to peace. How far this reversion to the past affected other countries it is difficult to estimate; as far as I can myself judge, the cult of the antique was pursued nowhere so devotedly as in England. It was characteristic that our illustrated weekly papers devoted at least a couple of pages in every issue to excavations, whether in our own country or in Egypt, Central America, or the Far East. Historical exhibitions of the art of various countries attracted huge crowds to Burlington House. Our musical life was characterized by a large number of revivals of old music; the movement may be said to have begun as far back as 1895, when Stanford celebrated the bicentenary of Purcell's death with a stage performance of *Dido and Aeneas*. The importance of that revival was that that opera, known for the previous two centuries only in concert mutilations, was brought back to its proper home, the theatre. Another landmark was the series of historical concerts and operas organized in 1914 for the congress of the old International Musical Society in Paris; that was really the beginning of the modern interest in the music of the early Middle Ages. Germany and Austria published innumerable volumes of *Denkmäler der Tonkunst*; France and Italy followed suit; while in England, especially at Oxford and Cambridge, there was a continuous practice of our own classics, notably the Tudor church music, the Elizabethan madrigals, and the works of Purcell both for the church and the theatre.

The early twentieth century was, of course, by no means the first era of excavation and adoration of 'the antique'; but whereas the archaeology of the Renaissance implied an immediate recognition of ancient art and literature and its ruthless adaptation to the practical needs of that day, and that of a hundred and fifty years ago, whether we take Winckelmann or J. R. Planché as typical figures, was essentially romantic, i.e. enthusiastic and by our own standards uncritical, the revivalist movement of the present age has been resolutely scientific in all its ramifications. The musical researchers, like the students of Byzantine or Medieval painting, have refused to regard the music of the centuries before Handel as merely primitive and unskilful; they have set themselves deliberately to train their imaginations to realize, as far as any later generation can, the emotional and poetic values of this art, as well as merely to decipher its notation. We may indeed be grateful to the Church of England for preserving unbroken the tradition of Blow and Purcell, of Greene, Battishill and Attwood; a consciously scientific enthusiasm restored Tallis and Byrd to practical performance, and at the present day it is possible for the ordinary concert-goer to hear even occasional performances of still earlier music. Indeed, during the last forty years or so many of us may well have had the impression that we were living, both auditively and visually, in the galleries of a museum.

It is a museum through which most of us wander rather aimlessly, conscious only too often of tired feet and museum headache; but there is one room which seems to be always full, both of silent readers and students, and of listeners to any performance that may take place there—the room devoted to the memory of Mozart.

It is a curious thing that Mozart, the bicentenary of whose birth is within ten years of its celebration, should have become the most popular classical composer of the present day. Fifty years ago his reputation was rather faded, although Hans Richter is said to have prophesied that he had a great future before him. The nineteenth century began by adoring Mozart as the fashionable novelty; within a few generations it had established him as a classic, and it ended by relegating him for the most part to the schoolroom as a composer of sonatinas for little girls to practise. In 1906 Leipzig celebrated the hundred and fiftieth anniversary of his birth with a Mozart Festival which provoked one of the younger critics to publish a curious and instructive little book called *Mozart-Heuchelei* ('Mozart-Hypocrisy', by Paul Zschorlich,

Leipzig, 1906). I came across this book accidentally in Germany many years ago and expected to read an attack on the modern cult of Mozart which was already under way; I was quite surprised to find that the author's rage and scorn were directed against survivors from a much older generation, trying vainly to preserve the worship of a divinity long extinct. This explosive young critic was in fact a full-blooded Wagnerite, but with a hearty contempt for those who were still at the stage of enjoying *Tannhäuser* and *Lohengrin*; at the same time he was furious with those whose reverence for the classics exalted *Don Giovanni* to the same level as *Tannhäuser*. Our modern devotion to Mozart is the result of an entirely different outlook on the whole of music. It would not be just to say that we regard Mozart's works, least of all his principal operas, as museum pieces; but our appreciation of him to-day is in many cases quite consciously a scientific appreciation, and even when it is experienced as a direct and natural enjoyment, that enjoyment is subconsciously due to a general background of musical education which fifty years ago hardly existed even amongst academically trained musicians.

Our modern opera repertory is in itself a museum repertory—or at any rate we should certainly describe it by that name if it was a drama repertory. Can anyone imagine a drama company, either in London or on tour, giving a different play every night, selected from, let us say, *Venice Preserv'd*, *The Rivals*, *The Lady of Lyons*, *Caste*, *Sweet Lavender* and *Peter Pan*? This might correspond very roughly to *Don Giovanni*, *The Barber of Seville*, *Lucia di Lammermoor*, *Carmen*, *La Bohème* and *Hänsel and Gretel*. Our ancestors, from Handel's day onwards, never wanted revivals of old operas; they wanted new operas, just as we normally want new plays. There were no classics in those happy days, except that the operas of Lully were kept up for a good many years in Paris, while in England our nearest approach to a repeatedly revived classic was *The Beggar's Opera*. After these Mozart is actually the first composer of operas to become a classic, and with the most disastrous results.

Not one of Mozart's principal operas enjoyed during his lifetime what a modern composer would admit to be a success. *Idomeneo* (1781) was revived privately in Vienna in 1786; between 1800 and 1825 it was given on a few other German stages, or as often as not in concert form—the worst way of confessing that an opera is no use for the theatre. Then in the 1840's come a few German revivals, going on at rare intervals to about the end of the century; Germany was obviously doing its pious duty to a classic, but *Idomeneo* never at any time became a regular repertory opera like *Don Giovanni*—it has always been what it still is, a magnificent museum piece. *Die Entführung aus dem Serail* (1782) had thirty-four performances, after which the German opera house for which it was composed was closed altogether. The same fate fell upon that English opera house which was inaugurated by Sullivan's *Ivanhoe*, commissioned, like Mozart's work, to be the new foundation of a national opera. *Die Entführung* has had many revivals in many countries and many different languages, but even though a single production may be acclaimed as a success, the opera has never attained real popularity anywhere, not even in Germany. It was given in London in Italian in 1866, but it was never given at all in Italy until 1935 and then only in German, at Florence. *Le Nozze di Figaro* (1786), probably the most popular by now of all Mozart's operas in most countries, had no great success at first, except at Prague. After it was translated into German it established itself firmly, but it never seems to have attracted French or Italian audiences to the same extent. French audiences probably preferred undiluted Beaumarchais; Italians, we may be quite sure, preferred Rossini's *Barber*. The English theatre in the days of Bishop and Planché solved the problem as usual by compromise, ingeniously combining the two operas. *Don Giovanni* (1787) has always been regarded as the most famous of all Mozart's operas, mainly because it was the one work of his which the Romantic movement could seize upon, interpret in its own way and claim for its own. One of the most curious things about the subsequent career of *Don Giovanni* in the German countries is that its libretto has baffled some fifteen or sixteen translators; all German critics are agreed that not one of them is really satisfactory. As far as Mozart's own lifetime was concerned, it was obvious that no opera in Italian could be really popular in a wide sense and in that adolescence of the German operatic stage there must have been very few German singers who could cope adequately with the vocal difficulties of Mozart's music. The third of Mozart's Italian comic operas to words by Da Ponte, *Così fan tutte* (1790), has had the oddest misfortunes of all; every theatre that gave the other two has taken it up on trial, but it has never had a real success until the present day, although it obtained some considerable popularity in London in English adaptations early in the last century. It is always gratifying to think that popular audiences in England enjoyed Mozart at a time when he was a comparatively modern composer; but we must not forget that his operas were mutilated and 'adapted' in a way that would now rouse universal indignation.

*Die Zauberflöte* (1791), being German to begin with, and, besides that, composed deliberately for a popular audience, naturally held the stage all over Germany as soon as the public's initial hesitation towards it had been overcome by persistent repetition. Here again England showed more appreciation of it than other countries; France started on the fatal policy of 'adaptation', and Italy, after a few early performances, decided firmly that Mozart was not for her in any operatic shape. *La Clemenza di Tito* (1791) was in itself such an anachronism, so belated a survival of the ancient 'dynastic' operas that one could hardly expect it to survive its own first production at all; but evidently there were still theatres in which *opera seria* was not considered altogether dead. It was the first Mozart opera to be produced in London, and appropriately enough, for Mrs. Billington's benefit, for she was a superb singer of the old school. For later generations it could only become even more of a museum piece than *Idomeneo*.

The general history of opera in the eighteenth century has been a good deal misunderstood owing to the fact that our popular textbooks have all derived their information from German sources; it has been the invariable tendency of all German historians to exaggerate the importance of Gluck under the impression that Gluck was a German composer. I do not for a moment wish to suggest that Gluck's achievement as a composer has been overrated; but it is completely erroneous to imagine that he destroyed the old-fashioned *opera seria* at one blow and prepared the way for Wagner and Richard Strauss. In the first place, Gluck was not a German at all; he was born of Czech parentage as a subject of Prince Lobkowitz, although his birthplace after Napoleonic times became part of German territory. He was educated at Prague and Komotau, as far as can be ascertained, and then sent to complete his studies in Italy. His early operas were all Italian and mostly written for Italian theatres. After he settled in Vienna, his duty as court composer was to provide French comic operas and Italian serious operas and what we should now classify in English as *masques* (in Italian) for the entertainment of the imperial family. Later on some of

his operas were performed in French adaptations in Paris, and a
few more were composed to French words for the same stage, if
composition is the right word for what were largely compilations
from earlier and forgotten works. Except for a few Odes of
Klopstock, Gluck never set a word of German to music in the
whole course of his life. As far as music was concerned, Vienna in
Gluck's day was an Italian city; the life of Mozart shows it all
too plainly.

The old *opera seria* represented by the musical dramas of
Metastasio had been pre-eminently a dynastic and aristocratic
entertainment. It may have enjoyed some popularity among the
middle classes in Italy, where its language was that of the people,
but north of the Alps it was supported entirely by the princes of
Central Europe, the Russian court and the English nobility.
A few members of these aristocracies may have understood Italian
and many more may have pretended to do so; but the main
function of the Italian opera (as in our own day too) was to be
expensive and exclusive. In Paris a national opera in French had
been created by Louis XIV, but after he grew old he ceased to
interest himself in it, and operatic activities were transferred
from Versailles to Paris and to private houses as well, as it became
more and more the amusement of the nobility and the new class
of wealthy *bourgeois*. In 1752 came the famous *Guerre des Bouffons*, a musical war that had a much more powerful influence on
French opera and on music in general than the more celebrated war
of the Gluckists and Piccinnists a generation later. The victory of
the *Bouffons* meant not so much the triumph of Italian music over
French as that of comic opera over serious opera. Europe in
general had grown tired of Metastasio; I name the poet rather than
any composer, for the composers were innumerable who set his
librettos, and those librettos imposed on the musicians a rigid
uniformity of style and plan. In all countries a new public for
opera was growing up; opera was no longer reserved exclusively
for royal weddings and birthdays. The new public did not want
to throw dynastic opera overboard all at once; what may be
called dynastic opera survived up to Mozart's *La Clemenza di Tito*
and in some places even into the following century. But the
number of comic operas produced between 1750 and 1800 is
enormously greater than that of the serious operas, and this is
true, not only for Italian opera, but for French, German, and
English as well. From the Italian point of view, the novelty of

Gluck's *Orfeo* (1762) lay in the attempt to impose a French structure on the traditional Italian style; all Calzabigi's innovations were borrowed from Paris—the mythological subject in place of a heroic one, the supernatural element pervading the whole, the literary forms of the verse, the liberal and conspicuous employment of chorus and ballet. The success of Gluck in Paris was due very largely to the personal influence of his former pupil, Marie Antoinette; the very choice of Piccinni as a rival to set up in opposition to him showed that the 'war' was not based on fundamental questions of musical or dramatic aesthetics, nor even on nationalistic grounds. Piccinni had made his great reputation, and indeed deservedly, on his comic operas; he had a cordial admiration for Gluck and was by no means anxious to enter into competition with him. Gluck's *Iphigénie en Tauride* is always supposed to have won that war with the complete rout of the Italian party; but various points may be noted. First, Gluck's next and last opera for Paris, *Echo et Narcisse*, was a complete failure, so much so that Gluck left Paris and went back to Vienna to take to his bed and die. Secondly, it may be observed that Piccinni's French operas are all decidedly French in manner; it is one of the most remarkable things about French music that although most of it seems—at any rate to a superficial observer from this side of the Channel—to have been composed by foreigners and not by Frenchmen, none the less the French tradition has somehow compelled all those strangers to adopt a style definitely French. Thirdly, Piccinni's *Iphigénie* came out two years after Gluck's and had quite a fair success; and most of the composers who followed up that success were Italians too— Salieri, Sacchini, Cherubini before the Revolution, and Spontini in the era of Napoleon. The French composers whose names have come down to posterity were chiefly occupied with *opéra-comique*, and the Revolution developed comic opera into romantic opera and melodrama.

Mozart's two serious operas, *Idomeneo* and *La Clemenza di Tito*, were anachronisms; they were museum pieces the moment that they were put on the stage. We have noted that almost all of Mozart's operas had some performances in Italy during the first twenty years or so of the new century; but we must remember that in those days Milan, Venice, and Florence were under Austrian domination and therefore in close contact with Vienna. One of Mozart's sons was in the Austrian Civil Service at Milan for most

of his life; he died there in 1858, but whether he had any influence
on operatic activities is not known.

Serious opera was still wanted in Italy at that date, and another
musical war was going on, though without any great publicity,
between the Italian composers (backed up, no doubt, by managers
and singers) who upheld the old traditions of *opera seria* based
mainly on a series of solo arias, and the modernists who wanted
to adopt the French type of libretto in which *ensembles* played
an increasingly important part. Moreover, serious opera was an
important export trade for Italy, as it has been now for over two
centuries. The London market was on the whole conservative
and thus could enjoy hearing Mrs. Billington in *La Clemenza*; but
Rossini swept all before him, and it was obvious that star singers
like Pasta and Catalani should prefer the more brilliant effects of
*Tancredi* or *Semiramide*. The Italians have shown quite plainly
for over a hundred years that they have no use for Mozart at all,
surprising as that may seem to his English admirers. The fate of
*Die Entführung* has already been mentioned. The Italian comic
operas were given a trial, and *Figaro* has reappeared from time
to time, even down to the present day, but the Italian public
obviously and naturally prefers Rossini. German critics, visiting
Italy in the first half of the last century, said that Mozart puzzled
and annoyed the Italian audiences because his duets and other
numbers often ended softly, so that the audience did not know
when to applaud; the opera continued without applause, and in
Italy an opera without applause, and violent applause too, must
be automatically a *fiasco*. For the comic-opera public Mozart was
much too complicated, and *Die Zauberflöte* in the standard Italian
translation dating from 1811 was even more incomprehensible
than in German. If its Masonic implications had ever been realized
in the Italy of Mazzini, the opera would certainly have been
forbidden altogether. Verdi summed up Mozart—for whom he
seems to have had no great interest—as *quartettista*, a composer of
chamber music, and for Italy in Verdi's day chamber music meant
one or two very exclusive and almost private quartet clubs, much
the same as the highly exclusive Musical Union started in 1840 by
John Ella in London.

For the nineteenth century then there are two separate aspects
of the Mozart cult; Mozart in German in Central Europe, generally
with not very accomplished singers, and with all recitatives turned
into spoken dialogue, and Mozart in Italian, not in Italy, but in

the Italian opera houses of Paris and London. The modern English reader may perhaps not be aware that Italian opera sung by Italians in Italian was cultivated pretty continuously in Paris from 1815 onwards, and that from 1841 to 1876 there was a flourishing Italian opera at the Théâtre Ventadour. This Italian opera had no connection with the Royal, Imperial, or National Opéra and Opéra-Comique, but like those two it received a large subvention from the Government. According to Alfred Bunn[1] the Royal Opera in the days of Louis Philippe received the equivalent of £32,000 annually, besides having the theatre rent free. Bunn does not state the amount of the subsidy to the Théâtre Italien, but its prices of admission were higher than those of the Opéra, and it was considered to be the more fashionable house from a social point of view. Italy supplied most of the singers, but not all. We learn from Liszt that in 1838 or thereabouts several of the star singers at La Scala in Milan were not Italian at all; and an article by G. A. Macfarren in *The Musical Times* of March 1869 says the same thing about the Italian opera in London:

'The majority of those who nowadays present themselves at the Italian Theatre in London are Germans, or Swedish, or French, or American or English, or in some other way foreign to the manner born of the text they have to enunciate. . . . The greater part of the vocalists, and nearly all of the best of them, who sing in Italian to London hearers, have the embarrassment, and make the consequent shortcomings, of contending with an acquired, and therefore to them unnatural, language.'

The situation has remained much the same from 1838 to 1938 but as the majority of the audience both in Paris and in London did not know more than a few words of Italian—generally nothing but the first few words of the favourite airs—the long-established and almost ineradicable tradition grew up that all opera librettos were nonsense and that it was really better not to know what they were about; and opera in English only confirmed this opinion. It can easily be understood that for such audiences *Il Flauto Magico* was nothing more than a display of exceptional voices; *Don Giovanni* and *Figaro*, the only other operas of Mozart performed with any frequency, naturally became treated more and more as 'grand romantic' operas, if only because the same singers were

[1] Alfred Bunn, *The Stage*, London, 1840.

roaring and screaming Donizetti and early Verdi for most of the season. It was only towards 1900 that Covent Garden began half-heartedly to adopt the principle of singing all operas in their original language, and this during one and the same season; in Victorian days there were occasional visits of German companies with German operas in German, but the regular seasons were entirely Italian, and French or German operas such as *Les Huguenots* or *Fidelio* were sung in Italian too.

Critics in the reign of George IV had talked of the 'craze' for Mozart in England, but although Mozart in English was steadily making its way, it was a very long time before any Mozart opera was given in English as the composer wrote it. Bishop arranged them to suit English taste, with a few songs of his own, and the singers had no scruple about introducing other songs wherever they thought they could win applause. Mozart and Rossini, in fact, were treated with the same freedom as modern composers of musical comedy are, except that modern copyright law can protect the composer of to-day from a good deal of the mutilation which Mozart had to suffer. We must not be too severe on Bishop for these 'atrocities'; he was sincerely concerned to raise the level of popular entertainment and to give the less cultivated classes an opportunity of enjoying cheaply what had hitherto been the exclusive privilege of the nobility and gentry at the Italian opera house.

In Germany the situation was a little better, because two of the operas had German words to begin with, and *Die Zauberflöte* soon established itself as a national classic; that meant, however, that it eventually became the sort of opera that was put on in a hurry without much rehearsal for the edification of children and Freemasons. Readers who are old enough to remember the Mozart revival at Munich in the 1890's must be reminded that these were quite exceptional performances of a 'festival' type and that they must on no account be regarded as typical of the German stage in general, even twenty or thirty years later. Outside Munich in the days of Possart and Levi there was hardly a theatre in Germany which ever attempted to sing the recitatives in *Figaro* and *Don Giovanni*; they were always given with spoken dialogue, like the two German operas.

But there was another and a much more powerful reason for the neglect and misunderstanding of Mozart during the nineteenth century—the gradual rise first of Beethoven and then of Wagner.

It was obvious that any society, in England, Germany, or any other country, which was learning to enter into the new outlook on the relation of music to life and thought represented by these two composers should turn away with horror and contempt from the frivolities and insincerities of Italian opera. There could be no compromise between *La donna è mobile* and *Freude, schöner Götterfunken*. We may feel nowadays that Beethoven and Wagner have given us a new outlook on Mozart; Beethoven has taught us to play his instrumental music seriously and Wagner has given us an altogether new attitude towards the theatre. But the tendency for the whole century was towards ethical aspiration and towards what may be called, according to the reader's individual taste, either megalomania or monumentalism. Among Mozart's operas there are only two which could be monumentalized and which indeed positively call for monumentalism— *Idomeneo* and *La Clemenza di Tito*, both of which had by that time been consigned to oblivion. To-day we can appreciate those tragic grandeurs which are no less characteristic of Mozart than they are of Handel or Rameau; fifty years ago or more they were ignored.

The romantic movement in Germany was intimately connected with the theatre, and with the theatre of Schiller, the theatre of moral grandeur and ethical aspiration. The opera was naturally affected by this influence. We see it in Beethoven's remark that he could never write an opera on such frivolous and immoral subjects as those of *Figaro* and *Don Giovanni*. It was further affected by the rise of the typical German dramatic soprano singer. She might have been appropriate to some of Gluck's operas, but these were very seldom performed in German until much later; musically she is the creation of Cherubini, whose romantic operas, beginning with *Lodoïska* (1791) were much more popular in Germany than in France. His *Faniska* (1806) was composed for Vienna, and never performed in France or Italy at all; the heroine, like Beethoven's Leonora of the preceding year, is typical of the new German dramatic style. The interpreters of this style might perhaps be traced to the famous Corona Schröter, singer and actress too; she acted Goethe's Iphigenia in a noteworthy performance of 1779, Goethe himself acting Orestes. Mara, well-known in England about the same time, may have owed her impressive style to her German birth, but she was always a singer of Italian and English. Milder-Hauptmann, for whom Beethoven wrote the part of Leonora, was typical of the new direction in German opera, and she was followed by Schröder-Devrient, Tietjens, and a continuous train of others down to the Wagner singers of our own day. They were almost invariably massive in figure, if not positively ungainly, often plain of features, with voices tending towards harshness; but they all threw themselves into such parts as Leonora with such tense sincerity and devotion that their physical unattractiveness was forgotten in the overwhelming emotional effect of their interpretations.

To the special art of such singers Mozart was forced to conform. Pamina in *Die Zauberflöte* was indeed the sort of *deutsches Mädchen* who might ultimately develop into a Leonora; it was less justifiable to impose the Leonora type on Donna Anna or the Countess in *Figaro*. There was always a strong sense of moral virtue in the German theatre; it had come from France of the Revolution, but Germany claimed it as essentially her own. It was only much later in the century that the unvirtuous heroine of opera, such as the Traviata and Carmen, found a responsive echo in German hearts, and it was long indeed before that type of heroine could be presented as a German by birth and education.[1] Heinrich Bulthaupt, whose *Dramaturgie der Oper* (1887) is a very illuminating study of standard German opera, is perpetually concerned to insist upon the 'chastity' and 'purity' of Mozart's music, even in the most erotic situations; at the same time he is anxious not to deny Mozart a certain quality of 'warmth,' but justifies it as appropriate for characters already married or on the immediate verge of legitimate union. As the century proceded, Mozart was interpreted more and more in the spirit of Beethoven and Wagner; all music had to be treated as philosophy and religion, until the even more devastating period of psychoanalysis arrived to insist upon the 'problematic' and 'daemonic' aspects of sex. It has been for our own century and for the generation of the present day to rediscover Mozart, not as the expression of an imaginary age of innocence, still less as the musical illustrator of an equally imaginary century of rococo artificiality, but as the completely mature creator of music that we can still enjoy as a thing of delight for its own sake.

[1] The unvirtuous heroines in modern German opera are mostly supposed to be French, Italian or Spanish. The first German composer to make a really German woman unvirtuous seems to have been Alban Berg. Marie in *Wozzeck* is pitiable rather than vicious, but Lulu is the real thing.

## 2

# THE EARLY OPERAS

THE century into which Mozart was born was dominated throughout by the influence of Italian opera. There is no need to quarrel with the consensus of opinion that has placed Handel, Haydn, and Mozart on a higher level of greatness than Leo, Pergolesi, and Jommelli; but it is most important to remember that the great Germans, however sincerely they may have felt that they were bringing about a reaction from the Italian supremacy, were all the time subconsciously expressing themselves in a musical language that was essentially Italian. Vernon Lee has well pointed out[1] that 'throughout the eighteenth century the evolution of the musical phrase, the evolution of what I should like to call *melodic form*, took place in Italy. . . . Musical style, in its musical essentials, was unaltered by Gluck's reforms.' But it was not merely the characteristic shape of an eighteenth-century tune that was Italian, but the forms in which all music was written. Composers all over Europe were trying to convey for different surroundings and for various instruments what they had heard sung in the Italian opera. The classical sonata-form was not invented by serious-minded Germans; it was taken over by them from the normal scheme of the operatic aria. The classical symphony, as is well known, was derived from the Italian operatic overtures; and since the early symphonies were composed mostly for the entertainment of German princes and archbishops during dinner, they were based on or imitated from the tunes of the popular comic operas, just as monarchs or prelates of the early twentieth century might dine to selections from the last new musical comedy. The Germans, being a nation of instrumental players rather than of singers, proceeded to develop instrumental, and especially orchestral, music on these lines for its own sake. This symphonic point of view, however, could only be reached by climbing the ladder of Italian opera. The ladder once climbed, young Germany very characteristically kicked it down, and a later generation pretended that there had

[1] *Studies of the Eighteenth Century in Italy*, Preface to the second edition, 1907.

never been any Italian ladder there at all. But the eighteenth century could not be deceived in this way. Its audiences were enveloped in an atmosphere of perpetual Italian song, just as modern audiences are haunted by the unending strains of Puccini in tea-shops and wherever 'light music' is habitually played. It was this subconscious memory of Italian opera that enabled audiences to follow the thought of the symphonic composers; it is a memory that we of to-day have lost, but if we can set ourselves to cultivate it we shall discover new and illuminating lights on the poetry of classical instrumental music. Austria, Germany and England were swarming with Italian musicians of all kinds; both literally and figuratively Italian was the language of music. Hardly a court was without its Italian opera, and there was hardly a place where Dr. Burney did not find Italian the most convenient medium of conversation. At the same time, the men who were colonizing that 'greater Italy' north of the Alps were themselves often susceptible to native influences, and the very fact that Italian was the universal musical language made for a certain cosmopolitanism which became still more marked as the century drew to its end.

Of all cosmopolitan eighteenth-century musicians, Mozart is the chief. His fame as an infant prodigy had caused him to begin his travels at a very tender age. His father was indefatigable in showing off his talents to everybody within his reach, and kept him as closely as possible in touch with all the new music of the day; indeed, to us modern amateurs who have been trained from childhood on 'the classics', and largely on the works of Mozart himself, his musical education seems curiously superficial. Leopold Mozart, although always held up to admiration as the most devoted of fathers, had a very repellent side to his character. He was a musical workman rather than an artist, and the way in which he regarded his son's abnormal gifts is made unpleasantly clear by a passage in a letter which he wrote on the subject of the journey to Italy projected in 1767. The performance of Wolfgang's opera *La Finta Semplice* at Vienna, a performance promised, but never carried out, would, he thought, be a sufficiently public recognition of the boy's talent to make an impression on the Archbishop of Salzburg and induce him to give permission for the Italian tour on which Leopold had set his heart. Leopold had had enough of Salzburg; is he to sit there, he asks, and let himself and his children submit to the Archbishop's whims till he is too old to undertake a journey, and 'until Wolfgangerl has reached the age and the stature which will deprive his accomplishments of all that is marvellous'?

The musical profession had its shady side in the eighteenth century no less than in the twentieth. Doubtless Afflisio, the manager of the Opera at Vienna, was a thorough scoundrel; but if Leopold's letters are to deserve credit, there was hardly a musician in Vienna or anywhere else who was not a monster of jealousy and intrigue. We may be fairly sure that a man who could write with such unfailing bitterness, even about men whose characters are fortunately known to us from other sources, was disagreeable enough in personal intercourse to encourage rather than disarm hostility from his brother musicians. Wolfgang was to be forced upon the world as a miraculous prodigy, and the iron was to be struck while it was hot; there was no reason to suppose that after he was grown up he would be anything more than a respectable professional musician like his father. Was it surprising that the men who were in possession of public favour should refuse to fall prostrate in admiration, or even to accept him as an equal? Burney, who had been in a very good position to judge of the boy's earlier attainments, had every reason to put faith in the letter of his anonymous Salzburg correspondent, who said of Wolfgang at sixteen: 'If I may judge of the music which I heard of his composition, in the orchestra, he is one further instance of early fruit being more extraordinary than excellent.'

At the age of eight he was in Paris writing harpsichord sonatas, which Leopold sent off at once to the engraver, so as to excite the jealousy of Schobert and the other Italianized Germans who were then fashionable in France; in London he was writing his first symphony to compete with Abel and J. C. Bach. He probably heard some of Rameau's music in Paris, if only owing to the friendly interest of Jelyotte, the great hero of Rameau's operas, and he undoubtedly heard a good deal of Handel's music in England. But Leopold had no great opinion of Handel, and was better pleased to think that 'Wolfgang at the age of eight knows all that could be expected of a man of forty'. Apparently all that Leopold expected of a man of forty was that he should have enough technical skill to write successful and effective drawing-room music. We have only to read his letters to his sister to see how hard his father kept him at work, not only playing and listening, but composing as well. No wonder he complains of headaches and tired fingers, and repeats again and again that Italy is a country where one always wants to go to sleep! That he speaks of his own music in the most perfunctory manner is perhaps a good sign; he shows not the least consciousness of being a genius, although he takes it as a matter of course that he is always among grown-up musicians,[1] nor is there the least trace of nervous or emotional exhaustion in connexion with music.

The first really strong and lasting musical impression that the child received was in all probability the influence of Manzuoli, a famous Italian singer, whom he often saw and heard in London. Manzuoli, although no longer young when he came to London, enjoyed an enormous popularity there; he was a frequent visitor to the Mozarts and gave Wolfgang lessons in singing. They met again in Milan in 1771, when Manzuoli took the leading part in his serenata *Ascanio in Alba*. Mozart's letters show not only that he was much attached to him, but also that he associated with his name a very definite sense of style. Along with Manzuoli must be mentioned another friend of Mozart's childhood, John Christian Bach, the completely Italianized youngest son of John Sebastian, known as the London Bach. He was one of the principal exponents of what was called the *galant* style—an essentially Italian instrumental style which was the result of a reaction against the severer manner of the Handelian period. It was a style which naturally appealed to a clever child like Wolfgang and it was some time before he was able to make it subservient to his own personality. Although more noticeable at first in the instrumental music of the period, the *galant* style was not confined to that branch of the art, and it led gradually to a certain lowering of operatic standards. It is amusing to read the patronizing and 'up-to-date' comments of Wolfgang, aged fourteen, on Jommelli's *Armida*, an opera which combined the severity and dignity of Leo with the picturesque orchestration of Rameau and an almost modern German sense of romance: 'Beautiful, but too careful and old-fashioned for the theatre!' The glorious days of Italian opera were indeed coming to an end; the stately eloquence of Metastasio, Jommelli and Hasse belonged to a past generation, and the sentimental humour of Piccinni's *La Buona Figliuola* had set a fashion destined to rule the musical world until Mozart himself was in a position to lead a new movement.

[1] He had at any rate one friend of his own age, Thomas Linley, whose name and features are familiar to all lovers of Gainsborough.

Yet only a few months later another force made itself felt in the boy's musical development. The summer of 1770 was spent at Bologna, where he underwent a long course of instruction from Padre Martini. Martini, although one of the most learned musicians of his own or of any other time, was no dry pedant, but a man of singular amiability with a strong sense of humour. Burney says of him: 'He joins to innocence of life and simplicity of manners a native cheerfulness, softness and philanthropy. Upon so short an acquaintance I never liked any man more; and I felt as little reserve with him in a few hours as with an old friend or beloved brother.' We have only to look at his portrait,[1] with its droll smile and twinkling eyes, to understand how Wolfgang soon developed a lasting affection for him, an affection no doubt deepened by the regular lessons in counterpoint which he received from him. If most young musicians find the study of strict counterpoint detestable in the extreme, it is due mainly to the incompetence of their teachers. Wolfgang worked through a good many exercises from Fux's celebrated treatise under the tuition of his father; but the rigid disciplinarian who could write of his own exercises for the violin, 'the more unpleasant they are found, the better I shall be pleased—I intended them to be so', was not likely to understand the value of strict counterpoint in awakening a pupil's sense of beauty and style. To Martini, on the other hand, it was a living language, saturated as he was with the knowledge of the great composers of the polyphonic period, and the result of his teaching was that Mozart eventually obtained a mastery of counterpoint such as has been rare even among composers of the first rank. There was hardly ever a period at which he did not make a point of employing contrapuntal methods, not as a mere display of learning, but as a means of poetic expression; and the consequence was that his polyphony, instead of sounding forced and archaistic, as it frequently does in Beethoven's late works, is always essentially Mozartian and imaginative.

During the months that were spent at home or at Vienna in the intervals between his Italian journeys the influences on Mozart were of a different character, but still fundamentally Italian. At Salzburg opera was practically non-existent; but there were a few Italian musicians there, including Brunetti the violinist and Ceccarelli the *castrato*, and Italian was the language of the court.

[1] A very characteristic portrait of him is reproduced in Vernon Lee's *Studies of the Eighteenth Century in Italy* (second edition).

The chief opportunities for composition were afforded by the
services of the Church and the entertainments of the Archbishop
and the nobility. Almost the whole of Mozart's church music
belongs to the period between his Italian travels and his final
breach with the Archbishop in 1781, and to the same period
belongs an enormous quantity of instrumental music now seldom
remembered. There was not the same distinction in those days
that there is now between symphonic and chamber music, and
neither symphony nor quartet had at that time acquired the
peculiarly serious quality that we have attached to those forms
since the later days of Mozart and Haydn. Any work in a series
of movements for three strings or any larger combination might
be called a *divertimento*,[1] and in practically all cases that name was
appropriate enough to the poetic content of the work, whether it
were actually named symphony, serenade, *notturno* or *cassation*.
It was from this long and regular routine that Mozart learned to
think symphonically, to conceive of music, not as a solo against
a neutral background, nor yet as the contrapuntal interaction of
equal and independent forces, but as a complex organization in
which various types of players sank their individualities to co-
operate in giving life to the most direct expression of the
composer's brain.

Italian opera, Italian polyphony and Italo-German symphony
—these three early influences were fundamental and permanent
throughout Mozart's life. But to the end of his days he was
experimenting, and experimenting with a practical knowledge of
his surroundings, so that the course of his development is very
different from that of men condemned to a life of solitude and
isolation like Beethoven, Domenico Scarlatti, and J. S. Bach.
Such men present in some ways a simpler artistic life-story; the
foundations of musical character once laid down, the rest is all
self-development from the inside. In considering Mozart we are
confronted all along by merely external considerations—the
exigencies of patrons, the peculiarities of individual executants,
as well as the direct influences of other composers' works. What
the musician of to-day can learn best from Mozart rather than
from any other composer of the past is that pride in craftsmanship
which enables him to adapt himself to the conditions of the
moment, to rewrite and rewrite again to suit the convenience of a

---

[1] All Haydn's quartets, even the latest, are entitled *Divertimento* in the autograph MSS.

singer or the necessity of the stage, and in every case to preserve and even to intensify his own individuality.

Mozart's early efforts at dramatic composition do not call for detailed analysis here. Judged in relation to his entire artistic output, they contribute their share to the gradual growth of his musical personality; but if we look at them merely as forerunners of the operas which still hold the stage we can find little in them that is of permanent or first-rate importance. The two childish entertainments *Die Schuldigkeit des ersten Gebotes* and *Apollo et Hyacinthus* may be dismissed at once. Wolfgang's first real opera, *La Finta Semplice*, was composed at the age of twelve. Leopold had taken him to Vienna in January 1768 and had worked his hardest to get the child's talents recognized both at court and among the aristocracy, but without much success. Fired by a suggestion thrown out by the Emperor probably as a jest, Leopold made up his mind that Wolfgang should write an opera. The Imperial Opera was in the hands of an Italian, Afflisio by name, under terms that enabled him to do as he pleased without reference to the Emperor's wishes. He was approached by various influential people, who put it to him that even if the music was poor all Vienna would flock to the theatre to see a little boy of twelve conduct.[1] Despite difficulties with the poet and the singers the opera was finished in the course of the summer and put into rehearsal, but by the middle of September it became clear that Afflisio had no intention of producing it. Leopold was furious, and set out a long complaint of his ill-treatment to the Emperor; the Emperor was powerless, and Afflisio merely replied that he would perform the opera if Leopold insisted, but would at the same time organize a parody of it and make the whole thing a ridiculous failure.

Afflisio had his public to consider and probably saw that his chance of a financial success was small. Is there any London manager of to-day who would risk the production of a 'musical comedy' by a boy of twelve? If he were a genius of the calibre of Mozart at twelve his work would probably be too musicianly, and if he were merely a mediocrity he would not even have the advantage of a trustworthy name and a practised hand for writing what the public wanted. Leopold had to give in, and the opera was eventually performed at Salzburg. There is nothing remarkable

---

[1] He would not have conducted in the modern way, but would have directed the opera sitting, or possibly standing, at the harpsichord.

about *La Finta Semplice* except that it was the work of a boy. It is just an ordinary Italian *opera buffa*; the libretto, based on one of Goldoni's comic operas, is farcical and absurd, but not more so than many others by the same author, and certainly no more absurd than the plots of modern musical comedies. It is characteristic of Germany in the 1850's that Otto Jahn does his best to make out that Mozart's music is a work of genius hampered by an unworthy libretto. Wolfgang knew better; for him it was obviously an entertainment of a stock pattern. Its characters were not individuals, but regular types of *opera buffa* represented by regular types of singers, and no more. He had been taken frequently to the opera and had seen *La Buona Figliuola*,[1] Giuseppe Scarlatti's *La Moglie Padrona*, and Gassmann's new opera *La Notte Critica*;[1] these showed him at once what sort of music to provide. Florian Gassmann, another Austrian pupil of Padre Martini, is an interesting forerunner of Mozart. Like Mozart, he puts a good deal more work into his score than the Italians, but, not having the inventive genius of the fully developed Mozart to carry it off, his opera is often rather heavy in style. The following example (pp. 21–3) will give an idea of his manner, and I quote it in preference to an extract from Mozart, because Gassmann represents a mature type of music which Mozart at that time was merely imitating without contributing anything new of his own. The situation (not unlike the opening scene of *The Barber of Seville*) is as follows: Leandro has been serenading Cecilia, but can get no answer. His servant Carlotto undertakes to arrange matters through Marinetta, the lady's maid, while Leandro is to wait at the Caffè della Luna. Leandro starts to give Carlotto very precise instructions, but finds that he is paying no attention to him. The two themes 'Tu dirai a Marinetta' and 'Dove sei? più non ti trovo' are the two subjects of the conventional sonata-form; they are contrasted and alternated with very humorous effect, leading to the climax of rage 'O che smania al cor io provo' which is repeated after the regular Italian fashion.

The general effect is on the whole spirited and amusing, though the themes of the voice part are not particularly notable. The interesting feature is the treatment of the orchestra, which is much fuller and more varied than in most Italian operas. The instrumental themes are indeed more individual than those of the voice—this strikes us at the very start—and the alternating use

---

[1] Both those librettos were by Goldoni.

of oboes and horns in the last four bars of the second extract shows that the composer had a vein of humour that was definitely symphonic in character.

To the same year as *La Finta Semplice* belongs *Bastien und Bastienne*, a one-act operetta with German words, acted at Vienna in the garden of Dr. Anton Mesmer, the discoverer of 'animal magnetism'. The libretto is derived from that of Rousseau's *Le Devin du Village* (1752); the music is an agreeable trifle more or less in the French style. It is sometimes performed nowadays, and is very suitable for puppet theatres, but it owes its fame less to its intrinsic merits than to the name of Mozart and to the comical coincidence of its first theme with that of the *Eroica* symphony.

Wolfgang and his father set off on their first Italian tour in December 1769. We possess a large number of letters written by him to his sister, which give us a good idea of his impressions. He was fairly fluent in the Italian language when he started, and was consequently ready to assume an Italian point of view as soon a he reached Verona. Through the good offices of Count Firmian, the governor of Lombardy, he was engaged to write an opera for the next season at Milan; this was *Mitridate Re di Ponto*, composed during the autumn of 1770 and performed on December 26. *Mitridate*, an imitation of a tragedy by Racine, had been written by Vittorio Amedeo Cigna-Santi three years earlier for Quirico

Gasparini of Turin, a composer of purely local importance. It fell far short of the literary beauty of Metastasio's opera books, but it at any rate provided composer and singers with well-contrasted dramatic effects. Mozart was not yet temperamentally equal to the treatment of such a subject. It is a mistake to suppose that all Italian operas of that period were merely displays of vocal virtuosity. Metastasio had a very clear idea of fusing music and poetry into a dramatic whole, although his conventions make it difficult for a modern audience to appreciate the complete results. Something which we perhaps feel to be vital was indeed sacrificed; it was sacrificed, not to virtuosity, but to classic dignity. We miss the sense of humanity in the music; the audiences of those days were concerned, not with men, but with heroes. No wonder then that Mozart at fourteen was unable to realize the greatness of his task. He adopted the Italian style with extraordinary fluency; his natural genius added to that a sense of beauty and a wealth of detail that separate him at once from the average run of Italian composers; but it is only in situations depending on some quite simple and obvious emotion that his music can be considered really moving and expressive.

The opera was successful enough for Mozart to be commissioned to write music for a *serenata* in honour of the marriage of the Archduke Ferdinand with Maria Beatrice of Modena in October 1771. This was a much easier problem; *Ascanio in Alba* had nothing dramatic about it at all, and may be conveniently described as a mixture of ballet and cantata, not unlike an English *masque*. Its one and only business was to be decorative and charming, and Mozart had no difficulty in producing music admirably suited to the occasion. Between *Ascanio in Alba* and the next opera, *Lucio Silla*, also composed for Milan, a full year elapsed, and it was a year of some importance in Mozart's life. It was a year of continuous hard work at Salzburg, and the year too in which a new Archbishop, the notorious Hieronymus Colloredo, had been enthroned to the formal and uninspired strains of Mozart's *Il Sogno di Scipione*. It was also the year which marked definitely in the young composer the change from boyhood to manhood. A new note of passion appears in the slow movements of his quartets and sonatas, which are often quite romantic in character. There was a wave of romanticism passing over all Germany at the time, felt not only by Mozart but by the older Haydn too, as we may see in his pianoforte sonata in C minor (1771 or 1772), an emotional outburst that seems to foreshadow the *Sonata Pathétique* or the C minor Symphony of Beethoven.

It was perhaps just the moment for Mozart to compose an opera, had he been provided with the right libretto and the right occasion. But *Lucio Silla* was a frigid piece of formality in which only one character, the heroine Giunia, had any semblance of life.

The libretto was by Giovanni di Gamerra, who acknowledges in his preface the kind help of Metastasio himself in making improvements; Gamerra survived Mozart and made the standard Italian translation of *Die Zauberflöte*. Wolfgang could find little to interest him beyond the work of providing the singers with the kind of music that suited them, and Leopold naturally thought that that was all there was to be done in any opera. The work was performed at Milan on 26 December 1772, under rather trying circumstances; the archduke of the moment kept everybody waiting for three hours before he was ready for the opera to begin, and one of the tenors, a church singer secured in a hurry as a stop-gap, was unaccustomed to the stage and over-acted so energetically that the audience burst out laughing at the most tragic moment. The *prima donna* was much upset and sang badly all the evening, the more so as she was very jealous of the *primo uomo*, who had been applauded by the archduchess the moment he came on the stage. Such is Leopold's account, and he goes on to say that in spite of these mishaps the opera was a great success. Of course it was—being Wolfgang's; it had in fact over twenty performances. But it is a significant fact that this was the last occasion on which Wolfgang was ever invited to compose a work for the Italian stage.

The plain truth was that *Lucio Silla*, taken as a whole, was a mediocre opera, not even as good as *Mitridate*. It is unequal in style, with no conception of dramatic unity. The majority of the airs are very difficult, and probably more difficult than effective. There are, however, two scenes for Giunia alone which rise to really tragic heights—her invocation to her father's shade in Act I, and her determination to face death herself in Act III. There is also a remarkable scene, modelled to some extent on Gluck's *Orfeo*, in which Giunia, accompanied by a chorus of mourners at her father's tomb, encounters her lover Cecilio. In these scenes we see something of the real Mozart—indeed, of a Mozart perhaps more real than we shall ever see again, after *Idomeneo*, until quite the end of his career.

*Lucio Silla*, in spite of its defects, had shown the young composer what were the possibilities of Italian *opera seria*, and from this date to the close of his life *opera seria* became his most absorbing passion—a passion, however, destined never to find a satisfactory outlet. He returned from Italy to Salzburg and devoted himself once more to writing symphonies; to the same

year also (1773) belong the first sketches for the incidental music
to Gebler's play, *Thamos, König in Ägypten*, which brought
Mozart for the first time into contact with the mystical ideas
embodied in Freemasonry. How much of Gebler's inner allegory
Mozart understood at this date we cannot attempt to guess; but
the noble dignity of this music, completed in 1779, shows at least
that he was profoundly impressed. The next year (1774) brought
about a certain reaction from this serious style. Mozart was
commissioned by the Elector of Bavaria to write a comic opera for
Munich, and the lengthy visit to that small but lively capital seems
to have given him a definite turn in the direction of fashionable
elegance and virtuosity of style. *La Finta Giardiniera* is a
conventional *opera buffa* of the stock Italian pattern. It had been
set to music hardly a year before by Pasquale Anfossi for performance at Rome, and very soon it was being performed all over
Europe. There can be no doubt that Mozart was acquainted with
Anfossi's music, though his own is widely different. Anfossi and
the rest of the Italian writers of *opera buffa* were skilled trades-
men, supplying what the public wanted with a minimum of
labour on their own part and exacting a minimum of labour on the
part of their audiences. They produced simply effective airs, with
accompaniments that were adequate and no more. Mozart, on
the other hand, had accustomed his mind to thinking in terms of
the symphony, conceiving voices and instruments all as
component parts of an organic whole; they were there, all of them,
not merely to amuse the public, but to make music. The curious
result is that although Mozart's voice parts are less obviously
vocal than Anfossi's his opera gives a much more vocal impression, because it is a much more musical impression. As
Wyzewa and Saint-Foix neatly express it: 'Voix et orchestre, on
a l'impression que tout parle, et souvent très-agréablement ou
très-spirituellement, chez Anfossi, mais que, chez Mozart, tout
chante.'

La Finta Giardiniera was produced at Munich in January 1775
and after being translated into German was given by a travelling
company in several German cities. The following April saw the
performance of another *serenata* at Salzburg. *Il Re Pastore*, a
string of arias written with an unfailing sense of grace and beauty,
but without the least suspicion of dramatic power. It was a long
time before Mozart had another opportunity of writing an opera.
He was now a grown man, with a just sense of pride in his own

powers and at the age when the petty tyranny of home life naturally became intolerable, all the more so in the provincial atmosphere of Salzburg. He pours out his woes in a long letter to the man whom he knows to be his best friend, the one man whose musical opinion he really values—old Padre Martini at Bologna.

'I live in a place where music has very little luck, although, besides those who have left us, we have still some very good musicians, and especially composers of sound learning and taste. As far as the theatre is concerned, we are in a bad way for want of singers. We have no *castrati*, and shall not have them so easily, since they want to be well paid; and generosity is not our national failing. So I amuse myself at present by writing for the chamber and the church.'

The days of *opera seria* were practically over, and *opera buffa* did not employ *castrati*, although they were always required for the churches. But church *castrati* were naturally drawn only from the inferior quality. Gluck's *Alceste* had been interpreted mainly by singers of the comic opera type. It is interesting to see that Mozart at this date had no objection whatever to *castrati*; in fact he evidently regarded them as the only possible interpreters of heroic opera.

Even Leopold saw that under the new Archbishop's régime Wolfgang could find no suitable scope for his genius. Hieronymus, Count Colloredo, was indeed a most unpleasant character. He was seriously interested in music and played the violin himself, but none too well. That he was an aristocrat and an autocrat was all in the natural order of things; but he was also a deeply religious man and a stern disciplinarian, bent on effecting all sorts of reforms. Among other things he demanded a simpler and severer type of music for the Church, and to his narrow-minded taste, or lack of it, Mozart was obliged to give way.

After some trouble with the Archbishop, he was finally allowed to leave Salzburg in September 1777. Leopold however would not allow him to travel alone, and since he could not accompany him himself, as he had done on all previous occasions, he sent his wife to take care of Wolfgang and see that he paid due heed to the paternal warnings against alcohol and doubtful company. The long winter spent at Mannheim, although most important in his general development, brought him no chance of appearing as

a dramatist. At Munich there was a faint chance, but it came to
nothing. Writing about a German version of Piccinni's *La Bella
Pescatrice*, he goes on to say: 'They have no original pieces. They
would like to have a German *opera seria* here soon, and they would
like me to compose it.' But he adds that it was all mere talk and
no more. Piccinni's opera had excited his brain for the moment,
he admits, and he plans the sort of contract he would like to make
—four German operas a year, some serious, some comic,—'and
how popular I should become if I were to help in raising the music
of the German national stage!' All mere talk! His old friend
Misliweczek, whom he visited in hospital, told him to go to Italy—
'there one is properly appreciated!' 'And he is quite right', adds
Mozart. 'I have never had so much honour and appreciation
anywhere as I had in Italy, and one gets some credit for it if one
has written operas in Italy, especially at Naples.' He forgot that
he was no longer an infant prodigy.

Misliweczek had had the offer of an opera for Naples, and, not
wishing to go there again himself, was ready to hand over the
engagement to Mozart, knowing that his own reputation at Naples
was good enough guarantee for the ability of any younger composer whom he chose to send instead. Mozart was all for accepting
the offer. 'I have an unspeakable desire to write another opera.
. . . If I only hear an opera mentioned, if I only go inside a theatre
and hear them tuning, I am quite beside myself.'

At Mannheim he heard Holzbauer's *Günther von Schwarzburg*
(1777). He rightly criticizes the libretto as being unworthy of the
music, which was extraordinarily vigorous considering the
advanced age of the composer. And he had a good word too for
Schweitzer, another German composer, whose two operas *Rosa-
munde* and *Alceste* he heard. But German opera in general was in
a bad way, and although these works are considered to be land-
marks in its history, they have not held the stage. The singers
were miserable, Mozart says, and it was hardly ever possible to
get a serious German opera performed. He gave up all hopes in
this direction. Leopold wrote to tell him that the Emperor intended to establish permanent German opera at Vienna, but
Wolfgang was quite angry and indignant at the idea of his taking
part in the scheme. He knew that it only meant comic opera, and
he had put that away with childish things: 'Some people think
one remains twelve years old all one's life!' 'Don't forget my wish
to write operas! I am envious of everyone who writes one; I could

positively cry with annoyance when I hear or even see an aria. But it must be Italian, not German, an *opera seria*, not *buffa!*'

A few days later, writing about the project of going to Paris, he brings up the subject again, with the same conditions: 'French rather than German, but Italian rather than either German or French.' The nearest he could get to Italian opera was writing concert arias for Raaff the tenor, Aloysia Weber, and other singers; he rejoiced at the prospect of Paris and the *concert spirituel*, because the French appreciated good choral music such as he loved composing. Rameau had set a high standard of choral music and Piccinni's *Roland* had been unfavourably criticized because its choruses were weak. Paris, however, was little better than Mannheim. He wrote a ballet, *Les Petits Riens*, for Noverre, and there was some talk of a grand opera, but again it came to nothing. Leopold had told him that he was to stay in Paris until he had established a reputation there; but matters went ill with him. He did not obtain the success that he had expected, and he disliked both Paris and the Parisians. On 3 July his mother died, and he was looked after to some extent by Baron von Grimm. Grimm and Mozart had started as good friends, but Mozart soon began to resent the older man's interference, and he was glad enough when his father told him to leave Paris, although he did not look forward with any pleasure to taking up his residence in Salzburg again.

He left Paris towards the end of September, having been there six months. It is difficult to form a complete judgement of the impressions that he received there. He was no doubt well informed on all the details of the great war of the Gluckists and Piccinnists, and it must be remembered that at the time when Mozart arrived in Paris the battle was still undecided. Gluck's *Armide* had not obtained the success of his previous operas, and Piccinni's *Roland*, which the composer himself expected to be a failure, turned out a success. Mozart had always had a great admiration for Gluck, but his natural sympathies were with Italian music. Moreover, since Rameau there had been no great French composer of serious opera, and even the comic opera of Paris, where real French music was seen at its best, was none the less under strong Italian influences. There was another reason too why Mozart was not likely to be much attracted by serious French opera, and that was because the performances, if we may trust the accounts of Italian and English visitors, were indescribably horrible. To

English as well as to Italian ears, French opera was simply not music at all, but just *un tintamarre du diable*. French comic opera was primarily a spoken play with songs, and even in the most famous examples the music seems to be rather a secondary consideration, judged by the comic operas of the Italians, to say nothing of the standards of Mozart.

The interactions of French and Italian opera during the third quarter of the eighteenth century are complicated and difficult to analyse. Fortunately, we need not take German opera into consideration at all; it exhibited three types; first, the *opera seria*, generally composed to librettos of Metastasio, in Italian, by Hasse and others; secondly, the abortive attempts at *opera seria* in German, with librettos modelled on Metastasio, set to music by Schweitzer and Holzbauer; and, thirdly, the German *Singspiel* or comic opera with spoken dialogue, the triviality of which is for the most part beneath contempt. In France no native successor to Rameau appeared to carry on the superb style of the *tragédie lyrique*. Even in the hands of Rameau himself it had degenerated into the *opéra-ballet*, in which, as the name implies, spectacle and ballet became more important than serious drama. Gluck, whom we must regard as an Italian composer, was influenced by French technique in the first version of *Orfeo* (1762), but what he brought to Paris was a more Italian outlook on the typical French lyric tragedy. This was continued in Paris by the two Italians, Piccinni and Sacchini; but their operas are of no great musical value compared with those of Rameau and Gluck. They had their vogue, even in London too, but they were very quickly forgotten, and a study of their scores does not encourage a desire to revive them. Much more interesting, even to us of to-day, are the operas of the Italian Traetta, composed for Italian and German stages, but making use of librettos translated or adapted from the French, indeed sometimes previously set by Rameau himself. Whether Mozart ever came across any of them may be doubted; Traetta worked mostly at Parma, Venice, and St. Petersburg, visiting Vienna only for performances of operas by him in 1759 and 1760, when Wolfgang was hardly of an age to go to the theatre.

It is clear from Marmontel, opera poet and literary critic as well, that the chief characteristic of French opera was *le merveilleux*, the supernatural element. Tragedy, he says, is concerned with realities, with the passions and sufferings of human beings; epic poetry introduces *le merveilleux* as a decorative accessory, describing it in words, and opera puts it all visibly on the stage. He cites the story of Armida and Rinaldo as an example, evidently regarding Armida, viewed as a figure of tragedy, as nothing more than a queen of unusual beauty and fascination; the supernatural element is introduced through Tasso's epic, and it is presented before our eyes in the operas of Lully and Gluck. Italian opera, on the other hand, started with mythological subjects, but very soon discarded them for purely human ones; and, of course, for Marmontel, writing in the second half of the eighteenth century, the typical Italian opera is that of Metastasio, who both directly and through his predecessor Apostolo Zeno had been greatly influenced by the spoken tragedy of Racine. The Italians used just as elaborate scenery as the French; indeed, the Italians were the inventors and pioneers of scenic engineering; but no Italian opera ever attempts to describe in instrumental music the storms or earthquakes that may be taking place on the stage. Descriptive music in opera is purely French; Locke and Purcell made some attempt at it, but under French influences. The descriptive music of Weber and Wagner is derived from that of the French Revolution composers such as Méhul and Lesueur; there is hardly a trace of it in Mozart. As we shall see when we come to analyse *Idomeneo* and *La Clemenza di Tito*, the instrumental commentary may suggest the feelings of the characters, but hardly at all the visible or audible phenomena of nature. In *Idomeneo* we have a storm and the arrival of a monster; in *La Clemenza* a conflagration. One can imagine how Wagner would have described them in terms of the orchestra; Mozart is concerned only with the moral effect that they have on the characters of the drama. Nor must we expect from Mozart that philosophical attitude to the stage inaugurated by Beethoven and indefinitely extended by Wagner. Leonora and Florestan in *Fidelio* are not so much individual characters like Electra and Idomeneo as projections of Beethoven's own personality; Beethoven starts to compose an innocent French rescue-story and before he is halfway through the first act he is involved in a discourse on justice and liberty. Tristan, Parsifal, and the characters of *The Ring* are even more obviously projections of Wagner himself; we only perceive them through the smoke-screen of the orchestra, whereas with Verdi we realize at once that Falstaff is a character in his own (or in Shakespeare's) right. Verdi makes us feel that when Falstaff walks on to the stage his presence creates the music, causing the orchestra to sound as his own will causes his own voice to utter words and notes. It is Wagner's own thoughts and emotions which materialize dimly as the half-imaginary figures of his music-dramas, and even they cannot materialize except through the preliminary suggestion of the orchestra. With all this nebulous philosophizing—the reader is welcome to accuse me of it rather than Wagner—Mozart has nothing whatever to do. Perhaps he opened the door to it in *The Magic Flute*, but death cut him off before he could pass through it himself.

## 3

## IDOMENEO—I

MOZART left Paris in September 1778 and returned home by way of Mannheim as before. The attraction at Mannheim was, of course, the Weber family; Mozart had fallen violently in love with Aloysia, the eldest daughter, and hoped that the time had now come to make her his wife. But it was a different Mannheim to which he returned in 1778; the electoral court had been transferred to Munich, and with the court went most of the musicians and actors, including the Webers. He found an excuse for going to Munich in January 1779 and presented Aloysia with the finest of all the arias that he wrote for her—*Popoli di Tessaglia*; but she had changed her mind and would have none of him, although she kept the song, and was often associated with him musically in later years. It was a very discontented Mozart that settled down again to the drudgery of a cathedral organist at Salzburg. He hated the Archbishop, he hated the Salzburgers generally, and could find pleasure only in the society of his father and sister, though we may be sure that Leopold got on his nerves fairly often in spite of all his affection. The chance of writing a serious opera seemed further off than ever. The only break in the monotony of Salzburg life was the visit of Schikaneder's theatrical company, which performed Gebler's *Thamos, König in Ägypten*. Mozart took up the music which he had written for Gebler in 1773 and recast it with additions. The principal interest of *Thamos* for us is its connexion with *Die Zauberflöte*, and we must leave to a later chapter the story of Mozart's friendship with Schikaneder and his interest in Egyptian mysteries. *Thamos* was not a success. Mozart evidently set some value on the music, for he mentions it again in a letter to his father from Vienna in 1783: 'I am very sorry that I shall not be able to make use of the music to *Thamos*. The piece has a bad reputation, since it did not please and is not performed any more. It could only be performed for the sake of the music, and that is hardly likely—it is a pity indeed.'

Another dramatic work which must also be left to a later chapter is an unfinished German opera which appears to have been begun with a view to performance in Salzburg. The libretto was by the Mozarts' old friend Schachtner, to whom posterity is indebted for a good many reminiscences of Wolfgang's earliest childhood. This libretto has for the most part disappeared, and not even the title of it is known. The music has been published under the name of the heroine, *Zaide*. Nothing is known about the circumstances under which it was written, but since it makes no great demand on either singers or orchestra, we may well suppose that Mozart, driven to desperation by the dreariness of life at Salzburg, planned an attempt at organizing some sort of operatic performance with such modest forces as he could raise among his personal friends. The composition was probably interrupted by the invitation which he received in the summer of 1780 to write a serious opera for Munich.

Here at last, it seemed, was Mozart's great opportunity. The libretto was to be written by the Abbé G. B. Varesco, chaplain to the Archbishop of Salzburg, so that composer and poet might work together with greater facility. Unfortunately, the Archbishop's chaplain had no sense whatever of the stage. Mozart, as usual, left the greater part of the opera to be composed during the last few weeks of rehearsal, and then wrote from Munich to say that various scenes must be altered. Varesco was highly indignant at this mutilation of his masterpiece and insisted that if Mozart cut down his verses his drama should at least appear complete in print.

The general scheme of *Idomeneo, Re di Creta*, modelled on a French libretto by A. Danchet, set to music by Campra in 1712, might have provided excellent opportunities for a poet who understood the requirements of the theatre. Varesco had no doubt read his Metastasio, but he must have read him with the eyes of a sermon-writer, not those of a dramatist. Metastasio understood better than anyone that an opera libretto, even in the grand manner, must be concise and direct. Varesco is verbose and sententious; he never seems to have imagined for a moment what the effect of his lines would be when set to music and presented on the stage. He seems also to have been a very difficult and disagreeable person to deal with. Wolfgang never corresponded with him directly, but made use of his father as an intermediary; we gather from Leopold's letters that the reverend gentleman not only objected very much to making alterations, but expected to be paid extra for them, like a printer.

There were further difficulties with the singers. The title-part
was taken by the tenor Raaff, an excellent singer but no actor;
moreover, he was at that time a man of sixty-five. As might be
expected, he was only too glad to give Mozart the benefit of his
long experience of the stage—in other words, to obstruct the
young composer as much as possible whenever his genius led him
into unexpected paths of originality. Panzacchi, the other tenor,
was a decidedly good actor with some skill in singing, but as he
too was of senior standing he had to be given more opportunities
for display than were appropriate to the part of a mere confidant.
The worst stumbling-block was Dal Prato, who took the youthful
part of Idamante. 'My *molto amato castrato* Dal Prato', as Mozart
called him, could have given no trouble from being too old and
experienced, for he was a mere boy and had never been on the
stage before. His voice was either badly trained or not trained at
all, and he had no intelligence for music or for anything else.
Mozart seems to have shown endless patience in teaching him,
and we gather from his letters that he could suffer stupidity of
this kind better than the conceit of those who professed to be
connoisseurs. Luckily, the female parts were taken by Dorothea
and Elisabeth Wendling, who weie capable singers and gave the
composer no trouble.

The general outline of the plot is as follows: Idomeneo, King of
Crete, has taken part in the Trojan War, but for many years has
not returned home. He has already sent to Crete a number of
Trojan captives, including Ilia, daughter of Priam, who falls in
love with Idamante, the son of Idomeneo. Idamante returns her
passion, but this is not made clear to her for some time after the
opera begins, owing to the very involved language in which
propriety compels him to conceal his feelings. Moreover Ilia has
a rival, Electra, daughter of Agamemnon, who has taken refuge
in Crete after the murder of her mother. At the beginning of
Act I the returning fleet of Idomeneo is sighted and Idamante
celebrates the happy day by releasing the Trojan prisoners. Just
as the ships near the harbour a storm arises, and the King only
reaches safety by a miracle, having vowed in his distress to
sacrifice to Poseidon the first living thing that he meets on landing. Naturally, the first person he encounters is his own son,
whom he does not recognize, having been away some twenty
years. On discovering his identity, he does not dare tell him of
his vow, but hastens away, forbidding his son to follow him. The

act ends with a chorus and dance of the population welcoming the soldiers of Idomeneo.

In Act II Idomeneo attempts to evade his vow by sending Idamante to escort Electra back to Argos. This confirms Ilia in the idea that Idamante loves Electra, and increases Idamante's bewilderment at his father's strange conduct towards him. They prepare to depart, but another storm arises and a fearful monster issues from the sea, convincing the people that some particular person must be guilty of having offended the god. Idomeneo confesses himself to be the man and expresses his readiness to die. The act ends with the chorus fleeing in terror from the monster.

In Act III Idamante determines to kill the monster himself or die in the attempt. This leads at last to a clear understanding between him and Ilia, but their expressions of love are interrupted by the entrance of Electra, always wild with jealousy, and the King, who bids his son leave the island at once. The people of Crete, ravaged both by the monster and by a pestilence, come to demand the necessary victim, and Idomeneo is compelled to disclose the name of his own son. The high priest is preparing for the sacrifice, when news is brought that Idamante has slain the monster. None the less, he is prepared to be slain himself in fulfilment of his father's vow, and the devoted Ilia insists on taking his place. The difficulty is solved by the voice of an oracle which proclaims that Idomeneo is to abdicate and that Idamante, united to Ilia, is to reign in his stead. After a final outburst of rage from Electra, Idomeneo formally renounces the throne and Idamante is crowned amid general rejoicing.

Mozart's letters to his father show that he at any rate had a thorough sense of the stage. Any musician might have complained when the poet put 'asides' into arias or made the sense of one line run over into the next—faults more unpardonable in those days than now, since the normal structure of the eighteenth-century aria would be destroyed by irregular verse construction, and an 'aside', if occurring in an aria, might have to be repeated in an inconvenient and undramatic way. But Mozart saw more essential things than these. His technical ingenuity might easily have overcome the problems of musical structure, though probably his elderly and experienced singers would have resented anything that they had not been accustomed to for the last forty years; but Varesco's dramatic blunders had to be corrected without any attempt at compromise. Varesco let Idomeneo make his first

entrance scrambling up the rocks at the back of the stage after
the shipwreck; Mozart and Quaglio, the scene-painter, saw that
this was undignified and ineffective, and caused him to enter with
some of his followers, whom he dismisses a few lines later, in order
to be alone when he meets his son. This next scene had to be very
much cut down (and for modern performance it needs still further
cutting), since both Raaff and Dal Prato were such bad actors as
to make the long dialogue in *recitativo secco* utterly intolerable.
The same applied to the dialogue between Idomeneo and the
confidant Arbace at the beginning of the second act. For the
chorus 'Placido è il mar' Varesco had written several stanzas;
Mozart reduced them to one. Between the storm chorus and the
final chorus of this act he had put in an aria for Idomeneo; Mozart
saw that this would destroy the whole dramatic effect and insisted
on having only a short recitative. The same thing had to be done
in the third act; Varesco expected that Ilia and Idamante should
sing a formal duet when on the point of being sacrificed. Had
Raaff's advice been followed, we should have lost the most
beautiful number in the whole opera, the quartet in Act III;
the worthy tenor considered that its place would be much more
effectively filled by an aria for himself. It becomes evident that
Varesco's plan was to follow the formal system of Apostolo Zeno
and Metastasio—to divide the libretto into what Continental poets
call 'scenes' and end each 'scene' with an aria on which the singer
made an exit. This was really a very practical arrangement,
because it allowed the audience to applaud as much as they liked
without appreciably holding up the progress of the drama. Mozart
evidently saw the stage from the standpoint of Gluck and the
French librettists. The Italian *opera seria* generally made little
or no use of the chorus; for the French the chorus was an indispensable factor in serious opera, and its value was that it allowed
the composer to build up a massive climax of sound towards the
end of an act. The Italian opera never attempted this; at the very
end there is what is marked *coro* in the score (Handel's operas
show easily accessible examples), but *coro* in most cases means no
more than the principal singers joining for a short movement in
block harmony. The elaborate finale which we find in such operas
as *Le Nozze di Figaro* and *Don Giovanni* is ultimately derived, not
from serious opera, Italian or French, but from Italian comic
opera; it begins with the quarrelling scenes for two characters such
as we find in the comic episodes of Alessandro Scarlatti's operas,

and gradually increases the number of its interlocutors until there may be six or seven of them, with a corresponding increase in length. But it should be noted that this sort of comic finale is practically never choral, any more than it is in the majority of Handel's operas; the dramatic chorus is a purely French invention.[1] Varesco had evidently studied his Greek plays as well as his more recent models; his 'dramatic irony' and his 'recognition scene' are only too tedious a homage to the classics. But, like the very earliest Italian librettists, he followed classical tradition in assigning a really important dramatic part to the chorus, and Mozart was quick to take advantage of it.

It seems to have been Mozart's invariable practice—probably it was the regular practice of all operatic composers in those days —to compose about half of an opera on receipt of the libretto and to postpone composing the rest until rehearsals had already begun. Indeed, librettists were often dilatory and did not always give their composers a complete book of words at once. Singers, as all composers must have known by sad experience, were more likely to be troublesome than not, and Mozart spent much of his time in accommodating his operas to suit their requirements. The result of this system is that when we come to put Mozart's operas on the modern stage we find that in every one of them the later acts show evidence of alteration and patching, and the modern producer is confronted by the most curious problems in attempting to reduce them to some sort of dramatic unity and continuity. It was the third act of *Idomeneo* that gave Mozart the most trouble. Varesco seems to have been very vague about the changes of scene required. According to the score, there are three separate scenes: the royal garden, for the scene between Ilia and Idamante, the great quartet, and Arbace's soliloquy; then the exterior of the royal palace, for the High Priest's address and the chorus of Cretans; lastly, the exterior of the temple of Neptune, which apparently serves for the interrupted sacrifice, the outburst of Electra (although she ought to have the whole stage to herself) and the abdication of Idomeneo. From Mozart's letters it would appear that there was actually no change of scene at all at the first performance. Arbace sang his aria and in accordance with Italian operatic etiquette left the stage at the

[1] I am speaking here of opera in the eighteenth century; the functions of the chorus in French, Italian, and English opera of the seventeenth are too complicated a matter to summarize shortly in this place.

end of it; but Varesco directed him to be on the stage with Idomeneo at the beginning of the High Priest's address. 'How can he be there again at once?' asks Mozart. 'Luckily he can stay away altogether' (he has nothing to say in this scene) 'but in order to be on the safe side I have written a rather longer introduction to the High Priest's recitative.' The next scene presented a similar difficulty. 'After the chorus of mourning, the King, the whole people, and everybody all go away, and in the following scene stands the direction, "Idomeneo on his knees in the temple". That cannot possibly be so; he must come with a complete train; so then there must of necessity be a march there, and I have written a quite simple march for strings and two oboes which is played *mezza voce* while the King comes in and the priests prepare the things for the sacrifice; then the King kneels down and begins his prayer.' It must be remembered that in *opera seria* great personages were always expected to be accompanied by considerable trains of supers, and the huge size of Italian theatres required a good deal in the way of processions and so forth to fill the stage.

As regards change of scenery, scenes in those days could be changed very quickly and in view of the audience by the system of wings and a backcloth. The front curtain did not fall; it is difficult to establish the exact date at which the main curtain first fell at the end of each act of an opera. It is probable that in *Idomeneo* the main curtain never fell at all until the very end of the opera, judging by what happens on the stage; on the other hand, it seems certain that the act drop must undoubtedly have fallen at the ends of the acts in *Le Nozze di Figaro* and *Don Giovanni*, although one can point to comic operas by Leo and Pergolesi (about 1730–40) in which the elaborate finales are ingeniously planned so as to get the characters gradually *off* the stage (as well as *on*) leaving the chief *basso buffo*, generally the angry old man, to make his effective exit by himself. The wings were shifted by a mechanism under the stage which is still to be seen in a few old German theatres;[1] with one movement of a lever all the wings receded and another set were pushed forward; the backcloth would be drawn up on a roller at the bottom—it was not until about 1800 or later that backcloths could be lifted completely out of sight without rolling. On the English stage there was often no backcloth, but a pair of wide flats joining (or sometimes not

[1] It is—or was recently—in working order at Ludwigsburg near Stuttgart.

joining properly) in the middle. This system of quickly shifting
wings no doubt explains the changes of scene in the third act of
this opera, changes which become much more difficult under
modern conditions.

*Idomeneo* owes both its failings and its merits to the fact that it
is a mixture of two types of opera, Italian and French. Varesco
took a French libretto as his foundation and, probably without
considering dramatic effects at all, turned it into as close an
imitation of Metastasio as his dull brain was capable of conceiving. Mozart in setting it to music was French by deliberate
intention, but Italian by natural instinct. Modern audiences,
acquainted to some extent with the works of Gluck, are naturally
moved most by the French moments of the opera—that is, by
the great choruses, the instrumental marches and interludes, and
the noble accompanied recitatives, which are closely modelled on
those of *Alceste*. We require a greater effort to focus our minds on
the beauties of the Italian scenes. A modern audience has a
horror of *recitativo secco*, and well it may, if it knows it only as it
is delivered by our orthodox oratorio singers. It is an exclusively
Italian method of treating words. Purcell's dramatic recitatives,
whether accompanied or not, are always strictly rhythmical and
their rhythm is determined more by the normal rhythms of music
than by those of English prose or blank verse. Moreover, the
varying quantity of English syllables requires the composer to use
a variety of time-values, crotchets and semiquavers as well as
quavers, whereas Italian recitative seldom employs any unit
except the quaver. French recitative, depending on the natural
rhythms of French verse, utilizes the three time-values in even
more generous mixture than English, and with a style of declamation that is generally more excitable than our own. Italian keeps
to the quaver unit, although Italian verse is theoretically more
varied in quantity than French; in practice it means that the
singer is allowed a great deal more rhythmical latitude. Italian
critics always said that French opera consisted entirely of recitative, and it is a fact that the French *air* approximates closely to
recitative while the recitative itself tends to approximate to the
inflections and rhythms of the *air*. In Italian the contrast was
extreme, and it was only in rare moments of accompanied recitative that the Italians approached an *arioso*. As the Italian arias
were generally the expression of one single emotion, all the
dramatic element, by which I mean the interaction of one character

with another, to say nothing of the indispensable moments in which mere information has to be given to the audience, had to be expressed in *recitativo secco*; the more there was of these elements, the more recitative there had to be, and the more necessity there was for getting through it quickly. The Italian recitative, accompanied only by chords on the harpsichord, accomplishes this admirably, provided that the singers deliver it at the normal pace of speech.

The ordinary Englishman of to-day has probably begun his operatic education either with isolated songs from various operas, perhaps heard on gramophone records, or with musical comedies and light operas in which the business of the play, sentimental perhaps, but certainly not poetical, is carried on in spoken dialogue. He probably associates sung recitative exclusively with oratorio. But we must remember that opera originally began with recitative alone; recitative was the main, indeed the only, reason for its creation, and as late as the days of Pepys there was in England a positive craze for 'recitative musick'. This accounts at once for the survival of recitative in Italy down to our own day; it had become so established a convention that no Italian could conceive of spoken dialogue in opera, however closely the declamation of comic recitative must have approximated to it.[1]

Recitative of any kind, and *secco* all the more, must inevitably be boring in the extreme to audiences which do not understand Italian. It was often boring to the Italians themselves. Rousseau admits this in his *Dictionnaire de Musique*, although he shows his invariable enthusiasm for everything Italian and his contempt for everything French:

'Démosthène parlant tout le jour ennuieroit à la fin; mais il ne s'ensuivroit pas delà que Démosthène fût un Orateur ennuyeux. Ceux qui disent que les Italiens eux-mêmes trouvent leur *Récitatif* mauvais le disent bien gratuitement; puisqu' au contraire il n'y a point de partie dans la Musique dont les Connoisseurs fassent tant de cas et sur laquelle ils soient aussi difficiles. Il suffit même d'exceller dans cette seule partie, fût-on médiocre dans toutes les

---

[1] In the nineteenth century all German operas, such as *Der Freischütz* or *Fidelio* had to be provided with sung recitatives in place of spoken dialogue, when performed in Italian, whether at Milan, Paris, or London. For Weber's *Oberon*, composed originally to English words, Benedict wrote Italian recitatives for later revivals at Her Majesty's Opera; but to my astonishment, the Rome Opera revived it in 1938 with spoken dialogue. It was the first time that I ever heard spoken dialogue on the stage of an Italian opera house.

autres, pour s'élever chez eux au rang des plus illustres Artistes, et le célèbre *Porpora* ne s'est immortalisé que par-là.'

Whether Rousseau was well informed as to the last sentence may be doubted, but apart from this exaggeration he probably spoke the truth for his date (1768). Rousseau divided recitative into three categories—*récitatif* (i.e. *recitativo secco*), *récitatif accompagné*, which is much the same as *secco*, but accompanied by held chords played by the strings, and *récitatif obligé*, which is his name for the sort of accompanied recitative that was being developed about the middle of the century.

'C'est celui qui, entremêlé de Ritournelles et de traits de Symphonie, *oblige* pour ainsi dire le Récitant et l'Orchestre l'un envers l'autre, en sorte qu'ils doivent être attentifs et s'attendre mutuellement. L'Acteur agité, transporté d'une passion qui ne lui permet pas de tout dire, s'interrompt, s'arrête, fait des réticences, durant lesquelles l'Orchestre parle pour lui; et ces silences, ainsi remplis, affectent infiniment plus l'Auditeur que si l'Acteur disoit lui-même tout ce qui la musique fait entendre.'

This is the definition of a Frenchman with a passion for all Italian ideas; an Italian perhaps would hardly have admitted that an Italian could become speechless—or songless—with passion. And accompanied recitative (as we and the Italians called it), in the hands of a second-rate composer, soon became as dull and conventional as *recitativo secco*. In Germany it led to the practice—momentarily fashionable in Mozart's days—of what was called *Melodram*, an alternation of instrumental commentary with spoken recitation. German composers, perhaps influenced by this, and certainly influenced by their habitual tendency towards an instrumental rather than vocal outlook on music in general, were tempted to let the orchestra and singer carry on a sort of *stichomuthia*, monotonous in rhythm and really destructive of the dramatic effect for which it was intended. We see it in such composers as Holzbauer, but also in Gluck and occasionally even in Mozart himself.

The aria is another form which modern audiences, especially those brought up on Wagner, profess to find undramatic. Yet if they would confess the truth honestly, it is the arias, or the movements of aria character, which have secured the immortality of all the favourite operas. Historians reprint and reprint again the preface to Gluck's *Alceste*, but what draws the public to hear

*Orfeo* is the agreeable melody of *Che faro* and the dignified grace
of the ballet music. It is naturally difficult for us to put ourselves
back into the days of the Handelian *da capo* aria, but by the time
Mozart was a mature composer the *da capo* aria was completely
obsolete. As we shall see in the next chapter, the middle section
of the old ternary aria had been dropped and the first part of it
had been extended into something like what is called sonata-form.
That form had become the standard form for practically every kind
of music, vocal, dance, or symphonic, apart from the strict fugue, and
even fugues were often influenced by sonata-form in their construction. And by the time of Mozart the serious opera, thanks to Gluck,
had begun to absorb certain features of the comic opera, the most
important of which was the *rondo*, exemplified in *Che farò*, with
its threefold appearance of the initial simple tune. There is
another type which we find in the first air of Orpheus, alternating
three repetitions of a simple melody in 3/8 with two intermediate
*arioso* sections in 4/4; this is almost a throwback to the refrain-
recitative-refrain alternation of the well-known *Lamento* in
Monteverdi's *Arianna*. The plain *da capo* form is to be seen both
in *Orfeo* (Act III; aria of Eurydice) and even in the famous
*Divinités du Styx* of *Alceste* itself.

Still more troublesome to a modern audience are the long
instrumental introductions to many of Mozart's arias in his early
operas, especially those which make a *concertante* display of
individual instruments. One has to admit that Mozart sometimes
committed errors of judgement in his desire to please his professional friends. In the operas of Gluck the introductions are
often intensely expressive, and still more the little instrumental
solos, especially for the oboe, which enter into a sort of dialogue
with the singer in certain arias. Mozart is aiming at the same
type of expression, but he was a much more accomplished composer for the orchestra than Gluck, even at the age of twenty or
less, and he had had far more practice in the composition of
symphonies and concertos. This fluency and ease in purely
symphonic composition tempts him at once to combine the
spontaneous and perhaps even crudely expressive instrumental
solos of Gluck with the finished elegance of an instrumental
concerto, especially as he was often on terms of personal friendship with the players and took a pleasure in showing them off.
Add to that Mozart's incomparable 'Mozartian' (there is no other
possible epithet) grace of pure melody, and the whole aria, the

voice framed in its inseparable orchestral setting, becomes a display of serene and exquisite musical beauty that quite eclipses the human passion which it is primarily intended to express. In his later operas Mozart discarded these *concertante* accompaniments; the only later suggestion of them is in *Die Zauberflöte*, where the magic flute and the magic bells have to be played visibly by the actors on the stage and are integral features of the drama itself. But other composers, notably Méhul and Cherubini, continued systematically to show off the solo instruments in their operas; we find plenty of examples in Spontini and Meyerbeer, and in Donizetti and early Verdi as well; there was no doubt that audiences enjoyed them, as indeed they do still, if the virtuosity is sufficiently obvious.[1]

Lastly, we must in listening to *Idomeneo* try to forget the hurry of modern existence and surrender ourselves to a sense of leisure such as our ancestors were happily able to enjoy. Even at the first performance *Idomeneo* had to be cut down; but I cannot think that that audience was haunted all through the last act by the fear of missing the last public conveyance to Schwabing or the Isarthal. *Idomeneo*, perhaps better than any other opera, illustrates the fact that the course of an opera is like a stream running for long stretches in a narrow channel, hidden perhaps for moments underground, dashing suddenly over a precipice and at frequent intervals broadening out into a vast and tranquil lake. The forms are various which it presents, as are the types of landscape with which it is associated; nevertheless, broad or narrow, shallow or profound, it is always moving onwards and gathering force until it reaches its ultimate goal.

[1] For the sake of accuracy, I must not forget the *obbligato* for the *corno di bassetto* in *La Clemenza di Tito*.

## 4

## IDOMENEO—II

THE first thing that strikes us about *Idomeneo* is the nobility and dignity of its entire conception. The overture alone is enough to show the exalted view which Mozart took of *opera seria*, and never for a single moment in the whole opera does the composer relax his intense seriousness. Nor is *Idomeneo* merely a cold and stately succession of formal movements. That description might perhaps fit *La Clemenza di Tito*, the product of Mozart's last physical exhaustion, but never *Idomeneo*. In his early attempts at serious opera, Mozart had been more concerned with providing what his audiences and singers wanted, but he was now a man of twenty-five who had had enough experience of life to be able to enter intimately into the personalities of his stage figures. There may not be here the delicate psychological detail that we find in *Figaro* and *Così fan Tutte*, or the sublime naturalness and simplicity of *Die Zauberflöte*—these would both have been completely foreign to the general style of this opera—but there is a monumental strength and a white heat of passion that we find in this early work of Mozart's and shall never find again. *Idomeneo* is the first and last *opera seria* that represents the complete and mature Mozart. The modern student of Mozart has unfortunately very few chances of ever seeing *Idomeneo* on the stage, but without a careful and devoted study of this opera there can be no complete understanding of Mozart's other works, especially of his works for the theatre. The theatre is the sphere in which Mozart is most completely himself; his concert works—concertos, symphonies, quartets, and sonatas are all fundamentally evocations of the theatre. And in the theatre itself a thorough knowledge of *Idomeneo* is indispensable because it is the one opera which can really give us a standard of dignity and grandeur. People who regard *Figaro, Don Giovanni, Così fan Tutte* and even *Die Zauberflöte* as 'grand operas' simply do not know what they are talking about. If they had any understanding of *Idomeneo* they would be compelled to admit at once that the four popular operas are not only packed with trivialities, but that there are hardly any isolated numbers among them which could possibly claim affinity of style to that of *Idomeneo*. I write the word 'triviality' with deliberation; Mozart's trivialities, even those of *Die Zauberflöte*, are his own, and they are appropriate enough to their situations as well as the delight of all who listen to them. Even the most solemn numbers of *Die Zauberflöte* could hardly have found a place in *Idomeneo*; they breathe the atmosphere, not of classical tragedy, but of religious mysticism.

It is absurd to talk of Mozart as a man who remained a child throughout his life, or as a polite composer who never sought to do more than please an aristocratic audience with a succession of graceful frivolities. Only in one sense can he be said to have been a child all his life, and that was in his passionate seriousness, in a complete self-abandonment to emotional impulse which at times (as in the Requiem) becomes positively hysterical. Both Stendhal, in his *Letters on Haydn*, and William Gardiner, his English translator, writing in the second decade of the nineteenth century, compare Mozart to the painter Domenichino.[1] Stendhal, indeed, says: 'As for Mozart, Domenichino should have had a still stronger cast of melancholy to resemble him completely.' In another passage, he expresses the view that to him, contrary to the opinion of all Italy, the first serious opera extant is not Cimarosa's *Gli Orazii e Curiazii*, but either *Idomeneo* or *La Clemenza di Tito*. We must make certain allowances for the romantic sentimentality of an Italianate Frenchman in the age of Byron, and we shall see, when we come to consider *Don Giovanni*, that even the early nineteenth century is not always a safe guide to the interpretation of the music of the eighteenth. But there can be no doubt, even to a cold-blooded critic of the twentieth century, about the intensity of emotional expression in such works as the G minor quintet, the fugue in C minor for two pianofortes, the fantasia in F minor for a mechanical organ, and many of the later pianoforte concertos, to mention only such works as are fairly well known to modern amateurs. These, it is true, are almost all products of Mozart's later life, but we can trace the germs of this characteristic emotionalism even in some of the often despised sonatas for pianoforte, as the following examples will show:

---

[1] To realize Stendhal's point of view one must remember that he compares Pergolesi and Cimarosa to Raphael, Handel to Michael Angelo, Haydn to Tintoretto and Gluck to Caravaggio.

The player, I need hardly say, must remember to consider the music as the recollection of a singer's voice.

It is, however, to *Idomeneo* that we must turn to see the young Mozart at his greatest heights. The opening bars of the overture indicate at once the heroic plane on which the drama is to move. It starts with a dignified assertion of the chord of D major, but the frequent use of minor harmonies, and a second subject in the minor instead of in the more usual major mode of the dominant, prepare us for tragedy. The construction is further unusual in that the second subject is not repeated after the return of the first, and its place is taken by a long and expressive coda based on a short and characteristic theme which reappears several times in the later course of the opera. It enters first near the beginning of the overture—a cry of flutes and oboes against the creeping approach of the strings:

A *crescendo* of the same two themes leads to the return of the first subject, and the coda, first on a dominant pedal, then on a tonic pedal, develops it still further, supported by a bold progression of harmonies:

The throb of the double-basses dies away, the strings and the solitary oboe settle quietly down in a couple of sighing phrases on to the chord of D; the curtain has risen, and we see Ilia, a lonely little figure in the vast perspectives of the royal apartments. We must imagine the scene not after the latest archaeological excavations, nor even as it might have been visualized by Leighton or Alma-Tadema, but in that delightful mixture of modern and baroque which we find in the frescoes of Tiepolo. Her first phrase shows us her character:

Ex. 5.

Quan - do av - ran fi - ne o - ma - i? l'as - pre sven - tu - re
*When will my woes be end - ed? when shall I cease to*

mi - e? I - lia in - fe - li - ce!
*suf - fer? O wretch-ed I - lia!*

Andantino.

Gentle and yielding by nature, she tries by the recollection of her race's overthrow to work herself up to the desire of due revenge upon Idomeneo and the Cretans. But other feelings are at work upon her; she cannot forget the King's son Idamante, who saved her from drowning. She has never dared reveal her love, and she fears that his is given to Electra, the terrible woman—a Greek too—who knows no obstacle to the fulfilment of her desires. She feels herself surrounded by enemies, torn by conflicting emotions; the recitative rises to its climax, and the two conventional chords of cadence by a stroke of genius fall into place as an integral part of the introduction which leads straight into her aria. Varesco has here provided ideally suitable words for the composer's purpose:

'Padre, germani, addio!
Voi foste, io vi perdei.
Grecia, cagion tu sei,
    E un greco adorerò?
D'ingrata al sangue mio
So che la colpa avrei;
Ma quel sembiante, oh Dei!
Odiare ancor non so.'

The lines fall into two groups, forming the 'first and second
subjects' for the aria; and while the second quatrain divides into
two long and flowing phrases, the first is broken up into several
short exclamations. The dramatic advantage is obvious to any
reader without the music; the musician will see how such short
groups of syllables, depending for their expression, not on continuous melodic beauty, but on well-marked rhythm and contour
of declamation, provide the composer with opportunities for free
harmonic treatment, and consequently for a heightening of the
emotional effect, when the subject returns according to rule
halfway through the aria. If the reader will have the patience to
analyse this one aria in detail, both from the technical and the
emotional standpoint, he will understand the formal principles
on which the expression of any aria of Mozart is based. We must
note the dramatic outburst on the word 'Grecia', and observe
how its effect is intensified on its reappearance by the movement
of the harmony; we must note also the recurrence in the bass of
the figure quoted in Ex. 3 and 4 at the words, 'D'ingrata al
sangue mio'. There is no reason to call it a *leitmotiv* or give it a
Wagnerian name; we shall find it in various places, always at
moments of tragic import, and generally connected with the love
of Ilia and Idamante.

Ilia's aria, it will be noticed, has no introduction beyond a few
chords, no instrumental interludes and no coda; it is not until the
action has got well under way that Mozart broadens out his arias
into a more imposing symphonic construction. Ilia has hardly
had time to finish her concluding shake before she sees Idamante
approaching and breaks off into recitative. Idamante speaks to
his attendants as he enters, and the accompanying chords are
purposely disconnected from what precedes. But as soon as he
turns to speak to Ilia, the chords fall again into the key in which
she left off. Mozart has done his best to make the two characters
distinct—Ilia passionate and agitated, Idamante self-possessed

and dignified. He indicates his admiration in rather formal terms; Ilia thinks it her duty to repel advances from her hereditary enemy. Idamante replies in a rather conventional aria; but if he here presents himself as a soprano hero of eighteenth-century opera, we must admit that he is at any rate as fine a specimen of the tribe as we shall be able to find.

The Trojan prisoners are brought in; the fleet of Idomeneo has been sighted, and the King's return is to be celebrated by their liberation and their reconciliation with their captors. Trojans and Cretans unite in a chorus of rejoicing, to the indignation of Electra, who enters at this moment. She is interrupted almost at once by the news, brought by Arbace, that Idomeneo has been shipwrecked off his own coast. Idamante, Ilia, and the people hasten to the shore, while Electra remains behind to give vent to her fury. She fears that if the King is dead there will be no authority to prevent his son from giving his hand to the despised captive, the daughter of Priam.

Mozart had a great admiration for Gluck's *Alceste*, and *Alceste* is obviously the model for many scenes in this opera; but for the recitatives and arias of Electra Gluck could provide no example— the wildest outbursts of Armide and the Furies seem almost childish in comparison with the utterances of Electra's savage jealousy. Mozart adopts Gluck's declamatory, almost barbarous and unvocal style of phrase, but whereas Gluck's rhythm nearly always becomes monotonous, and his management of purely musical technique often fumbling and helpless, Mozart's complete mastery of symphonic resources enables him to pile up his phrases to a well-defined climax, to contrast the brute force of diatonic harmony with the anguished wail of gliding chromatics. This first aria of Electra's is in the usual binary form; but how unearthly is the effect when the first subject returns, not, as we should expect it, either in the tonic, D minor, or even in the dominant or relative major, as often happens, but in C minor, a completely foreign key, a whole tone lower than the tonic! The transposition is dictated by the compass of the voice; but it also brings about a dramatic effect—the darkening of the key-colour, and the additional step upwards in the sequence of piercing cries. The climax is thus much more powerful than it would have been if it had started from the tonic, with two steps instead of three.

The binary form of aria, based like a sonata movement (in fact, the instrumental sonata is derived from it) on two subjects of contrasting character, often exposed the weakness of an inferior composer, while to a clever and ingenious one it offered great opportunities for dramatic effect. It is obvious that if the second subject suits a certain type of voice when it appears first in the dominant, it will probably be either too high or too low when it returns according to rule in the tonic. A careful composer will at least take the precaution of designing his second subject so as to be more effective in the later key; but the man of genius, such as Mozart, will be able to make it appear thoroughly effective on its first entry and then enhance its expressiveness by some unexpected modification of it when it comes back the second time. The casual listener may not notice these things and may even resent having them pointed out to him; but the serious student of music ought to realize that conscious ingenuities like these are essential to sound workmanship and also serve a genuinely poetic purpose.

Electra leaves the stage at the end of her aria, but the storm of her passions grows in the orchestra to the representation of a real tempest. The scene changes quickly and we are transported to the seashore. The music runs on without break into a chorus of men imploring the mercy of the gods, echoed by a distant chorus of shipwrecked sailors, the first accompanied by restless figures for violins, the second by smooth scale passages for wood-wind. Four horns are also employed in this scene; it is very rare to find more than two in any opera of this period. And the four horns interlock so ingeniously that it is a matter of great difficulty to reduce them to two for the resources of a small theatre. It was Varesco's intention that the storm should be made to subside by the appearance of Poseidon himself, Idomeneo's appeal to him being indicated in dumb show. Mozart, possibly on the advice of Quaglio the scene-painter, disregarded this direction altogether; the few bars between the end of the chorus and Idomeneo's landing would hardly give time for a representation of this kind. The division of the chorus into two groups was entirely Mozart's idea. The storm is short, but very vividly depicted; as the chorus disperse and the waters subside the King lands from a boat with his attendants, whom he dismisses at once. No sooner has he explained in a soliloquy the nature of his unfortunate vow than Idamante enters. It is this dialogue between father and son which Mozart felt obliged to cut down owing to the incompetence of the singers.

The scene is certainly long, but Leopold was perhaps not in the wrong when he urged Mozart not to shorten it, since in the hands of good actors the gradual development of the dramatic situation would be extremely moving. In Handel's *Jephtha* the unhappy father sees his daughter approaching, drives her from him at once, and is obliged to explain everything at once to the other characters. Varesco here lets the audience into the secret at once, but keeps the other characters in the dark until the end of the opera. He seizes very happily on the fact that Idomeneo and Idamante have not set eyes on each other since the son was an infant. They meet as strangers, and the sight of even an unknown man is enough to make Idomeneo begin to realize the horror of his position. Idamante laments the loss of his father whom he believes to be drowned; Idomeneo feels himself more and more drawn to the youth, until he suddenly discovers him to be his own son. The emotion is too strong for him (it is at this moment, of course, that Mozart brings in the orchestra to accompany the recitative); he cannot help revealing himself, although he realizes, directly the words have passed his lips, that by doing so he has cut off his only chance of saving his son's life. He turns in horror from his embrace and warns him never to approach his presence. Idamante is distracted. No sooner has he found his father than he has lost him; what can have caused his anger? Can it be Idamante's love for the Trojan captive? The aria with which the scene closes is more characteristic than that which Idamante sang at the beginning of the act; the feeling expressed is more human and direct, and Idamante has by this time become a more definite individual.

The Cretan warriors disembark to a brilliant march followed by a long choral movement headed *ciaccona,* a sudden transition from Italian to French procedure, for the *chaconne* is a favourite device in the operas of Rameau and Gluck for bringing an act to an animated conclusion. The whole was probably designed less as a formal dance than as a representation of a magnificent religious ceremony.

The second act opens with a scene between Idomeneo and Arbace. The King discloses his secret and the wise councillor advises that the prince be sent to some other country; Idomeneo decides to evade his vow by letting him escort Electra back to Greece. This scene was put in mainly for the benefit of Panzacchi, who sang the part of Arbace, and ends with a very conventional aria for him. He then departs to make the necessary arrangements, and Ilia enters. Idomeneo assures her of his friendship and of his desire to make amends for all that she has suffered. In an aria of singular beauty she replies that she has found a second home in Crete and a second father in the King. Mozart, like Beethoven, had very definite associations with certain keys. All readers will recall that for Beethoven C minor seems to have a peculiar character of its own—we need only think of the three pianoforte sonatas in that key, the violin sonata, the early pianoforte concerto, the early string quartet and above all the C minor symphony. For Mozart the best-defined keys are G minor and E flat major. The two great symphonies may illustrate them; we may note also the string quintet and pianoforte quartet in G minor, as well as Pamina's aria in the second act of *Die Zauberflöte*, while for E flat major we may study the overture and concluding chorus of that opera, the violin sonata, the Countess's first aria in *Figaro* and the slow movements of the symphony and the quintet in G minor. These last show the two keys in close conjunction, and it is the same sort of connexion that we can observe between this aria of Ilia and that with which the opera opens. When she first appears, gentle and unhappy, conscious of her utter weakness in the presence of an overmastering fate, Mozart chooses for her the key of G minor; he takes E flat major to paint the same gentle heroine after Idomeneo has given her a sense of serenity and confidence in the future.

For the sake of his friends in the orchestra Mozart has accompanied this aria with four solo wind instruments. The aria itself is an exquisitely finished piece of construction, besides being full of real poetic feeling. But considered as an episode in an opera, the long introduction, necessary as it is to introduce the *concertante* soloists, and still more justified by the new interest given to their phrases in conjunction with the voice, is something of a hindrance to the drama. No doubt Mozart did not feel the inconvenience of this as we do to-day, and his audiences would be quite accustomed to it. Yet Mozart knew how to turn the most unexpected things to dramatic account. As Ilia leaves the stage, Idomeneo ponders on her words; it flashes upon him that she loves his son, that her love is returned, and that Poseidon will have not one victim, but three, since neither he nor Ilia can bear to live without Idamante. His recitative is marked *in tempo dell' aria*

and opens with a theme that we have just heard played by the
solo wind instruments, given now to the strings.

Its harmony is given a more threatening colour, and the change
of rhythm points to a relation with the theme that we have already
noted in the overture and in Ilia's first aria.

Idomeneo's aria which now follows is the great show-piece of
the opera, in which Raaff was to do his best to live up to the
triumphs of his youth. The old gentleman expressed his complete
satisfaction with it, and Mozart writes that he was so much in love
with it that he sang it over every night before he went to bed and
every morning as soon as he woke up! He had indeed reason to
be pleased with it, for it was evidently composed with the greatest
care and ingenuity; it is designed to show off Raaff's technique
and style to the best advantage without ever putting too great a
strain upon him. The modern opera-goer has little chance of
hearing any aria of this type sung as it ought to be. This particular example is not incredibly difficult; it seldom requires even
the ordinary high G, its *coloratura* is smooth, and it lies very
conveniently and easily for the voice. But *coloratura* for men has
gone out of fashion, thanks to Wagner, and, thanks to the late
Madame Patti, *coloratura* for women has become associated with
the frail type of heroine rather than the heroic. In the eighteenth
century and especially in the earlier half of it, the grand period of
*opera seria*, *coloratura* was almost invariably heroic in character
and chiefly associated with the *castrato* singer who represented
the great figures of antiquity. Donizetti's Lucia is paired off with
a flute. Handel's heroes compete with a trumpet. The heroic

aria for Idomeneo comes in very appropriately at this point in
the drama. Idomeneo has escaped the storm at sea, but Poseidon's
anger still threatens him and a far worse storm is raging in his
own breast; Mozart's music might at first sight seem to express
anything but such a situation. Yet Mozart knows what he is
doing; first he is giving every satisfaction to old Raaff and Raaff's
faithful admirers in the audience, and he is also expressing the
indomitable dignity, pride, and courage with which the King
faces his tragedy.

A short scene for Electra follows; the prospect of happiness has
made her forget the past, and she presents herself almost in a new
character. Words and music seem here indeed incompatible.
Varesco has surpassed himself in obscurity; Mozart has simply
seized the dramatic situation and, since no one could possibly
follow the sense of these words when sung, not even an Italian of
Varesco's own day, he is content to provide Electra with an aria
of unexpected serenity and charm. It is accompanied by strings
only, so elegantly and ingeniously treated that we never become
tired of them. The technical reason for this becomes at once
apparent; there is no coda to the song, but on the last note of the
voice there break in, on her ear as well as on ours, the strains of
a distant march calling her to the harbour to embark for Greece.
As with the more familiar case of the wedding march in *Figaro*,
Mozart makes this one start in the middle, returning later to what
is really its beginning. It is played first by wind instruments, very
softly, so as to sound a long way off; Mozart has been saving them
up for this unexpected effect. While they are playing, the strings
rest and have time to put on mutes, for they join the wind in
repeating the march. The brass and drums are muted already;
but Mozart wishes the march to grow louder and louder until the
scene has been changed, and therefore he provides further rests
now and then during which both brass and eventually the strings
too can remove their mutes so as to open the new scene with a
sonorous burst of music.

We are at the harbour again; the ship is waiting and the people
invite Electra to embark with the well-known chorus, the one
movement of the opera generally familiar in this country, *Placido
è il mar, andiamo*. This is one of Mozart's great moments of
cosmopolitanism; we have a stage picture worthy of Rameau, an
Italian melody that makes us visualize the scene as a mixture of
Naples and Venice designed by Tiepolo, with that German sense

of pure musical thought that gives the whole its unearthly and magical beauty.

Idomeneo enters with Idamante; he and Electra take leave of the King in a trio. Electra has a strange sense of foreboding; Idamante is parting from Ilia without having dared to reveal his love, and he is still conscious of the shadow between him and his father. Idomeneo can only hope against the inner conviction of his conscience. With a sort of half-frightened resolution the music quickens up as they move towards the ship, when suddenly without warning there comes the crash of a storm. A monster rises from the sea; the terrified populace know then for certain that they are under a curse of heaven. 'Who is the guilty one?' they ask, and three times the scream of the wind instruments echoes the cry. Idomeneo fearlessly admits that the guilty man is himself; he is willing to offer himself as a sacrifice, but he knows that it will not be accepted. He does not tell the people of his vow; in fact, he completely ignores the people at this moment and addresses himself directly to the god. It is not until the next act that the people themselves begin to take action and insist that the King should take some step to relieve their agony; at this juncture fear is their only emotion. Idomeneo defies the god and accuses him openly of injustice. The orchestra rises to an outburst of rage; Idomeneo knows that he is blaspheming, but love is more to him than religious obedience. The people, understanding nothing, disperse in terror as the storm continues, and the curtain falls on Idomeneo standing at bay before the angry sea.

The third act begins with a soliloquy of Ilia. As with Jephtha's daughter in Handel's oratorio, her character can be seen developing in the course of the opera; the same thing happens to Pamina in *Die Zauberflöte*. Ilia in the first act was a Trojan princess bound in duty to hate her Cretan captors; in the second she began to realize that Idomeneo and Idamante might bring her more happiness than she had ever known in Troy. We see her now given up wholly to her love. She has not yet declared it, but she has admitted it to herself, and it now possesses her so completely that she has forgotten to be jealous of Electra. There is a maturity and emotional depth about this aria which was not present in those of the preceding acts; the best illustration of it will be seen in the concluding phrase of the second theme, beautiful enough in its simple form, but made more intensely human by the warm chromatic harmonies which accompany its repetition.

Ex. 7.

che    mi  ser - bi   il   cor........   fe - del,
bid   him  ev - er   be   true.....   to   me,

che    mi  ser - bi   il   cor........   fe - del. ............
bid   him  ev - er   be   true ......   to   me. ............

This is the purest Mozart; no Italian composer would ever have thought of so delicate and so poetical an effect; or if anyone had vaguely imagined the feeling which it expresses, he would have interpreted it by a melodic variation of the vocal line, not by a change of accompanying harmony.

Idamante enters to take leave of Ilia; he is going out to slay the monster, perhaps to be slain himself. Ilia is led to declare her love, and the inevitable duet follows, the best part of it being the slow introduction in which we hear yet again an allusion to that theme of the overture which recurs so frequently throughout the opera. The lovers are interrupted by Idomeneo, followed closely by Electra. Once more Idamante begs his father to tell him the reason of his estrangement; once more Idomeneo hints darkly at the wrath of Poseidon, and bids his son depart never to return. The thought begins to take shape in Ilia's mind that it is she who has aroused the anger of the god by winning the love of Idamante. Electra realizes that her last chance has gone, and her smouldering hatred begins to glow once more till it finally bursts into flame. Idamante must go. Ilia, in a burst of emotion, says that she will go with him; he gently puts her from him—

> 'Farewell, live happy!
> Remote, alone, I'll wander,
> Seeking for death in exile
> Till he releases me.'

Here follows the great quartet, for which Raaff wished an aria
for himself to be substituted. Mozart, however, seems to have
thought it the best movement of the opera, and we may well agree
with him, for it is perhaps the most beautiful ensemble ever composed for the stage. Electra's fury, Idomeneo's despair, the tender
resignation of the youthful lovers, all find utterance in it, now
sharply individualized, now grouped in contrasting pairs, now
joining all together in the united expression of that experience
fundamental to tragedy, the sense of oppression by mysterious
powers beyond human control, beyond even human approach.
The strictly symmetrical form gives the movement its classic
dignity, and the necessity of considering the compass of different
voices leads to modulations of startling expressive power. At the
end a series of hurried imitative phrases piles up the harmony to
a climax; then after a pause Idamante repeats his first words—
*andrò ramingo e solo*—his voice breaks, he turns away, and the

- rir, mio ben, vogl' i - o,          Deh   res - ta, o ca - ra,      e vivi in
*die, dear love, with-out thee.*          *Nay,   let me  go,....   once more fare -*

pa - ce, ad - di - o !          *Allegro.*
*well,    live happy!*

An - drò...... ra -
*A - lone ....    for*

- min - go e          so - - - - - - - lo,
*e'er       I'll       wan - - - - - - - der,*

orchestra in a few sobbing phrases brings the movement to a pathetic close.

We may well give a moment's consideration to the aesthetic and dramatic significance of such movements as this. The first composer to unite voices in a formal movement at a moment of high dramatic tension seems to have been Alessandro Scarlatti.[1] But his successors had little sense of its value; Handel shows only rare examples, and the Neapolitan composers made use of the device mainly for comic effects. Average singers, as we can see in the case of Raaff, were not in favour of an episode which demanded so much preliminary rehearsing and gave so little opportunity for individual display. This type of ensemble, which I have called the 'ensemble of perplexity', must be carefully distinguished from the concerted finale which we find at the end of an act, especially in comic operas, as in *Figaro*, *Don Giovanni*, and *Così fan Tutte*; but later composers were not so clearly aware of formal constructive principles as Mozart was. The best modern example of a serious ensemble is probably the quintet which precedes the death of the heroine in *La Traviata*. It is a device peculiar to the musical drama; the action is suspended and a tableau is formed which can be maintained just so long as the composer can sustain the musical interest. It is often a great relief, after the struggle of rising to a dramatic climax, to reach a sort of plateau, a point of repose at which we may contemplate the dramatic situation, as it were, from outside. Opera has indeed had a recognizable influence on later dramatic technique; there are moments in Goldoni's comedies which at once suggest an operatic ensemble such as he might have planned for an opera libretto, and the operatic ensemble is certainly the origin of the *tableau* which is the characteristic invention of Pixérécourt, the creator of French melodrama. There is another value in the operatic ensemble, and that is the peculiarly musical one, quite impossible to describe in words, of four or five solo voices joining together in harmony. Verdi is one of the greatest masters of operatic ensemble and at the same time perhaps the worst of all offenders in this respect when he has no scruple (as elsewhere in *La Traviata*) about making three male characters sing three completely different sets of words expressing completely different emotions to one and the same bass part, and

[1] See my *Alessandro Scarlatti*, London, 1905, and two papers by me on 'Ensembles and Finales in Eighteenth-century Opera' in the *Sammelbände der Internationalen Musikgesellschaft*, Leipzig, 1910.

that the sort of bass that would most properly be given, not to a human voice, but to a bombardon.

With Idamante's silent departure this scene should properly end, and Varesco intended a change from the garden to the front of the palace, where Idomeneo should be discovered seated on a throne, attended by the High Priest, facing the assembly of the people. But there was some misunderstanding between Mozart and Varesco, due probably to the claim of Panzacchi, the second tenor, to be allowed an important aria in the character of Arbace. Mozart, always desirous of obliging his singers, here provides Panzacchi (who indeed deserved it on grounds of merit) with an elaborate recitative of outstanding beauty, followed by a very dignified aria. The audience of those days may have listened to these with pleasure, but for a modern revival one can only recommend their excision. The scene forms a lamentable anticlimax to the quartet and delays the action of the drama just at the moment when it is urgent to quicken the pace.

The change of scene is ushered in by a short instrumental movement of changing paces separated by pauses; it obviously represents some sort of action in dumb show, but we have no stage directions. Probably the people, who are supposed to be dying of plague—such of them, at any rate, as have not already perished in thousands 'buried before they died within the ample and filthy stomach' of the sea monster, as Varesco elegantly expresses it, make some sort of a demonstration before the King; after this the High Priest begins his allocution, evidently inspired by the similar scene in Gluck's *Alceste*, the same orchestral figure appearing in both operas. If Idomeneo was Italian in Act II, here he is completely French. We see before us not the individual singer but the whole stage picture, the High Priest threatening (priests in opera are always odious, and Mozart certainly had the best of examples before him every day), the King confessing before an excited and agonized crowd of suffering people. The people have come into the play; they form the last great force which has been brought into action against Idomeneo's irresolution; it is they who compel him to fulfil the horrible sacrifice which he has so long tried vainly to escape. Yet they suffer as much as he does at the thought of what is to take place; only at the end of the choral movement, as they disperse, a sudden little gleam of sunlight makes itself perceptible for a moment in the orchestra, before the priests enter to a subdued and solemn march. The King begins the ceremony with a fervent prayer to Poseidon, answered in a strange monotoned chant by the ministrants at the altar. The scene must have been still fresh in Mozart's memory when he composed *Die Zauberflöte*.

A sudden burst of trumpets and a shout of voices is heard outside. The prince has killed the monster and the people hail their deliverer with rejoicing. Idomeneo's gloom only deepens—by the slaughter of the monster, sacrilege has been added to sin. Idamante is led on in triumph; but he has heard the story of his father's vow at last and now of his own accord presents himself for sacrifice. The long recitative which follows is masterly both in declamation and in characterization; the serene yet youthful gravity of Idamante suggests what Tamino was to be in later years. It contrasts well with the passionate outbursts of Idomeneo, for it is this rash impulsiveness of Idomeneo that has brought about the whole tragedy, and it is the self-control, the childlike simplicity and directness of Idamante that is to save the tragedy from its dreadful completion.

Here again Varesco's unpractical libretto caused trouble. Idamante must naturally sing an aria before he is slaughtered, and when the self-sacrificing Ilia rushes in at the critical moment and insists on dying instead of him, their affectionate protestations must be elegantly disposed into a formal duet. Mozart cut the duet out at once, but he set the first aria—*No, la morte io non pavento*; after rehearsal he cut this out too. On 18 January 1781 he writes to his father:

'The rehearsal of the third act went off splendidly. People think that it is far superior even to the other two. Only the libretto is far too long, and consequently the music is too, as I have been saying all along; so Idamante's aria must be cut out—and in any case it is not in the right place there. But the people who have heard the music are groaning over this, and still more over the fact that Raaff's last aria is cut too; but one must make a virtue of necessity.'

It is interesting to observe how Mozart himself seems to make no complaint at all about the cutting of his own music; he thinks only of the stage and the general dramatic effect. Beethoven would have been furious and obstinate to the last ditch if a bar of his own music had to be cut, regardless of what the singers might think. Mozart is his own physician and surgeon.

As soon as Ilia has thrown herself at the foot of the altar a mysterious noise is heard and the oracle delivers judgement. Here again Mozart writes: 'The speech of the oracle is also much too long; I have shortened it, but Varesco need not know anything about this, since everything will be printed as he wrote it.' There are in fact three versions of the oracle's pronouncement, one obviously much too long, another cut down to the shortest possible limits. It is not clear which version was actually performed.

Following the example of Gluck, Mozart accompanies the oracle with trombones. Since the days of Rossini and Spontini, the trombones have been regarded as normal constituents of every orchestra, to be used mostly for adding to the total strength of a *fortissimo*. But just as we find Alessandro Scarlatti using the horns as exotic instruments only to be used on the stage itself for special local colour, so we find that in Mozart's day the trombones are always regarded as being outside the normal orchestra, and generally suitable only to the expression of the supernatural. To Mozart's audience, the mere sound of trombones would be unfamiliar, unless they had heard them in a church; a modern audience derives the same sort of impression from the unexpected sound of an organ in the theatre.[1] As Meyerbeer and Wagner use the organ in the theatre, so Mozart uses the trombones in all his operas exclusively for religious and mysterious effects. It is in the same sense that we must understand Beethoven's trombone parts, especially in the C minor, Pastoral and Choral Symphonies; their function there is always to emphasize the essentially solemn and religious character of the movements in which they are introduced.

A curious and very impressive feature of Mozart's trombone chords accompanying the oracle is the grouping of them in threes, each with a pause and a *crescendo* and *diminuendo*; this is what Italian singers called the *messa di voce*. It seems to suggest the miraculous animation of the statue of Poseidon, as its huge breast of bronze begins to heave, and then, after the climax of its utterance, lapses once more into rigidity when the god no longer breathes into its nostrils the breath of life. And as the statue ceases to breathe, those who stood breathless before it come back to life, with little broken phrases of wonder and joy.

[1]This statement is now out of date, as the cinema has now given the organ a popularity which it had not enjoyed since the days of tavern organs in the sixteenth and seventeenth centuries. It is curious to note that organs on a large scale are often to be found in Canadian hotels.

The simplicity of the treatment is most moving; an aria or even a more developed recitative would be out of place. It is only Electra, her hopes now shattered for ever, whose jealousy and rage must find their last volcanic outlet, her harsh voice breaks in rudely on the holy calm of the others as she calls upon the Furies to let her share the torments of Ajax and Orestes; she rushes away, the orchestra closing with a passionate distortion of the sighing phrases which ended the overture, and we see her no more.

The last scene opens with a solemn and gracious phrase in the violins, alluding once again to that characteristic figure of the overture which we have so often noticed in the course of the opera; it is imitated canonically by each of the other strings in turn. Idomeneo ascends his throne for the last time and addresses his assembled subjects. He presents to them formally their new ruler, with his royal bride, in a dignified recitative, the accompaniment of which is, as often happens, skilfully developed out of the figures of the introduction. *O Creta fortunata! O me felice!* Happy Crete, happy Idomeneo! His conscience is at peace, his mind unburdened, and he feels like some old tree when the spring has wakened it into leaf once more.[1] And so he takes leave of his

---

[1] This beautiful aria had to be cut out at the first performance owing to the great length of the third act.

people, while they celebrate the accession of Idamante and Ilia with songs and dances. The High Priest, it may be noticed, takes no part in this scene; after the capitulation of the oracle—no doubt stage-managed by himself—he probably thinks it would be more prudent to keep out of the way.

## 5

## DIE ENTFÜHRUNG AUS DEM SERAIL

D URING the eighteen months that elapsed between *Idomeneo* and Mozart's next opera three important events took place in the composer's life—his rupture with the Archbishop of Salzburg, his separation from his father, and his betrothal to Constanze Weber. His marriage indeed took place within a month of the production of the new opera. The real turning-point in his career was, however, *Idomeneo*; it was *Idomeneo* and the success which it encountered that made Mozart realize fully that he was a composer with a future before him and a right to his own independence. Hitherto he had borne the tyranny of his father and the insults of the Archbishop as best he could; after *Idomeneo* he could endure neither any longer.

The Archbishop summoned him from Munich in March 1781 to attend upon him in Vienna with the rest of his suite. Mozart was in no mood to return to the humble position of former days. At meals he had to sit with Ceccarelli the *castrato* and Brunetti the violinist, above the Archbishop's cooks, but below the Archbishop's valets: 'Well! I could almost think I was in Salzburg.' Ceccarelli's society could be just tolerated, but Brunetti was uneducated and mannerless; Mozart was ashamed to be seen about with them.

Schubert would have felt more at home in such company, at any rate if the Archbishop had brought any maidservants with him. Mozart was soon able to make friends among the music-loving nobility of Vienna, but the Archbishop put every possible hindrance in his way and would not even allow him to play at a concert for the benefit of musicians' widows. He was obliged to give in, however, since Starzer, the organizer of the concert, appealed to Prince Galitzin, who, with other members of the aristocracy, could put pressure on the Archbishop to change his mind. Mozart played for the widows and naturally made a huge success; but his right reverend lord absolutely refused to let him give a concert on his own account. He sent in his resignation, but it was not accepted, for the Archbishop expected that Leopold would prevail upon his son to withdraw it. Wolfgang had no intention of withdrawing it, and after much trouble in obtaining an audience of the Archbishop he was finally kicked out of his ante-chamber by Count Arco, the chamberlain.[1]

Old Leopold (he was now sixty-two) was very much shocked and grieved, not so much at the treatment to which his son had been exposed as at his son's resentment of it. He was quite content to be a servant of the Archbishop himself and he could not understand why Wolfgang should be so rebellious. He was inwardly convinced that what really governed his son's actions was a love of pleasure and dissipation, and that once set free from paternal discipline he would merely lead a life of self-indulgence and extravagance. Wolfgang, being at last independent, had to find new lodgings, so he went to live with his old Mannheim friends, the Webers. The father was dead, and since Aloysia was now engaged at the Opera and married to the actor Lange, the widow and her three remaining daughters had settled in Vienna. The voice of scandal soon made itself heard and even reached as far as Salzburg; Leopold, always ready to believe anything to the discredit of his own son, returned to his letters of reproach. Wolfgang had already thought it advisable himself to look for lodgings elsewhere. He protested that he had no intention of marrying any of the Weber daughters, whatever people might say, and begged his father not to listen to malicious gossip. This was in July. But by December he had changed his mind and was definitely engaged to the second of the three, Constanze. Leopold had always viewed the Webers with suspicion, even in their Mannheim days, and was convinced that they were bent on entrapping Wolfgang into marriage. Wolfgang was naturally indignant at this, and furious at hearing that Peter von Winter had called Constanze a *Luder* and had in fact asserted to Leopold that she was Wolfgang's mistress. Winter had never forgiven Mozart for scoffing at the pompous manners and clumsy playing of the Abbé Vogler,[2] of whom he was a very devout pupil. If we read Wolfgang's letters to his father we can have not the least reason to doubt that his attachment to the girl was absolutely sincere and genuine—we know that he was devoted to her all his

[1] The English translatrix of Jahn discreetly says that Count Arco 'pushed him towards the door with his foot'.

[2] Robert Browning's *Abt Vogler*.

life—or that his conduct had been as chaste as he protests.[1] But chastity, male or female, was never very much of a Viennese virtue, and it is clear that his intimacy with Constanze had led people to take it for granted that he had seduced her, otherwise her guardian would hardly have forced him to sign a document promising either to marry her or to pay her an annuity of 300 florins. No sooner was the guardian out of the house than Constanze snatched the paper from her mother's hands and tore it up. Mozart must have remembered this episode when he was composing Le Nozze di Figaro.

Leopold for a long time withheld his consent. Old Madame Weber was intemperate in her habits, as Wolfgang had to admit, although he said that he never saw her absolutely drunk. Constanze's own behaviour sometimes shocked even Wolfgang himself, who considered that a girl who was engaged to be married ought to be more careful.[2] Constanze was indeed very far below the level of her husband. Even during their engagement he describes her in no very attractive terms. 'She is not ugly, but certainly anything but beautiful—her entire beauty consists of two little black eyes and a good figure. She is not clever, but has sound common sense enough to be able to fulfil her duties as wife and mother.' Her spelling was indeed deplorable, and she felt quite ashamed of herself when she had to write to her future father-in-law. She was said to be a good housekeeper, and she had need to be, considering the circumstances of her married life; her common sense may have fitted her for the duties of a wife and mother, but her health certainly did not. Madame Weber's tendency to drink seems to have increased rapidly during the year 1782, and Constanze was treated very badly by her. The performance of Mozart's new opera in July brought him and his affairs into some prominence, and the situation was not improved

[1] 'In the first place I have too much religion; secondly, too much altruism and sense of honour to seduce an innocent girl; and, thirdly, too much horror and disgust, revulsion and fear of diseases, too much care for my own health to play about with whores. So I can swear that I have never yet had any doings of this sort with any female. If I had, I would not conceal it from you, for to err is only human nature' (Mozart to his father, Vienna, 15 December 1781).

[2] Mozart scolded her severely for having allowed a gentleman to measure her calves in a game of forfeits. That might be all very well for a child, but not for a grown-up woman, still less for one who was engaged to be married. If she could not avoid paying the forfeit (she had apparently excused herself on the ground that in society one must do as other people do), she ought to have taken the tape from the gentleman and measured her calves herself (letter to Constanze, 29 April 1782).

by his attempt to place Constanze under the protection of Baroness von Waldstätten, a lady of kindly disposition and more than doubtful reputation. Madame Weber threatened that if the Baroness did not give up her daughter she would send the police for her. This was towards the end of July. Leopold, despite all Wolfgang's entreaties, still refused his consent, and refused to take any interest in the success of *Die Entführung*. Finally, Wolfgang took the matter into his own hands and married Constanze on 4 August, his father's consent reaching him, as a matter of fact, a day after the ceremony. Leopold further informed him that since he himself could not expect to be helped by his son out of the awkward position in which he had placed himself on his son's account, Wolfgang was therefore not to expect any financial assistance from him either now or in the future.

Such were the domestic difficulties with which Mozart had to grapple during the composition of *Die Entführung aus dem Serail*. Needless to say, it has often been maintained that Constanze Weber was the inspiration of the opera, since Constanze is also the name of its heroine; but if Mozart had not been so much distracted by the painful circumstances of his engagement, he might very possibly have produced a work that was better planned and more consistent in style.

The Emperor Joseph II had been seized with an enthusiasm for developing the national drama, and had begun in 1776 by doing away with the old system of letting the Imperial Theatre to private managers; he established it as a court and national institution. The movement had been a pronounced success; the theatrical company included various names that are now famous in the history of the German stage, and with the co-operation of eminent authors both as playwrights and critics the Viennese public were gradually educated up to a high standard of appreciation and interest in the drama. The next step was to nationalize the opera. The old Italian opera and ballet were abolished and in February 1778 the *National-Singspiel*, as it was called, began its career with a little one-act comic opera by Umlauf, *Die Bergknappen*. The members of the company were almost all actors rather than singers, and the repertory consisted mainly of translations from French and Italian comic opera. Perhaps for these very reasons the *National-Singspiel* prospered, and eventually a company of genuine German opera-singers was assembled. German comic opera had hitherto been limited chiefly to North Germany; it was really the northern composers who founded that school of German song which culminated in Schubert and Brahms. But the northerners never found much appreciation in Vienna, and their singers too were considered too 'Lutheran' for an audience which from geographical and historical causes had always been much more under Italian influences.

The moment could hardly have been more favourable for Mozart. He had hoped to get *Idomeneo* performed in German, but this plan fell through; *Zaide*, the unfinished score of which he had brought with him, was apparently condemned on account of its libretto, although the plot of *Zaide* was actually much the same as that of the opera he was now about to write. But it showed at any rate what he could do, and the inspector of the German opera, Gottlob Stephanie, always known as 'Stephanie the younger', promised him a libretto of his own. Stephanie and his elder brother were at this time both well known on the Vienna stage. The elder was a sound actor and a writer of some merit; Gottlob, who had lived an adventurous life, was a notoriously untrustworthy character—'the evil genius of the Vienna stage, envious, avaricious, restless and quarrelsome'.[1]

This libretto, called at first *Belmont und Constanze*, was not an original work; it was adapted with slight alterations from a libretto by one Bretzner, who had written it only that same year for the composer André. In those days librettos seem to have enjoyed no copyright. Bretzner was very indignant at the alterations made by Stephanie and Mozart and published a protest in 1782 against the bad verses which they had inserted in it. But he had no very sound claim to originality himself, for his play was imitated from an English comic opera, *The Captive*, performed in 1769 with music by Dibdin and others; and this in its turn had been adapted, probably by Isaac Bickerstaffe, from Dryden's play, *Don Sebastian*, as the English libretto admits. Another English play with songs, *The Sultan, or a Peep into the Seraglio*, by Bickerstaffe (Drury Lane, 1775), contains scenes between a custodian of the harem called Osmin and an English lady called Roxelana. This play had been adapted from the French of Marmontel. Besides these, there were various Italian plays and comic operas on similar subjects.

The plot of the opera as finally set by Mozart is as follows.

[1] *Allgemeine Deutsche Biographie.*

Act I: Constanze, a Spanish lady, has been captured by the Pasha Selim, who wishes to make her his wife. Her Spanish lover, Belmonte, has discovered her whereabouts through his former servant, Pedrillo, who has also been captured by the Turks and is now head gardener to Selim. Belmonte hastens to her rescue and first encounters Osmin, head of the Pasha's household, who is very suspicious of him, as he is a friend of Pedrillo; Pedrillo has aroused Osmin's jealousy with regard to Constanze's maid, Blonde, an English girl. Pedrillo presents Belmonte to Selim as an architect, and, despite the protests of Osmin, he is admitted to the palace. Act II begins with a scene for Blonde and Osmin in which the lady insists on being treated with the respect due to her nationality. Selim renews his advances to Constanze, even threatening her with torture; she again refuses. Pedrillo reveals to Blonde that Belmonte is planning to rescue her and Constanze; he then proceeds to make Osmin drunk, after which the ladies return to the stage for a quartet. Act III begins with the elopement, which is intercepted by Osmin and slaves. The Pasha, on discovering that Belmonte is the son of his worst enemy, determines to set an example of magnanimity, and sends all four prisoners home, the opera ending with a quintet and chorus in praise of his generous action.

The original libretto was no more than a play with songs. The entire action of the play took place in spoken dialogue and every song might have been omitted without damage to the drama. This was the general principle of comic opera in the earlier years of the eighteenth century in all countries, for even if the Italians sang their operas all the way through, the dramatic action took place in the recitative and not in the musical movements. Even as late as Cherubini's *Les Deux Journées* the necessary explanations are spoken; but it is in the French Revolution operas that we first see the beginnings of dramatic development in the course of a movement. It is obvious that the dramatic interest of a play will generally depend on some complication of intrigue, and the more complicated this intrigue is, the more explanation will be required at the *dénouement*, the point at which the knots are finally untied; the more complicated the explanation has to be, the more obviously it must be made in plain speech or at most in very plain recitative. Some of the ensembles and finales in Mozart's later operas seem to give the impression of carrying on the drama; but if we consider the amount of dramatic action in comparison with the length of the musical movements we shall find that the action represented is extremely small; the bulk of all these movements is occupied with the mere expression of feeling.

Mozart felt from the first that an opera, comic just as much as serious, must be a continuous piece of music as far as possible. He had no intention of following the example of popular composers like Hiller and André, who merely provided trivial ditties that had no real connexion with the drama. For him an opera was always a 'music-drama'. His letters about this very opera leave no doubt on this point.

'In an opera the poetry must be the obedient daughter of the music. For why do the Italian comic operas succeed everywhere? with all the wretched nonsense of their librettos—even in Paris, as I saw myself? Because the music has the upper hand completely, and people forget everything on that account. And so an opera ought to succeed all the more when the plan of the piece has been well worked out, and the words written simply for the music, without putting in words or whole stanzas that destroy a composer's entire idea just for the sake of a miserable rhyme.'

Another letter shows how he set to work to get the play modified to suit his ideas.

'The opera began originally with a soliloquy for Belmonte, and I asked Herr Stephanie to make a little arietta out of it, and also that instead of the two chattering after Osmin's song there should be a duet. . . . Osmin in the original libretto had that one song to sing and nothing else, except in the terzetto end of Act I and the finale. He has therefore been given an aria in the first act, and will have something in the second. I have given Herr Stephanie the aria complete, and most of the music was ready before he knew a word about it.'

Stephanie must have found Mozart a thorough nuisance, for he was always wanting to have the libretto altered, or even altered it himself when he considered Stephanie's language unsuitable for musical setting. The result was an opera which is a succession of masterly and original numbers, but taken as a whole has no unity of style. German critics would no doubt maintain that *Die Entführung* is just as popular as *Figaro* or *Don Giovanni* and probably more popular than *Così fan Tutte*; but although I cannot bring forward any statistics, I can only state from my own experience that *Die Entführung* during the last fifty years has been very seldom performed, even if it is performed oftener than *Idomeneo* and *La Clemenza di Tito*. It requires singers of exceptional compass, but so does *Die Zauberflöte*, which is quite definitely a popular opera, even in Germany; if singers exist for the one, they can sing the other. German critics have also insisted vehemently on the importance of *Die Entführung* as being essentially a German opera. To this matter of nationalism in opera I shall return later; the real fact is that for various reasons *Die Entführung* is singularly difficult to make convincing on the stage.

The opera begins with a bright and cheerful overture, to which triangle, big drum, and cymbals give a conventional but picturesque 'Turkish' colour. In the middle of it there is a slow movement in the minor mode; the overture then returns to its first subject and passes without stopping into the arietta for Belmonte mentioned in the letters just quoted. This arietta is more or less a major version of the minor movement in the overture. It is quite short and makes an admirable opening to the drama. Belmonte has travelled to Turkey in search of his captive beloved, and is now standing in the garden of the Pasha Selim, in whose harem she is confined. Osmin, whom we might describe in Biblical language as 'chief butler' to the Pasha, is standing on a ladder gathering figs; he begins to sing to himself about the best way to make sure of one's wife. Belmonte tries to speak to him, but he takes no notice and goes on singing until Belmonte bursts out with some annoyance. A duet follows; Belmonte asks first if this is the house of Selim and then if he can speak to Pedrillo, formerly his own servant, now Selim's gardener. Osmin is in a very bad temper; he hates Pedrillo because Pedrillo is always running after Blonde, whom Osmin desires for himself, and he does his best to get rid of Belmonte. The duet is an admirable piece of comic music, more or less in the Italian *buffo* tradition, but it also has curious anticipations of *Die Zauberflöte*. Whether Mozart consciously remembered this former German opera of his when he was composing his last opera one cannot attempt to guess; but throughout *Die Entführung* we shall find several scattered moments that remind us of Monostatos and Papageno, as well as a few that suggest Tamino and Pamina. A good deal of the resemblance is due simply to the metrical structure of the libretto, which is often exactly the same as in *Die Zauberflöte*. Moreover, once we begin to look for anticipations or resemblances, we can just as easily remind ourselves of *Figaro* and *Don Giovanni*, and at a few moments of *Idomeneo* as well. These similarities are not of any vital importance, but they are helpful to anyone who wants to make a really careful study of Mozart, as they may give us some indication of the way in which his subconscious mind worked. They may also have a dramatic value; they may show us, for instance, that Osmin has something in common both with Monostatos and with Don Giovanni too.

After a short dialogue which tells us nothing more than that Osmin cannot bear the sight of Belmonte, Osmin breaks into an aria of considerable length. It is a masterpiece of comedy, with its two codas separated by a few spoken words, the singer's anger and malignance rising in grotesque vehemence; but we see at once that Mozart has already yielded to his besetting temptation —the tendency to make all his arias too long. This tendency in fact becomes more and more disastrously pronounced as this opera proceeds. We shall find indications of it again in *Così fan Tutte*, but there it is less obvious and there is more justification for it. On the other hand, it is to be observed that in *Don Giovanni* Mozart is much more concise, perhaps more consistently so than in any other opera; and that, of course, at once explains why *Don Giovanni* holds the attention and keeps the spectator strung up and excited the whole way through—a quality for which *Don Giovanni* is almost unique among operas of all periods.[1]

Osmin leaves the stage; Pedrillo enters, recognizes his master, and proposes to introduce him to the Pasha as an architect, as the Pasha has the craze of an eighteenth-century German princeling or archbishop for building palaces and laying out gardens. This is quite the appropriate moment for Belmonte to sing an aria of the devoted and adoring type, just as Tamino does when he first sees the portrait of Pamina. But Tamino gets through his devotions in half the time. Like Sarastro, the Pasha arrives supported by a chorus, who sing his praises with very effective local colour. With the Pasha is Constanze; they have just come back from an outing on the water. Selim, again like Sarastro, says that he will not force her to love; but he ardently desires to make her the first favourite among his wives. This sentiment is conveyed in plain prose; Selim never sings at all throughout the

---

[1] The only other opera which seems to me to share this peculiar quality is *Il Trovatore*.

whole opera. Constanze, however, requires a full-dress aria to tell him that she is already pledged to someone else. During this song, according to the stage direction, the Pasha walks rapidly to and fro; we can hardly be surprised, if we try to put ourselves in his place, but if we have to stage-manage the opera, we shall certainly not allow him to set such a bad example to the audience. The aria is in the grand manner, with copious *coloratura*. If the singer is equal to her task we shall no doubt listen to her with admiration, but all the same we shall have to admit that the aria is on the long side, and, worse than that, it has the leisurely quality of a concert aria without the tragic depth of feeling which justifies the length of such arias in *Idomeneo*. After the aria, Constanze leaves the stage just as she would in an opera of Metastasio; Pedrillo presents Belmonte to Selim as an architect and Selim takes a fancy to him at once; but Osmin, as soon as the Pasha has gone in, prevents the two from entering. This provides a little trio to bring the act to an end. It is a very spirited piece of Mozartian music, but much too self-consciously developed. If it was a purely instrumental concert piece, we should admire its economy of material and its ingenious development of two or three short and incisive themes. But on the stage this means that two or three short exclamatory phrases are repeated and repeated over and over again. The words will not bear it, all the less since they in every case suggest stage action. In some theatres we may see the three men stand perfectly still throughout the trio, performing perhaps a little stage business as the curtain falls on the instrumental coda; in others, if there is a modern-minded producer, there will be a continuous battle spread over a hundred and thirty bars. It may be argued that the finales of the Italian comic operas are far longer; but then far more people take part in them and far more real drama is unfolded on the stage.

Act II introduces us to Blonde, the English waiting-woman, who starts off with a very attractive little song; the part was sung by Therese Teyber, and Mozart has done his best to show off her exceptional high compass. She has evidently been having some trouble with Osmin, who now takes up the quarrel again in dialogue; a duet follows. It is a little on the long side, but so spirited and amusing that we should be sorry to have it shortened. The arrangement of the next few scenes is confusing, and they have been treated in various ways. Constanze enters and sings a very beautiful and expressive recitative and aria, recalling

Belmonte and her happiness with him, and deploring her enforced separation. The aria bears a remarkable resemblance to the aria of Pamina—*Ach, ich fühl's*—in the second act of *Die Zauberflöte*, all the more so as both are in the key of G minor; but, as with Tamino, Pamina takes very much less time to pour out her griefs. The Pasha enters, and again presses his suit, this time with some peremptoriness and the definite threat of torture. Constanze seizes on his words—*Martern aller Arten* (tortures of every kind)—and embarks on an enormous aria which is by many connoisseurs regarded as the main feature of this opera. It ought never to have been put into the opera at all; it is completely a concert aria, written solely to please the singer, Madame Cavalieri, and would have been out of place in any opera on any subject.

Considered simply as a piece of concert music and as a display piece for a *prima donna*, it is magnificent, and its splendour is enhanced by its construction as a sort of concerto for four solo instruments, flute, oboe, violin, and violoncello. They develop a long and elaborate *concertante* introduction and enter into brilliant and ingenious conversation with the singer all the way through. Donald Tovey pointed out many years ago that the form of Mozart's pianoforte concertos is derived from the Italian operatic aria, the solo instrument taking the part of the voice; here we see an operatic aria deliberately constructed on the model of an instrumental concerto. On the stage it is simply impossible. The most obvious criticism to make is that it follows directly, separated by only two or three short sentences of dialogue, on the previous long recitative and aria for Constanze; one can only imagine that either the one or the other aria was in practice omitted. What makes this great aria ludicrous on the stage is the modern practice, initiated by some over-ingenious German *regisseur*, of filling out the sixty bars of leisurely introduction by making Selim go through an elaborate conversation with Constanze in the gesture-language of the classical ballet, as if they were both of them deaf mutes. It is often solemnly protested by these producers that Mozart's music really does mean all that these gestures are supposed to convey; but the modern interpretations of Brahms's symphonies as Russian ballets are plain common sense compared to these pantomimic absurdities. Besides, what can Selim and Constanze possibly 'say' to each other in gesture during these sixty bars beyond what they have already made

perfectly clear to the audience in the previous two sentences of
spoken dialogue?

After the aria Constanze, of course, leaves the stage. Selim,
left alone, recovers his voice and speaks the following soliloquy:

'*Selim.* Is this a dream? Whence does she derive all at once the
courage thus to oppose my wishes? Well, what threats and
prayers cannot bring about, cunning must accomplish.'

This cryptic sentence suggests that some new intrigue will be
developed in the third act; but the crisis of the elopement takes
place perhaps before the Pasha has had time to think out how his
cunning is to be employed. Blonde now gets another pretty little
aria, more or less in rondo form; the rondo was a favourite form
for Italian comic opera, the point of it being that it started with
a very simple little tune that anyone could remember and repeated
it at least twice again, if not more. This is followed by a very
similar aria for Pedrillo, another rondo, but more military in
style, with trumpets and drums. A German critic has suggested
that this 'military' effect is all intended satirically, Pedrillo being
a prototype of Leporello; and it seems to be an axiom of German
operatic sociology that a manservant is *ipso facto* a coward. There
is, however, nothing in the libretto to indicate that Pedrillo is
deficient in courage. The battle to which Pedrillo alludes is,
however, merely his intention of making Osmin drunk, and he
wins it without any difficulty. The little duet *Vivat Bacchus* is
a masterpiece, and well on the short side for once. Pedrillo pushes
Osmin into his house, and Belmonte at once enters. Pedrillo tells
him that Constanze is coming at once; he anticipates her arrival
with an aria rather like *Il mio tesoro* in *Don Giovanni* but more of
the rondo type in the extreme simplicity of its initial tune,
although it is not treated in rondo form. Constanze enters and
here begins the great quartet which ends the act. Each pair of
lovers falls into each other's arms; then there is a moment of
suspicion on the part of the men as to whether the women have
been faithful. Blonde boxes Pedrillo's ears (*cf.* Susanna and
Figaro), Constanze protests with tearful indignation, and all four
join in a curiously solemn little passage of block harmony, after
which the movement proceeds to the end in the conventional style
of a finale. There is an interesting section in which the men beg
for forgiveness while Blonde sings a lively and teasing counterpoint against them in 12/8. Sullivan must have known this

quartet, for he does the same thing in *The Gondoliers*; but Mozart never repeated the device, though he might have found many opportunities for doing so.

In the original libretto Act II ended with a song and the quartet came at the beginning of Act III. Mozart, writing to his father, calls it a quintet; but the only quintet in the opera is the *vaudeville* at the very end. Some of Goldoni's comic opera books have ensemble movements at the beginning of an act, and even some of his plays open an act with a group that suggests a musical ensemble. It was Mozart who insisted on transferring this quartet to the end of Act II to make a finale. It is not very suitable for a finale, but Mozart has worked it up to the conventional noisy end; 'noisy end' is his own expression about the terzetto in Act I, and he says that an act must always end with as much noise as possible in order to make the audience applaud. In the quartet the situation is very much the same as in the second act of *Figaro*, where the Count, after a scene of furious jealousy, begs for forgiveness and is reconciled to the Countess; but in *Figaro* this moment of affection is quite short and very soon interrupted by the entry of Figaro, which begins the real business of the con-certed finale. Here the reconciliation is the end, and it makes a very poor curtain; obviously Bretzner was right and the meeting of the lovers for the first time should have led on to the concerting of the plot for their escape—it is not an end, but a beginning. One can only pity the singers (especially Constanze) who have to take part in it; they repeat *Es lebe die Liebe* interminably, and the soprano part remains for several pages in the uncomfortable region between D and high A—indeed, mostly on the three highest notes. Mozart is always spoken of as one of the very few com-posers who knew how to write for the voice; but in his ensembles he is ruthless to his sopranos and when setting German words shows no consideration at all about difficult vowels and consonants.

The events of the third act remind one of *The Barber of Seville*, and as Beaumarchais is known to have taken his idea from the old Italian comedy of masks, we may well assume that a frustrated elopement by a ladder, with a magnanimous forgiveness to make a happy end, was a favourite device of the theatre. The scene is the outside of the Pasha's palace, with a view of the sea in the background—time, midnight. Belmonte begins with a long aria; it is Mozart at his loveliest, but exceedingly florid; it requires an immensely accomplished *coloratura* tenor to do it justice. Pedrillo

enters with a ladder, but must first serenade Blonde as a
signal. He sings three verses of a ballad which has a curious
modal character; it might be Neapolitan, but is probably intended
to suggest a Spanish and Moorish atmosphere. It is interesting to
compare this stroke of real genius with the trivialities provided
for the same situation by the three other composers who set the
same libretto.

The elopement is frustrated by Osmin; all this scene is in spoken
dialogue with a great deal of comic business on the stage. Finally,
the guards take the four lovers into custody and Osmin sings his
great song of triumph. For this song the words seem to have been
written by Mozart himself. It is a typical *buffo* song, except that
it makes a great display of the singer's lowest notes; Osmin is in
fact a much more exacting part than that of Sarastro, and in this
respect can be compared only to some of the low bass parts in the
operas of Berlioz, Halévy, and Meyerbeer. The scene changes and
the lovers are brought before the Pasha, who discovers that
Belmonte is the son of a man who had once done him irreparable
injuries. Belmonte and Constanze are then conveniently left alone
to sing a long recitative and duet expressing all the proper sentiments of resignation, courage, and devotion. The recitative, which
is almost more of an *arioso*, is deeply moving; the duet is a superb

piece of music, but enormously long for the type of opera in which it occurs. Those who regard *Don Giovanni* as a tragic opera and *Die Zauberflöte* as a 'grand opera' should try to consider them in relation to *Die Entführung* and *Idomeneo*. The situation of Belmonte and Constanze at this point is not unlike that of Tamino and Pamina before they pass through the fire and water, with this difference: that Belmonte and Constanze are supposed to be real people in a story that might conceivably be true, while Tamino and Pamina are never anything but characters in a mystical allegory. The unreal couple get through their business as quickly as possible, but with a simplicity and directness of expression that creates in us a feeling of profound sincerity and truth. The real couple, on the other hand, present themselves with every conceivable artifice of vocal virtuosity. If the duet were sung with the accomplishment and assurance that it demands, it would be a supremely beautiful piece of music, and although it could never give the impression of truth or sincerity except in the *arioso* and in certain isolated phrases of the *andante*, its masterly construction and craftsmanship could easily make us indifferent to those realistic virtues. It is much more tragic than anything in *Don Giovanni*, as well as much more ample and grandiose in style; at the same time it never quite reaches the monumentality of *Idomeneo*.

The opera now comes to its expected happy end. Selim returns and informs the lovers that he will set an example of magnanimity; a ship is waiting and they can all go home at once. Osmin objects to the departure of Blonde, whom he considers his own property; the Pasha tells him that if he insists, he will only have his eyes scratched out. The last words of the spoken dialogue will give the reader a very happy idea of its general literary level:

'*Osmin.* Poison and daggers! I am ready to burst!
*Selim.* Compose yourself! Those whom one cannot win by beneficence it is best not to detain by compulsion.'[1]

Here follows the *vaudeville*—that is, a finale in which each character sings a verse to the same tune followed by a refrain in chorus. It was a fairly common ending to French comic operas. Beaumarchais's play *Le Mariage de Figaro* ends with one, and so does Rossini's *Barbiere*; it also forms the conclusion of Gluck's

---

[1] English translation by the Rev. J. Troutbeck.

Italian *Orfeo* and is amplified in his French *Orphée*. Mozart expands the form very ingeniously; after Belmonte, Constanze, and Blonde have each sung a verse (Pedrillo is not given one) Osmin takes up the tune, but has to alter it on account of his compass and then extends it by a return to the outburst of fury which concluded his aria in the first act. This makes an admirable exit for him, after which the lovers join for a few bars of block harmony to observe that nothing is so ugly as revenge and that forgiveness is the sign of a great mind. This reminds us at once of the similar moral statements that are so frequent in *Die Zauberflöte*. Constanze then makes what the old French composers would have called a *petite reprise*, repeating the last four bars of the vaudeville tune, echoed by the others, after which the full chorus sings the praises of the Pasha, as in the first act. These two choruses are so much alike in style that one might easily think them identical; as a matter of fact, they have only one single bar in common.

*Die Entführung* is a jumble of incompatible styles. Mozart was unfortunate in having such unusually accomplished singers at his disposal, for they had all been trained to Italian opera and had achieved their reputations in that form of art. With his invariable readiness to oblige, he provided them with songs that were so much outside the scale of German *Singspiel* that the characters in the opera lose all individuality, with the exception of Osmin. The other four are simply *prima donna*, *soubrette*, first tenor, and second tenor. It is only for the short moment of the *arioso* of the duet in Act III that the noble pair become at all human. Are the characters in *Idomeneo* any more human? They are far more remote, because they are tragic heroes of antiquity. But their very names are enough to give them reality; they belong to the Homeric world, and Mozart has only to re-create them. Belmonte and Constanze are mere puppets; even if their story were a true one they exist only as characters for a comic opera. Osmin stands out alone; he is as complete a personality as Verdi's Falstaff. The unfortunate Pasha simply does not exist at all. A few critics seem to have imagined that Mozart deliberately deprived him of song for some special purpose; that is inconceivable—we cannot compare him with the dumb heroine of Auber's *Masaniello*, who carries on all her conversation in the language of the ballet. It was quite usual in old French comic opera for actors to take part who could not sing; in Gaveaux's *Léonore* (the original of *Fidelio*)

Pizarro never sings at all. But the airs of the French operas were always on a much smaller scale than those of the Italian, so that the difference was not so marked.

That modern critics in Germany should insist on the essentially 'German' character of *Die Entführung* is only natural. In all countries, even in our own, we find the same tendency to regard nationalism in music as a merit, with very little serious analysis of what really constitutes a 'national' type of music. For generations English people have been attracted by folksong of all nations except their own; the craze for Scotch and Irish songs in the days of Purcell was probably no less a delight in the exotic and picturesque as the later admiration for Italian, Bohemian, or Russian folk-tunes, or the interest that some of us take now in Indian or Chinese music. Towards the end of the last century it was discovered that England itself possessed a store of folksongs; they were assiduously collected and for a generation or so this movement had a very fruitful influence on the serious output of English composers. The folksong movement was certainly a landmark in our musical history; but it seems fairly clear that it is by now a thing of the past. It may be that the next generation of English composers will have absorbed it subconsciously, just as the German composers did their folk-music a century ago or more, with the result that to many English musicians these wretched trivialities have become 'classical' through the fact that we meet with them at odd moments in the works of Beethoven or Schubert. But there is another aspect of nationalism which we must take seriously in Germany as in all other countries—the national qualities that are subconscious and indefinable. Here they can only be suggested and scantily illustrated.

The fragments of *Zaide* that have survived show another jumble of styles, but the isolated numbers are interesting as experiments. Consider this example:

Ex. 12.
Andantino.

Flutes, Bassoons *sotto voce* and Strings.

No Italian could have written it; no Italian would have wanted
to obtain that peculiarly delicate intimacy of expression which is
its distinguishing feature. It reads more like chamber-music than
like opera; but it would certainly be suitable for a rather sentimental type of *Singspiel* in a small theatre. The same can be said
of this second extract:

Ex. 13. *Tempo di minuetto grazioso.*

This again is like chamber-music in the exquisite craftsmanship of the string parts and the melodious movement of the bass. The vocal line is melodious too, but extremely simple, and its simplicity follows the typically German metre of the words; it even recalls some of the little secular songs of J. S. Bach. And there is the strangest suggestion of Bach in the *arioso* of Constanze in Act II of *Die Entführung*:

'Was ist der Tod? Ein Uebergang zur Ruh,
Und dann an deiner Seite, ist er Vorgeschmack der Seligkeit.'

('What then is death? The door that leads to peace;
With thee to stand beside me, 'tis a foretaste of blessedness.')

The words might have come from a church cantata; how they ever came into the libretto of a Viennese comic opera is beyond guessing. But the notes which Mozart writes for them might have come from Bach too. It was a long time before German opera ever arrived at any sort of real stability of style. Not even Mozart was destined to achieve perfection; *Die Zauberflöte* laid firm foundations, but considered as a complete work it stands as definitely apart from the general operatic history of Germany as does *Der Ring der Nibelungen*. The fault lay not so much with the German composers as with their librettists. The poets had no idea of how to lay out a libretto and the composers seem to have been unable to give them any instructions. Schubert was hardly a man of letters, but Weber and Schumann were both writers of notable ability; yet Mozart, whose literary output was restricted to his private letters, had more practical common sense and literary sense too when it came to remodelling a libretto. All the same, there can be no doubt that the libretto of *Die Entführung* was the very worst that he ever had to set to music, and the whole story of Mozart's operatic life is a synopsis of what perpetually happens always and everywhere in the operatic world— making alterations in a hurry at the last moment. Nobody could think Mozart a great composer just for having composed *Die Entführung*, but most people are content to accept it uncritically as a great opera merely because it was the work of Mozart.

## 6

## LE NOZZE DI FIGARO—I

MOZART'S life was so short that musicians seldom think of dividing it into three periods as they habitually do that of Beethoven. But one can generally divide any creative man's life into three periods. In the first he is asserting himself and trying to obtain an audience; in the second he has obtained his audience and is trying to develop himself to the fullest extent compatible with remaining in touch with it; in the third he has become indifferent to his audience and writes only for himself. We may date Mozart's second period from the year of *Die Entführung*. Between that and *Le Nozze di Figaro* four years elapsed, and to these four years belong a large number of his best-known works. Among the symphonies the *Haffner* (1782) and the *Prague* (1785) are the only famous ones of this time; the three more celebrated symphonies date from 1788. But the six string quartets dedicated to Joseph Haydn were written between 1782 and 1785, and still more important are fourteen pianoforte concertos, some composed for pupils, but most of them for his own performance. We must never lose sight of the fact that the operas and the pianoforte concertos are the works in which we meet Mozart most closely; they are his most important creations and they are the ones which represent his individual personality most intimately and completely. It is necessary to emphasize this even at the risk of saying it too often, for we naturally associate Mozart inseparably with Haydn and Beethoven, whose creative minds really worked in quite different directions. The string quartet is practically the only ground common to all three. Haydn was always convinced that his operas were his greatest works, but recent attempts to resurrect them have only proved their insignificance; as a composer of concertos he is negligible. *Fidelio* is perhaps still the most deeply moving opera of the whole modern repertory, and all the more profoundly impressive because it is the quintessence of Beethoven, the culminating work of his second period; but in the general career of Beethoven it stands out as an isolated experiment. Like the concertos, it is great because it is the expression of Beethoven; but for complete mastery and supreme accomplishment in the handling of a definite form we must look to the concertos of Mozart as we do to the operas. The general doctrine of the nineteenth century was that the concerto was of its very nature morally inferior to the symphony; it was a display piece for a virtuoso, while the symphony—represented, of course, ideally by those of Beethoven—stood for the religious aspirations of a community. About Wagner people were still hesitating, and the representative figure of opera was Donizetti. To understand the relative values of all these types of musical creation, we have to put ourselves back into the days before the French Revolution. A hundred years ago that was too great an effort of the imagination to expect from any serious-minded listener; to-day, with our general tendency to repudiate the nineteenth century altogether, we can make an easier approach to Mozart and his environment.

It requires perhaps yet more historical imagination to understand Mozart's own approach during these years of development to the music of Handel and J. S. Bach, which he began to study carefully about this time under the influence of Baron van Swieten, who had been Ambassador at the Court of Berlin. To us in England now the styles of Bach and Handel are perhaps even more familiar than that of Mozart himself. Mozart had been an intimate friend of Bach's youngest son in London, and the other two sons, Friedemann and Emmanuel, were both still living in 1782, but to Mozart the musical atmosphere of Berlin must have been as strange as that of Moscow might be now to a young Spanish composer. It is hardly too much to suggest that the strongest bond of union between the northern composers and Mozart would be, not their common German blood, but their common Italian education. It was only because Mozart had been so thoroughly trained in fugue and its power of poetry by Martini that he was able to enter into the spirit of Handel and Bach and see how that power of poetry could be still further developed by the employment of a more ruthless musical reasoning. We may best judge the effect of this new influence on him by studying the fugue in C minor for two pianofortes, composed in December 1783. Considered harmonically it is cacophonous, but besides its clear and logical construction there is a vocal character in its themes which brings strength and beauty out of ugliness, such as Luca Signorelli could bring out of all the agony and torture of those devils and damned souls which writhe and struggle on the walls of the Cathedral of Orvieto.

Another aspect of Mozart's life must be mentioned here, though the full discussion of it must be postponed until later. At the time of his engagement to Constanze Weber he had been a sincere Catholic; his great Mass in C minor was begun definitely as a thank-offering for his marriage. He never finished it. Vienna brought him into a wider social circle, and it is curious to note that he became well acquainted with leading men of science. How this came about can only be conjectured—possibly through van Swieten, possibly through the Mesmer family. His intimate friend Gottfried von Jacquin was the son of a distinguished botanist and he also frequented the house of the Greiner family, a notable centre for music and for science and literature as well. In 1785 he became a Freemason. This must have brought him into close association with Ignaz von Born, one of the most eminent scientists of his time and a great leader in Masonic circles, and the result was that Mozart began to think seriously about problems the solution of which he had hitherto accepted unproved from the mouth of authority. For the present we must imagine him not as having cast off Catholicism—that step he never definitely took—but as being at that stage of intellectual development when he might well begin to realize that the religion of his fathers did not provide him with so complete a philosophy of life as he had been hitherto taught to believe. The abandonment of the Mass in C minor, which might, if completed, have been one of Mozart's greatest masterpieces, and one of the greatest settings of the Mass ever produced by any composer, here acquires a certain significance to which we shall revert more in detail when we come to consider *Die Zauberflöte*. After 1782 Mozart never wrote another note of church music until the *Ave verum corpus* of June 1791 and the Requiem which he did not live to finish.

The German opera at Vienna was given up in the spring of 1783 and its place was taken by a season of comic opera in Italian. Mozart expected that this too would come to grief, but he was mistaken. Salieri, who was in command of the Italian opera, was not merely a favourite of the Emperor, but was a very capable composer; he had secured a capable company of singers and an unusually capable poet as well. This was Lorenzo Da Ponte. Mozart met him first in 1783 at the house of Baron Wetzlar, a rich Jew with whom the Mozarts were then lodging.[1] Da Ponte pro-

[1] Wetzlar stood godfather to Mozart's first child, Raymund, who was called after him.

mised Mozart a libretto; 'but who knows whether he will be able
to keep his word—or be willing either? As you know, these
Italian gentlemen are very polite to one's face—we know all
about them! If he is in league with Salieri, I shall get nothing out
of him as long as I live.' And so Mozart, after reading through
over a hundred librettos by various authors, was reduced to
asking Varesco to write him a comic opera, if he was not still too
sore after the affair of *Idomeneo*.

Lorenzo Da Ponte is so important a factor in Mozart's development that it is worth while studying his personality in some detail.
He was born on 10 March 1749 at Ceneda, at the foot of the
mountains to the north of Venice. His father was a Jew, by name
Geremia Conegliano, by trade a *cordovaniere*, which may mean a
leather-dresser or a shoemaker.

Wishing in 1763 to take a Catholic as his second wife, he had
himself baptized with great solemnity along with his three sons
Emmanuel, Baruch, and Ananias, who received the Christian
names of Lorenzo, Girolamo, and Luigi respectively. According
to some custom of the time, Geremia, now Gasparo, assumed the
surname of the bishop who administered the sacrament, Monsignor Lorenzo Da Ponte. Our future poet was then fourteen; his
education till then seems to have been rather haphazard, and he
was known as *lo spiritoso ignorante*. Foreseeing that their father's
second marriage would probably lead to financial difficulties, he
and his brother Girolamo applied to the Bishop for admission to
the local seminary; not only were they admitted, but the Bishop
generously undertook to bear the cost of their maintenance. In
two years the brothers had made such rapid progress in Latin
that their father determined to make priests of them, although,
as Lorenzo tells us, 'this was utterly contrary to my vocation and
my character'. At seventeen he was still incapable of expressing
himself in Italian,[1] but he had considerable fluency in writing
Latin verse. Those who have had an English public school education will probably agree that this was no bad introduction to the
study of Dante, Petrarch, Ariosto, and Tasso to which he was
encouraged by one of his younger instructors. He quickly
developed a passion for poetry; he translated from Latin into
Italian and from Italian into Latin, acquiring a remarkable
facility in dealing with any kind of style or metre. On the death

---

[1] At home and in the seminary he would have talked the Venetian dialect;
possibly Hebrew to some extent at home and Latin in school.

of Monsignor Da Ponte he was sent to the seminary at Porto-gruaro, where he tells us that he began the study of mathematics and philosophy, but did not take much pleasure in them. In 1772 he was appointed professor of rhetoric and vice-rector of the seminary; on 27 March 1773 he was ordained priest. Some six months later he left the seminary and went to Venice to seek his fortune.

Venice at that date was an international pleasure-resort comparable with Monte Carlo in recent times; and it must further be remembered that in those days the ecclesiastical habit did not necessarily imply any great strictness of morals even in Rome itself. Peter Beckford, writing from Rome a generation later, says:

'As for the Abbés, they are not only men of intrigue themselves, but, as Falstaff says of his wit, are the cause of it in others. They are excellent at carrying a *billet-doux*, or presenting you to a female of easy virtue' (*Familiar Letters from Italy*, London, 1805).[1]

Lorenzo remained a year at Venice, and became involved in a series of disreputable adventures; in the autumn of 1774, he and his brother were summoned to Treviso to teach 'humanity', rhetoric, and grammar at the local seminary.

A poem which he wrote for public recitation, inspired by the doctrines of Rousseau, caused a scandal and he was dismissed in December 1776. The next two or three years were spent in Venice; he continued both his profligacy and his priestly functions until the autumn of 1779, when he was advised to fly from Venetian territory, and escaped just in time to Gorizia, where he stayed a little over a year. Here he saw an old friend, the poet Caterino Mazzolà, who was on his way from Venice to Dresden to be poet to the Italian opera at the Saxon court. Da Ponte asked Mazzolà to find a post there for himself too, and on receipt of an encouraging letter left Gorizia for Dresden probably in December 1780. On the way he stopped at Vienna, where he found the city in mourning for the death of Maria Theresa. This gives us an approximate date, as she died on 29 November of that year. Finding that there were no entertainments going on, he stayed no more than three days. On arriving at Dresden, he discovered that the letter of invitation was a forgery; an enemy in Gorizia had intercepted Mazzolà's genuine letter saying that there was no

[1] An experienced friend of mine said to me some fifty years ago, 'If you want a woman in Rome, follow a priest'.

opening for him, and in order to get him out of the way had substituted a letter promising an appointment. Da Ponte remained
about a year in Dresden and went to Vienna probably early in
1782. This is dated by the fact that he was introduced to Metastasio, who read a poem of Da Ponte's aloud at an evening party.
Metastasio died 12 April 1782. Mazzolà had given him a cordial
introduction to Salieri, and he even aspired to succeed Metastasio
as *poeta cesareo*; but he never achieved this honour. At this moment
he had never even attempted to write an opera libretto; but
Salieri evidently tested his powers by giving him plenty of work
in the way of adapting other operas for performance. In 1783 he
wrote *Il Ricco d'un Giorno* for Salieri, but Salieri put off the
performance till December 1784 on account of the arrival in
Vienna of Paisiello and the Abbé Giambattista Casti, who had
written the brilliant libretto of *Il Re Teodoro in Venezia* for him.
Paisiello was a formidable rival for both Salieri and Mozart, and
Casti an even more formidable rival for Da Ponte. They had spent
some time at St. Petersburg in the service of the Empress
Catherine and were on their way back to Italy.

Salieri was a pupil of Gluck, and his tragic opera, *Les Danaïdes*,
which was produced in Paris in 1783, was at first announced as by
Gluck himself, Gluck having been unable to fulfil his contract
through ill-health and wishing at the same time to give Salieri
the chance of making a name for himself in Paris. His best work
probably is *Axur*, composed first to a French libretto by Beaumarchais and afterwards remodelled for Vienna by Da Ponte.
*Il Ricco d'un Giorno* was not successful and of course the blame
was thrown on the librettist. The following example may serve
as a specimen of Salieri's style at its most attractive:

The first act ends with an enormous finale which is very spirited. The scene is Venice; two lovers are serenading the same lady; they quarrel, start their serenades again, and are finally discomfited by a storm, with choruses of gondoliers and frightened people. Salieri was hardly equal to dealing with this anticipation of *Die Meistersinger*. Salieri said that he would sooner cut off his fingers than set another line of Da Ponte's to music; his next opera was *La Grotta di Trofonio*, on an amusing libretto by Casti. Da Ponte tried his luck with the Spaniard Vicente Martín y Solar, generally known as Martini,[1] for whom he adapted a play of Goldoni (*Le Bourru bienfaisant*) written originally in French for Paris and successfully performed in a German translation at Vienna in 1772. This must have shown him the advantage of using a successful play as a basis for an opera-book. He did the same thing for Gazzaniga in 1786, adapting a French play.

But it was Mozart himself who first suggested turning *Le Mariage de Figaro* into an opera. The idea was partly due to the success which Paisiello had obtained with his *Barbiere di Siviglia* and in all probability still more to the public scandal which the second comedy had aroused both in Paris and in Vienna. It had been produced in Paris in 1784 after three years of the best possible advertisement—prohibition by the authorities. The play was still prohibited in Vienna as politically subversive, but Mozart probably foresaw that it might be possible to get permission for it in the shape of an Italian opera, and that as long as the play was forbidden, the opera would be certain to arouse curiosity.

Da Ponte and Mozart have been blamed, on the one side, for depriving one of the greatest of French comedies of all its savour, and turning a prophecy of revolution into a sordid intrigue; on the other, they have been commended for eliminating all that was political, satirical, and erotic in the original and turning all things

---

[1] Vincenzo Martini must be distinguished from Padre G. B. Martini of Bologna, the learned theorist and historian, also from G. B. San Martini or Sammartini of Milan, composer of instrumental music, and from Martini il Tedesco, composer of the popular song, *Plaisir d'amour*, whose real name was Aegidius Schwarzendorf.

to chastity, favour and prettiness. It is easy for those to whom both works are classics to pronounce such judgements. But in 1786 neither Beaumarchais nor Mozart were classics; to that Vienna audience, *Figaro* was a play of modern life, and although the scene was laid in Spain there was no great effort wasted on trying to obtain local colour. Anyone who takes the trouble to compare Da Ponte's libretto page by page with the original play will be surprised to see how closely the two correspond. One reason for this is that Beaumarchais himself had had some experience of opera, both as librettist and as composer. *Le Barbier de Séville* was originally intended as a comic opera, with music arranged by the author from his recollections of the songs and dances he had heard in Spain. It was refused by the Opéra-Comique and required very little alteration to transform it into a *comédie en prose mêlée d'ariettes* such as at that date was quite admissible at the Comédie-Française. The main outline of the story is stated in its simplest terms by Beaumarchais himself:

'Un grand Seigneur espagnol, amoureux d'une jeune fille qu'il veut séduire, et les efforts que cette fiancée, celui qu'elle doit épouser et la femme du Seigneur réunissent pour faire échouer dans son dessein un maître absolu que son rang, sa fortune et sa prodigalité rendent tout-puissant pour l'accomplir. Voilà tout, rien de plus.'

Beaumarchais's plan was to take an old-fashioned type of comic opera plot as a foundation and embroider satirical dialogue upon it, the conventional stage tricks appearing deliberately ridiculous in their new garb of fine literary artifice. It is a device with which the modern theatre has been made familiar enough, both in England and abroad. The danger of converting a play of this kind into a comic opera was that while the old tricks would remain as the foundation of the work, the flavour of the new dialogue, and, more important still, the new social point of view, would disappear entirely. But what Da Ponte was often obliged to sacrifice, Mozart could to some extent reconstitute in another medium; and in any case a dozen German translations of the play had been published by 1785, so that the audience which listened to Mozart could easily supply from their own recollection such matter as Da Ponte had thought it more prudent to omit.

Da Ponte as a librettist deserves to be taken seriously. The general tendency of English musicians is to take it for granted that

all opera librettos are rubbish, and they can always quote the
well-known remark of Figaro himself—*ce qui ne vaut pas la peine
d'être dit, on le chante*. Historians of literature almost invariably run away in horror from any drama written for the purpose
of musical setting, even when the poet is eminent enough to
command general respect. The three librettos which Da Ponte
wrote for Mozart are masterpieces of their own category, and his
work for other composers is no less interesting. To remodel
Beaumarchais's *Tarare* for performance at Vienna under the name
of *Axur* was no small accomplishment; there again it is worth
while going through the French and the Italian page by page. Da
Ponte was evidently quite seriously interested in his task as a
librettist and it is quite clear that he selected and planned his
librettos with a subtle understanding of the different temperaments
and abilities of the composers for whom he worked.

About the actual composition and preparation of *Figaro* there
is little known. There is a considerable gap in Mozart's letters just
at this time, and our principal source of information is the gossip-
ing Irish tenor, Michael Kelly, who had recently been engaged at
the Italian opera in Vienna. Kelly, whose anecdotes are so
amusing that they ought to be read in the original and not in the
few quotations for which space could be found here, deals mostly
with those eternal and trivial matters which play so important
a part in the autobiographies of all singers and managers; of what
was going on in the minds of Mozart and Da Ponte he can tell us
nothing. Da Ponte says that the music was composed in six weeks
and that the composition of the opera was kept a strict secret
until all was ready; but Leopold, in a letter to his daughter, gives
us to understand that there was no particular secrecy about it,
and that Mozart had some considerable trouble in getting the
libretto arranged to his own satisfaction as well as to that of the
censorship. The first performance took place by command of the
Emperor on 1 May 1786. Kelly considered that no opera had ever
had a better cast, and that no subsequent performance had ever
equalled it. The stories of the intrigues carried on by the Italians
against Mozart are numerous, but must be accepted with caution.
Kelly talks of himself as having been the only singer who appreciated the composer's genius and the only one who did not
join the cabal against him; but Kelly, like Da Ponte, put his
reminiscences together at a date when Mozart had become a
recognized classic. and was naturally anxious to make the most of

his connexion with him. I do not wish to cast any doubt on the sincerity of his admiration and personal affection, but from his description of the first full rehearsal it is clear that the singers were all doing their best, and that Benucci, who sang Figaro, threw himself into his part in a way that would hardly have been possible for a man who wanted the opera to be a failure. It is curious that the company were nearly all Italians, the only exceptions being Kelly, the Irishman, who doubled the parts of Don Basilio and Don Curzio, Nancy Storace (Susanna), of Italian origin, though practically an Englishwoman, and Nannina Gottlieb (Barbarina), who eventually sang the part of Pamina in the first performance of *Die Zauberflöte*.[1] That Madame Cavalieri took no part may have been due to her intimacy with Salieri; but it is strange that neither Therese Teyber nor Aloysia Lange were among the singers.

The enthusiasm aroused by the first performance was immense; but although the opera was performed nine times in the course of the season, its popularity was short-lived. Martín had already made a success with *Il Burbero di Buon Cuore*, and his *Una Cosa Rara*, produced in the following November, soon caused *Figaro* to disappear from the Vienna stage until the appearance of *Don Giovanni* brought Mozart once more into sufficient prominence to make it worth while reviving it.

[1] For a curious anecdote of Nannina Gottlieb in old age, see W. Kuhe, *My Musical Reminiscences*, London, 1896, p. 13.

## 7

## LE NOZZE DI FIGARO—II

*F*IGARO, if not the most celebrated, is at any rate probably the most often performed of Mozart's operas and also the most intelligently performed, since it presents no great difficulties of interpretation. Its plot is extremely complicated, but it is so admirably constructed that every event develops logically and falls into its proper place in the drama. There is, however, one drawback for the average modern opera-goer: *Le Nozze di Figaro* was composed, and the original comedy too was written, for an audience already familiar with the previous history of the characters. English audiences are not likely to have seen or even read Beaumarchais's comedy *Le Barbier de Séville*; still less likely are they ever to have heard of Paisiello's opera. They are, however, fairly familiar now with Rossini's *Barbiere*, but that is not really the right preparation for Mozart's *Figaro*. Paisiello based his opera on the play; Rossini based his on Paisiello. I do not mean that Rossini stole from Paisiello, or that an acquaintance with Paisiello's opera is in any way necessary to the enjoyment of Rossini's. But whereas Paisiello had to translate Beaumarchais into music for the first time, Rossini found the subject already familiar in his own language, so that he did not feel it necessary to make any effort to preserve the original literary character of the drama, but confined himself to enhancing its purely musical aspect. The result is that all the characters are rather overwhelmed with their own music, and the opera has tended to become more and more a show piece for singers. And when it is played as a comedy in a language understood by the audience it almost inevitably degenerates into slapstick farce.

Beaumarchais's play is, of course, itself more of a farce than *Le Mariage de Figaro*; the subject was a well-worn theme of Italian comic operas and was possibly chosen for that very reason, so that the audience might have the better chance of enjoying the witty dialogue and the picturesque Spanish effects of costume and music. By utilizing the same characters in the second play, the author saved himself the time and trouble usually spent on an exposition;

and hence arise the extraordinary complexity and fullness of detail which characterize it. When acted as a play, the spectator can easily follow its intricacies, even without a previous knowledge of *Le Barbier*; but the addition of music, and the necessary reconstruction of the play to make it suitable for music, place the operagoer in a less comfortable position, even if he hears the work in his own language.

The earlier play tells us how Count Almaviva succeeded in marrying Rosina, a young heiress, in the teeth of her guardian, Doctor Bartolo, who had intended to marry her himself. Doctor Bartolo imagined that he had taken every possible precaution, but Rosina was a typical young girl of the Latin race, quite ready for an intrigue with a strange young man, and knowing instinctively how to arrange all the preliminaries of an elopement, even if she had not knowledge enough of the world to foresee what the later results of it would be. One can hardly wonder at the state of her character after she has been brought up by the elderly duenna Marcellina and the hypocritical music-master, Don Basilio, for Marcellina is the half-discarded mistress of Doctor Bartolo and Basilio is a typical needy *abbé* such as Beckford describes, always ready to oblige the highest bidder. The principal agent in the intrigue is the barber Figaro, who by virtue of his profession knows everybody and has the entry to all houses.

When the curtain rises on *Le Nozze di Figaro* the Count and Rosina have been married for some time. The Count has rewarded Figaro by making him his valet and Don Basilio by appointing him organist of his private chapel.

He gives music-lessons when required, but his principal duty is to assist the Count in any little affair with another woman that may be on hand. Just at this moment the object of the Count's attentions is the Countess's maid Susanna, who is to be married to Figaro this very day. The Count has made a great point of abolishing voluntarily the so-called *jus primae noctis*[1] within his dominions, but counts on obtaining it with equal good will in this particular case. The first act begins in the room which has been assigned to the happy pair; Figaro is measuring the floor, to see whether it is big enough to take the matrimonial bed which the Count has promised as a wedding present, and Susanna is trying on her bridal headgear. She knows perfectly well what the Count's intentions are and has no intention whatever of gratifying them;

[1] On the *jus primae noctis* see note at the end of this chapter.

but Figaro has had too much experience not to be inclined to jealousy. The Count is still more inclined to jealousy, having had still more experience; and although he has ceased to care for his wife he is ready enough to suspect her of an intrigue with the page Cherubino, who is just young enough to be allowed still to take liberties, and just old enough to make the Countess's conduct at any rate, if not his own, suspicious.[1] Cherubino has a genius for being discovered in the wrong place. The Count has already found him making love to Barbarina, the gardener's daughter, and in this first act he discovers him hidden in Susanna's room after the boy has overheard his request for an assignation. The page must evidently be got rid of as quickly as possible, and the most convenient way is for the Count to give him a commission in the army. Figaro is not altogether sorry to see another possible source of danger to Susanna removed, and the act ends with the song *Non più andrai*, in which he describes to Cherubino the new life that he will have to lead as a soldier.

Act II introduces us to the Countess. Susanna explains the whole situation to her, and a plot is laid to rouse the Count's jealousy by an anonymous letter warning him that his wife has made an assignation with another man. Cherubino is to be dressed up as a girl and sent to meet the Count in the garden at night in place of Susanna. While he is having a dress tried on the Count suddenly demands admission. Cherubino manages to jump out of the window, and after the Countess has confessed his presence, both she and the Count are surprised to find only Susanna in the locked inner room. The situation is complicated by Antonio, the drunken gardener, Susanna's uncle, who complains that a man has jumped out of the window and damaged his flowers. Figaro on the spur of the moment says that it was himself and sustains the part with difficulty when confronted with the commission that the page has accidentally dropped. Lastly, Bartolo and Marcellina enter, accompanied by Basilio, to assert a claim that Figaro is legally obliged to marry Marcellina in compensation for a debt which he is unable to repay.

In Act III the case is brought before the Count for trial. He has already had another interview with Susanna and feels certain of success; but he suspects treachery when he overhears her say to Figaro that he has won his case before it is tried. At the trial,

[1] Cherubino is a page, but not of the Pickwickian type; he is a young gentleman of good family sent to serve in a noble household by way of education in manners.

which in the opera does not take place on the stage, as it does in the play, Figaro is condemned to marry Marcellina; but directly afterwards it is discovered that Figaro is the natural son of Marcellina and Bartolo, who thereupon decide to legalize their union. The Countess dictates a letter for Susanna to write, making an assignation for that evening, to which she herself will go dressed in Susanna's clothes. Cherubino once more makes an unexpected appearance, having been dressed up again as a girl, this time by Barbarina, who brings him as an imaginary cousin to present flowers to the Countess. The double wedding of Figaro and Bartolo gives occasion for a dance, in the course of which Susanna contrives to hand the letter secretly to the Count.

The last act takes place in the garden at night. Barbarina's simplicity has led Figaro to discover Susanna's assignation, which he believes to be genuine. All the characters arrive in turn and in the regular old Italian comic opera manner mistake each other's identity. The Count makes love to his own wife under the impression that she is Susanna, and catches Figaro making love to Susanna, whom he takes for the Countess; finally, after being obliged to confess himself in the wrong, he is graciously forgiven by the Countess and the opera ends with the usual chorus of rejoicing.

At the time when he wrote *Figaro* Mozart was a fully developed composer. He had no need to imitate the external effects of his predecessors. He had already shown that he was a complete master of the art of music in almost all its forms. If he had not yet created the new German opera, he had learned the tricks of old Italian musical comedy in the days of his adolescence, and he had been obliged to acquire the art of turning his hand to anything, an art which, although more important to the dramatic composer than to any other type of musician, is never acquired by those who after making an early and easy success content themselves with repeating the pattern for the rest of their lives. Even though he had not produced an Italian comic opera since 1775, he had had a fair amount of practice in that style. Twice he had taken up a comic libretto and left it unfinished; of *L'Oca del Cairo*, begun in 1783, he completed almost all the first act, and a few sketches remain of *Lo Sposo Deluso* (1784). Neither of these works is of any great importance, though foolish attempts have been made to add another opera of Mozart to the repertory by patching these and other fragments together on the basis of a new libretto. A similar attempt was made with the little entertain-ment *Der Schauspieldirektor*, composed for performance in the Orangery at Schönbrunn on 7 February 1786. It was merely an excuse for showing off the best actors and singers of the court theatres; the music consists of no more than an overture, two arias, a trio and a quartet. Apart from bringing in various actors and actresses who do not sing at all, the main idea illustrated is that of two *prime donne*, each of whom gives a separate exhibition of her powers. They quarrel, the tenor vainly endeavouring to pacify them, in a trio; the final quartet, in which another actor joins, serves as a cheerful concluding *vaudeville*. Towards the middle of the last century, when Mozart, like Pergolesi, Stradella, and Astorga, was being made the not very heroic hero of a number of absurd legends, this little piece was turned into an opera with Mozart, Schikaneder, and Aloysia Lange as the principal charac-ters. Jahn was very severe on the dishonour shown to Mozart's memory by presenting him in this not very creditable character; the real dishonour is the stringing together of isolated numbers in a *pasticcio* and passing off this jumble as Mozart, which could only tend to confirm people in the idea that a Mozart opera is no more than a concert of agreeable music with a more or less foolish play going on in the background. A much better adaptation of *Der Schauspieldirektor* is that of Mr. Eric Blom (*The Impresario*), who gives us Mozart's music with the minimum of dialogue necessary to hold the story together, retaining the original characters of an imaginary manager and two opera-singers.

Trifling as it appears at first sight, *Der Schauspieldirektor* is a work of remarkable beauty and finished craftsmanship. The overture is much more solidly constructed than one would expect; its themes are light and graceful, but the orchestration is unusually full, and there is a considerable development section. The whole movement is contrapuntal in spirit, and its fullness and sonority are due, not to the employment of more instruments, but to the independence and individuality of the part-writing. Even the vocal numbers are contrapuntal in character; Mozart had learned from the practice of the string quartet how to accompany a beautiful melody with a texture of dramatic counterpoint that gives the first aria especially a wonderful intensity and intimacy of feeling, suited not so much to the theatre as to the chamber. In general style the little piece is German rather than Italian, for it shows more affinity to *Die Entführung* and *Die Zauberflöte* than to the Italian operas, *Così fan Tutte* perhaps excepted; it is therefore of great interest as showing us what Mozart might have achieved with German opera at this period if he had been given another chance to write it.

In the style of Italian opera a marked change was taking place just at this time. During the interval between *Die Entführung* and *Figaro* three new Italian composers had made their appearance in Vienna—Giuseppe Sarti, Vicente Martín,[1] and Giovanni Paisiello. Of these the last is the best remembered at the present day, and the first is the most interesting. Sarti was a pupil of Padre Martini and himself the teacher of Cherubini. He was a man of fifty-five when he came to Vienna in 1784, which accounts for his not understanding Mozart's quartets, as his own style was fully matured and fixed. His opera *I due Litiganti*,[2] first produced at Milan in 1782, had met with great popularity in Vienna in the following year. It is a well-written work, suggesting Cimarosa in its general style, and showing the beginnings of certain effects, such as the famous *crescendo*, later developed by Rossini.

Paisiello was of a rather different type. His education had been Neapolitan, and in 1776, at the age of thirty-seven, he had been invited to direct the Italian opera at St. Petersburg. Sarti, it may be added, had lived for a long period at Copenhagen, and it may be that both composers were to some extent influenced by their northern environment. I cannot bring forward any evidence to trace Danish or Russian folksong in their melodies; much more probably it was merely the remoteness of the northern courts from the inner sources of Italian culture (however much they admired it) that led both Sarti and Paisiello to employ a more simple, naïve and almost childish type of melody than their predecessors such as Leo and Logroscino. Indeed, it was this exaggerated simplicity that made Paisiello's reputation, and it is amusing to find that he, who made the most scathing (and by no means unjust) criticisms on the mild sentimentality of Pergolesi, attained popularity by exactly the same means, though he had not the advantage of an early death.[3]

[1] Martín, although a Spaniard by birth, may be counted among the Italians, like his compatriots, Perez and Terradellas.

[2] The full title of the opera is *I Pretendenti Delusi, ovvero Fra i due Litiganti il Terzo Gode*, but it was generally known and referred to by the shorter name given above.

[3] For Paisiello's criticism on Pergolesi see the article *Pergolesi* in *Grove's Dictionary* (second and later editions).

Martín was a much younger man, only two years older than Mozart. His music seems nowadays empty and commonplace, and it is difficult to see what could have caused his extraordinary success in Vienna. His most noticeable characteristic seems to have been a facility for writing amiable melodies in 6/8 rhythm that recall *Here we go round the mulberry bush*.

Along with this exaggerated simplicity in the arias, the fashionable comic opera had greatly expanded the finale; but it is very seldom that these long finales contain music of real interest. Such passages as the following from *I due Litiganti*—

are the staple material of all of them and of Mozart's as well. Da Ponte in his memoirs describes the finale precisely:

'This *finale*, which has to be closely connected with the rest of the opera, is a sort of little comedy in itself and requires a fresh plot and a special interest of its own. This is the great occasion for showing off the genius of the composer, the ability of the singers, and the most effective "situation" of the drama. Recitative is excluded from it; everything is sung, and every style of singing must find a place in it—*adagio, allegro, andante, amabile, armonioso, strepitoso, arcistrepitoso, strepitosissimo,* and with this the said finale generally ends. This in the musicians' slang is called the *chiusa* or *stretta*—I suppose because it gives not one twinge but a hundred to the unhappy brain of the poet who has to write the words. In this finale it is a dogma of theatrical theology that all the singers should appear on the stage, even if there were three hundred of them, by ones, by twos, by threes, by sixes, by tens, by sixties, to sing solos, duets, trios, sextets, sessantets; and if the plot of the play does not allow of it, the poet must find some way of making the plot allow of it, in defiance of his judgment, of his reason, or of all the Aristotles on earth; and if he then finds his play going badly, so much the worse for him!'

When we consider that Da Ponte's first attempt at writing a finale was for Salieri in 1783, we may well admire his speed in acquiring craftsmanship, for his finales in the three operas written for Mozart are masterpieces. The whole scheme of Italian comic opera was in fact designed for inattentive and uncultured audiences; a few pretty tunes that anyone could whistle as he went home, and the physiological excitement of noise and rhythm to bring down the curtain. Nor were great demands made upon the intelligence of the singers; what the arias required most was personal charm, and the finales, being built up on easily-remembered formulae, gave plenty of opportunity, if not for fine acting, at any rate for hackneyed 'business' and any amount of jabbering and shouting.

The libretto of *I due Litiganti* was by Goldoni; it bears a certain resemblance to that of *Figaro* and Da Ponte probably found it a useful guide. There is a Countess who wishes to marry her maid Dorina to a certain Mingone, and a Count who wishes to marry her to his own servant Titta. The Countess, who thinks that her husband no longer loves her and is arranging Dorina's marriage with a certain ulterior object of his own in view, calls to her aid the *soubrette* Livia and the bailiff Masotto; Masotto manages everybody and everything and eventually obtains the hand of Dorina for himself. Beaumarchais's play was written in 1776, but not performed until 1784 and first printed in 1785; Sarti's opera came out in 1782. Obviously neither Goldoni nor Beaumarchais could have been indebted to each other; the skeleton of the plot probably goes back to the Comedy of Masks.

Mozart's recollections of the music are fairly unmistakable.

The following bars are from one of the airs of Sarti's Countess, but they might equally well belong to Mozart's—

and some of Masotto's songs have a clear suggestion of Figaro. e.g.:

We are oddly reminded of *Non più andrai* in a quartet for Dorina and her three lovers, although the *tempo* is slower—

and in the course of the first finale, which in its general scheme closely resembles the last finale of *Figaro*, we come upon a still more interesting anticipation—the model for *Deh vieni*:

Ex. 19.
*Larghetto.*

bel - la co - sa e - gli è far all' a - mo - re,...........

Quan - do si tro - va chi ci da nel

ge - nio...........................

We see from this what is the ancestry of Mozart's famous song; it is a direct descendant of the *canzonetta* which appears regularly in all the early Neapolitan comic operas as a type of popular folksong, and was carried on as a tradition, not only in the later Italian operas, but in the Viennese imitations of them composed by Fux, Gassmann, and other Germans.

Paisiello is familiar to us now only in the two little airs on which Beethoven wrote variations. The influence of his music on *Figaro*

is apparent mainly in *Voi che sapete*, which was very probably
intended as an improvement on the serenade of Count Almaviva
at the beginning of *Il Barbiere di Siviglia* (St. Petersburg, 1782;
Vienna, August 1783).[1]

If we look through the table of contents in a copy of *Figaro*, we
shall at once notice one respect in which that opera differs from
its contemporaries. In most Italian operas the principal form is
the solo aria; there may be an occasional duet, perhaps a quartet
or two and the usual finales, but arias will be in a large majority.
It is interesting to compare *Figaro* with Martín's *Una Cosa Rara*,
the libretto of which (in two acts only) is also by Da Ponte
(Vienna, 1786).

---

[1] I have left out the mandoline *obbligato* for the sake of clearness, as it is not
important in these bars. The introduction, in which it is prominent, is quoted
in score in E. Prout, *The Orchestra*, vol. i, p. 90.

|          |            | Act I | Act II | Act III | Act IV | Total | Martin's *Una Cosa Rara* (8 characters) |
|----------|------------|-------|--------|---------|--------|-------|------------|
| *Arias*  | Barbarina  | —     | —      | —       | 1      | 1     | —          |
|          | Bartolo    | 1     | —      | —       | —      | 1     | —          |
|          | Basilio    | —     | —      | —       | 1      | 1     | —          |
|          | Cherubino  | 1     | 1      | —       | —      | 2     | —          |
|          | Count      | —     | —      | 1       | —      | 1     | —          |
|          | Countess   | —     | 1      | 1       | —      | 2     | —          |
|          | Figaro     | 2     | —      | —       | 1      | 3     | —          |
|          | Marcellina[1] | —  | —      | —       | 1      | 1     | —          |
|          | Susanna    | —     | 1      | —       | 1      | 2     | —          |
|          | (9 characters) | 4 | 3      | 2       | 5      | 14    | 19         |
| *Duets*  |            | 3     | 1      | 2       | —      | 6     | 4          |
| *Trios*  |            | 1     | 1      | —       | —      | 2     | 2          |
| *Sextets*|            | —     | —      | 1       | —      | 1     | 1          |
| *Choruses*|           | 1     | —      | 1       | —      | 2     | 2          |
| *Finales*|            | —     | 1      | 1       | 1      | 3     | 2          |
|          |            | 9     | 6      | 7       | 6      | 28    | 30         |

We observe that although *Figaro* has more characters and fewer musical movements, the arias form just half the total, while in Martín's opera they amount to very nearly two-thirds. Mozart, like Verdi in *Rigoletto*, seems to have wanted to make his opera a series of duets. A duet in the old *opera seria* could only be an expression of the same sentiment by two persons; in the earlier *opera buffa* it was a vehicle of abuse. Pergolesi created the sentimental and conversational duet in *L'Olimpiade* (Rome, 1735); Mozart applied the technique for ordinary conversation, realistic, but not as a rule abusive. Thus Susanna has no aria at all in Act I of *Figaro*, but she takes part in three duets and a trio; she holds musical conversation with four separate persons—five if we count the conversation in *recitativo secco* with Cherubino. Her aria in Act II is practically a duet with Cherubino, for she is dressing him up and talking to him all the time, while he replies in action, if not in song. As the opera progresses we hear her in conversation with every other character in the play; it is not until the last act that her aria *Deh vieni* gives us a sudden revelation of her character in a new aspect. Mozart is always trying to carry on the action of the drama in definitely musical conversation. It is curious that Weber, writing thirty years later, should so com-

[1] In the Donaueschingen MS. (not autograph, but very early) Marcellina has another aria in Act I instead of the duet between her and Susanna. Dr. Alfred Einstein regards it as genuine Mozart.

In practice the number of arias in *Figaro* is still further reduced by the almost invariable omission of those for Basilio and Marcellina in Act IV; and occasionally those for Barbarina and Figaro are omitted too.

pletely miss this opportunity as he does in *Der Freischütz*; Agathe
and Aennchen sing together, but they do not converse, they
merely sing 'at each other', each going her own way. Weber and
his librettist (who was perhaps mostly to blame) leave the business
of the play to the spoken dialogue. Mozart too has by this time
acquired his peculiar gift for musical conciseness and compression;
Sarti, Paisiello, even Cimarosa and Schubert, take twenty bars
or more to say what Mozart can say in two.

Mozart and Da Ponte must soon have seen that an adaptation
of *Le Mariage de Figaro* was going to make a very long opera;
that is no doubt why it had to be in four acts, whereas the normal
number for comic opera was three, or even two. Four acts must
have caused some trouble in the theatre, for it is pretty clear that
*Don Giovanni* was first planned in four acts, like *Figaro*, and then
made into two, and *Così Fan Tutte*, another very long opera, was
probably planned in two acts to begin with. The length of *Figaro*
is due first to the enormous amount of drama that had to be
squeezed in, and also to the obvious insistence of the singers on
their statutory rights in the matter of arias, for it is obvious that
the arias for Basilio and Marcellina in Act IV are very much in
the way and contribute nothing to the drama; and they come far
too late to illustrate the characters of their singers—we were left
in no doubt about those in Act I.[1] Hence we may reasonably
imagine that Mozart deliberately kept a tight hand on that
luxuriance of invention which he allowed himself in *Die Entführung*, and the result is that *Figaro* is a masterpiece of comedy in
music such as had never been seen before. We may indeed wonder
whether it has ever been equalled by any subsequent composer.

Figaro and Susanna, being active-minded practical people not
much given to introspection, are presented to us at once in duets.
We see their action first on one another and then on the rest of the
characters. The Countess, on the other hand, makes her first
appearance with a soliloquy and has an even more important
soliloquy in Act III; she is a woman who from early childhood
has had nothing to do except think about herself. When she joins
in a trio or ensemble she is a different person; to the world,

---

[1] There are oddities about both these arias worth mention in a footnote. The
words of Marcellina's are a close imitation of Ariosto, *Orlando Furioso*, canto v,
stanza 1. In Basilio's aria, the words of which are also probably traceable to a
much earlier source, there is a conspicuous march theme near the end, in the
orchestra, which sounds like a deliberate quotation of some well-known tune.
I pointed it out to Dr. Alfred Einstein; he agreed with my view, but was equally
unable to identify it.

including her husband, she is Countess Almaviva—to herself, *la triste femme délaissée*. Cherubino, if less self-centred, is at any rate highly self-conscious, and therefore enters with a deliberate exposition of his own personality. His second aria—*Voi che sapete*—is not directly self-revealing, since it is a song which had been a song in the original spoken play. Writers of librettos often think it effective to drag in songs simply as performances of music into the course of an opera, but the device requires careful handling, because it upsets the balance of an opera if music is introduced as 'music', i.e. as an abnormal mode of expression, when the whole principle of opera is that music should be the one mode of expression that is consistently normal. The little duet for Cherubino and Susanna is admirably constructed; it is always Susanna who takes the lead, first encouraging (modulation to the dominant), then restraining (modulation to the subdominant). Only just at the end does Cherubino burst out into an amusingly passionate expression of puerile chivalry (transition to G minor), and practical Susanna ends the duet as it began.

The Count, as a man of intense energy, shows himself first in ensemble. One might say he has not time to sing an aria until the moment comes when he has to stop taking action and think over his position. When he does sing his aria it is a wonderful piece of self-revelation. It is closely related to the duet with Susanna which precedes it, as we can see from this phrase, half aside, half to Susanna—

Ex. 21.

Mi sen - to  dal con - ten - to  pie - no di gio - ia il cor,....
*Oh  joy past  all  ex - press - ing!  All  my de - sire  to ob - tain. ..*

and the fierce phrase of the soliloquy:

EX. 22.

Ve - drò ....mentre io so - spi - ro, .... fe - li - ce un ser - vo mi - o?
*Shall my .... de - sire be thwart-ed, .... while  serf  of mine re - joi - ces?*

At one moment he seems to have something in common with Bartolo, grotesque in his thirst for vengeance; at another he almost suggests the calculated cruelty of Beethoven's Pizarro.

The other characters are of less importance, but each is drawn with a firm hand. Even little Barbarina's one half-finished *arietta* has its function; her *naïveté* adds by force of contrast to the spirit of sinister intrigue that dominates the last act, perhaps all the more because we can never feel quite sure how far the *naïveté* is genuine. Bartolo is a relic of an older generation and is appropriately represented by a full-blown *buffo* song of the old-fashioned type. Marcellina and Basilio are seldom allowed to sing their arias in Act IV, and when they do they tell us little about them. They are both people to whom a certain artificiality of manner has become habitual, and we hardly recognize them when they throw off the mask, because there is more individuality in the mask than in the face behind it.

To the old-fashioned opera-goer the central feature of *Figaro* was *Voi che sapete*, and just subsidiary to that came *Dove sono*, the 'letter duet', and *Deh vieni*, with *Non più andrai* as the one concession to the male sex. I would rather suggest that the supreme moment of the opera is the sextet in Act III; I cannot think of any ensemble in any other opera which achieves—and by purely musical means too—the dramatic force and the irresistible comicality of 'His mother! his mother!', etc., passed from one voice to another. And there are so many delightful details besides —the geniality of Marcellina's first phrase, the absurdly rapturous exclamations, with the bewildered discomfiture of the Count and Don Curzio in the background; then the sudden entrance of Susanna, her complete misunderstanding of the situation, the ridiculously laborious explanations to her, and last of all the ravishing new melody of the last section (curiously anticipatory of Sullivan) with the Count and Curzio again venting their fury while the rest pause to take breath. Another magnificent number is the recitative and aria for Figaro in Act IV, sometimes, alas, omitted to save time. The opening of Act IV brings at once a complete change of temper. Hitherto the whole intrigue has been hardly more than a game of scoring points, with a game-player's amused satisfaction at every trick won; and now Barbarina—the last character one would expect to do so—sets the tone of sinister anxiety with the strange key of F minor.

Act IV is generally so much shortened in performance that few opera-goers really know what ought to happen on the stage. Barbarina is seen looking for the pin; then enter Figaro and Marcellina. Figaro has begun to take the situation seriously; after the dance and the episode of the pin, he has lost faith in Susanna and turns to his mother for consolation. She is a woman of practical experience; she tells *him* not to lose his head and jump to wrong conclusions, and she also tells *us* that whatever happens 'one woman must stand by another'. Here follows her aria in abuse of men, and her exit. Then, after Barbarina has returned to look for Cherubino in that left-hand arbour which is eventually to accommodate most of the cast, Basilio and Bartolo keep another appointment with Figaro, who has summoned them to the garden for a purpose of his own. I translate the original recitative:

'*Bas.* You asked us to come here, here we are.

*Bart.* Why are you scowling just like the villain in a play? What is the cause of this mysterious appointment?

*Fig.* You will see very shortly. You are invited here to witness the ancient privilege of the Lord of the Manor, granted by my virtuous wife.

*Bas.* Oh, shall we really? I see now how it stands: they've arranged it without employing me.

*Fig.* You will stay here and wait where no one can see you. I have to go and make further arrangements; I'll come back in a moment. Then when I whistle you'll all rush out together.'

Bartolo is completely puzzled; Basilio, the master of all intrigues, understands at once; he is rather annoyed at the Count's having managed the affair without his help, but delighted, as in Act I, at the prospect of an 'exposure'. This leads to his sententious fable-aria addressed to Bartolo, after which they both go into hiding. Figaro re-enters; all that has passed so far has been leading up steadily to his great recitative and aria in abuse of women, which he can now deliver with all the passion and complete sincerity of which he is capable. After the aria he retires, not to the back, but to the front of the stage, where he is supposed to be invisible to the Countess and Susanna, who now come on, but is actually visible the whole time to the audience, continuing to act his part and at the same time forming a link between the audience and the stage. He overhears every word of the women's conversation and every note of Susanna's aria; in fact, she knows he is there and intends him to overhear it. After Susanna's aria the finale begins, and the entrance of Basilio and Bartolo at the end is only to be rightly understood if we know already that they are in hiding to catch the Count and Susanna *in flagranti delicto*.

## NOTE TO CHAPTER 7

The following observations on the supposed *jus primae noctis* or *droit du seigneur* which plays such an important part in the comedy of Beaumarchais and in Mozart's opera are taken from a curious little book by one J. J. Raepsaet, *Les Droits du Seigneur. Recherches sur l'origine et la nature des Droits connus anciennement sous les noms de Droits des premières Nuits, de Markette, d'Afforage, Marcheta, Maritagium et Bumede*. Gand, chez tous les libraires, 1817 (*sic*). The date 1817 is a misprint for 1877; the outside covers of the book give the imprint at Rouen, J. Lemonnyer, libraire, 1 Rue des Carmes, 1877. Colophon: Achevé d'imprimer sur les presses de A. Lesguillon, Roubaix le 20 Novembre 1877. Pour J. Lemonnyer, libraire, à Rouen.

I should guess the author to have been a Flemish Jesuit, or at any rate a priest. The book takes a strictly Catholic point of view. It begins with an *Avant-propos*:

'Si ces droits ou redevances avaient existé dans le sens ou de la manière que des écrivains peu instruits ou peu sincères l'ont rapporté, il y aurait eu un temps et même une série de siècles où la fornication était un droit et la prostitution un devoir; où la foi conjugale devait être violée aussitôt que promise, et ou le lit nuptial devait être flétri avant de recevoir de légitimes époux.'

Many writers appear to have confused the *Marcheta* or *Maritagium* with the *jus primae noctis*. 'Le premier consiste en un bon maxime d'état, l'autre en un conseil évangélique.' In the Middle Ages, if the daughter of a serf wanted to marry a serf belonging to another lord, she or her parents had to pay her own lord some sort of compensation in view of the fact that by her marriage he lost both her services and the ownership of her offspring. This compensation took various legally recognized forms; but even M. Raepsaet hints that in certain cases it may have taken the form of a *défloration* by the *seigneur*.

The *jus primae noctis*, on the other hand, was an entirely different thing. At certain periods it was required by the Church that newly wedded couples should not consummate their marriage until a certain time after the sacramental ceremony, abstaining perhaps for the first night, or even for three days and longer.

Permission to consummate could be obtained by the spouses on payment of a sum of money to the Church, and this payment was often claimed by a priest before an ecclesiastical court.

The chief source of error, according to M. Raepsaet, was Hector Boethius, author of a History of Scotland in the sixteenth century. This is evidently not the more famous Boethius of a thousand years earlier, author of the treatise *De Musica*.

M. Raepsaet makes no mention whatever of Beaumarchais or Mozart.

## 8

### DON GIOVANNI—I

THOUGH the success of *Figaro* at Vienna was only momentary, there was at any rate one city where the opera was
appreciated to the full. Prague had already seized upon
*Die Entführung* with delight, and when *Figaro* was performed
there in the winter of 1786, enthusiasm knew no bounds. The
musical conditions of Prague were at that time quite different
from those of any other European capital. The Bohemians had,
and have still, a most remarkable natural talent for music, and
throughout the country, even in the poorest villages, music,
especially instrumental music, seems to have been regarded as an
indispensable part of elementary education, equally important
with reading and writing. Burney's description of his journey
across Bohemia in September 1772 gives an interesting picture of
the kingdom both from the artistic and from the economic point
of view:

'The country is flat, naked, and disagreeable to the eye for the
most part, all the way through Austria, Moravia, and Bohemia,
as far as Prague, the situation and environs of which are very
beautiful.

'The dearness and scarcity of provisions of all kinds on this road
were now excessive; and the half-starved people, just recovered
from malignant fevers, little less contagious than the plague,
occasioned by bad food and by no food at all, offered to view the
most melancholy spectacles I ever beheld.

'I crossed the whole kingdom of Bohemia, from south to north;
and being very assiduous in my inquiries, how the common people
learned music, I found out at length that not only in every large
town, but in all villages, where there is a reading and writing
school, children of both sexes are taught music. At Teuchenbrod
[Deutschbrod], Janich, Czaslau, Böhmischbrod, and other places,
I visited these schools; and at Czaslau, in particular, within a post
of Colin, I caught them in the fact. . . . I went into the school,
which was full of little children of both sexes, from six to ten or
eleven years old, who were reading, writing, playing on violins,
hautbois, bassoons, and other instruments. The organist had in

a small room of his house four clavichords, with little boys practising on them all. . . . Many of those who learn music at school go afterwards to the plough, or to other laborious employments; and then their knowledge of music turns to no other account, than to enable them to sing in their parish church, and as an innocent domestic recreation, which are, perhaps, among the best and most unexceptionable purposes that music can be applied to.

'It has been said by travellers, that the Bohemian nobility keep musicians in their houses; but in keeping servants, it is impossible to be otherwise, as all the children of the peasants and tradespeople, in every town and village throughout the kingdom of Bohemia, are taught music at the common reading schools, except in Prague, where, indeed, it is no part of school learning; the musicians being brought thither from the country.'

Burney tells us further that 'their first nobility are attached to the court of Vienna, and seldom reside in their own capital'; but Mozart seems to have found a very brisk social life going on there when he visited Prague in January 1787 at the invitation of his admirers there. His oldest friends in Prague were Franz Duschek and his wife, who had relatives in Salzburg, and had known the Mozarts since 1777. Duschek was a pianist of ability, and his wife a singer.[1] The Duscheks were very active in spreading the enthusiasm for Mozart's works, and he had another very influential friend in old Count Thun, whose daughter-in-law, the wife of Count Franz Josef Thun, was a great leader of musical society in Vienna, and had always done more than anyone else to forward Mozart's interests there.[2] We must imagine Prague as a capital of a very provincial type, very conscious of its own individuality, with a fairly numerous aristocracy, living in magnificent palaces dating mostly from the early years of the century, attended by suites of musical servants—a society wealthy and artistic enough to encourage a local Italian Opera, but not to maintain it on a very firm footing. The Opera was under the management of one Pasquale Bondini and had only recently transferred its performances from Count Thun's private theatre to the new national theatre built in 1783. Bondini's financial position was generally precarious, but the unprecedented success of *Figaro*, which came

---

[1] Franz Duschek seems to have been no relation to the well-known composer J. L. Dussek, despite the identity of name and country.

[2] The Thun palace at Prague is now the British Legation.

very near to having an uninterrupted run all through the winter,
fully re-established it. Mozart's visit in January 1787 naturally
increased his popularity; it was a round of social distractions, with
an occasional concert, at which he delighted his audience by
extemporizing on themes from *Figaro*. Bondini seized the moment
at which Prague was most delighted with Mozart and Mozart with
Prague to conclude an agreement with him for a new opera to be
produced in the following winter.

Mozart returned to Vienna in February and consulted Da Ponte
about a libretto. It was Da Ponte who suggested the legend of
Don Juan. With regard to the composition of the opera, we have
practically no information that is at all reliable, although no opera
has ever given rise to such a rich crop of fatuous anecdotes. Da
Ponte in his autobiography gives a very picturesque account of
his own fluency in composition, but we must read him with
caution, since the autobiography was written forty years later,
when *Don Giovanni* had become an accepted classic. Moreover,
it was written for an American public, just after Garcia had
produced the opera in New York. There is no doubt, however,
that the poet was extremely busy at this moment, as he had two
other librettos to write at the same time—*L'Arbore di Diana* for
Martín, and *Axur, Re d'Ormuz* for Salieri. The libretto which he
himself regarded as the best of the three was *L'Arbore di Diana*,
the theme of which was the dissolution of the monasteries and
nunneries by Joseph II, gracefully and amusingly represented by
a story of how Cupid and Endymion outwitted the goddess of
chastity and her secluded nymphs. This play was probably
original; the other two were not. *Axur* was a rearrangement in
Italian (but a very considerable rearrangement) of Beaumarchais's
*Tarare*, set by Salieri for production in Paris, but not very
successful there. *Don Giovanni*, as we shall see, was almost
entirely appropriated from the work of another librettist. We
may indeed not unreasonably suspect that Da Ponte suggested
the subject to Mozart not so much because he thought it appropriate to the composer's romantic temperament as because the
material happened to lie ready to his hand.

Mozart probably began on the work at once, as was his usual
habit, and then left the greater part to be finished at the last
moment. He went to Prague in September 1787 and lodged in a
house near the theatre; but he is said to have spent most of his
time at the Villa Bertramka, a little house in the suburb of

Smichow, on the west side of the River Moldau. The house is still standing, and Mozart's room still preserves its decorated ceiling, its dark green flowered wall-paper, and its parquet floor, just as they were in his day, though the surroundings were long ago transformed into an ugly workmen's quarter. Da Ponte arrived on 8 October, and the opera, after several delays, finally came out on 29 October. It is clear from Mozart's letters to Gottfried von Jacquin that it was ready for performance some time before; but the story of the overture having been written down so late that the band had to play it at sight is very possibly true. The amplifications of this story have no foundation and are probably the invention of that most unscrupulous and romantic journalist, Friedrich Rochlitz, author of the standard translation of *Don Giovanni* into German—a translation now condemned by every producer, but still firmly fixed in popular memory. There is also a story that Mozart composed three overtures to the opera and asked Duschek which he thought the best. These overtures were said to have been in E flat major, C minor (a free fugue), and D major respectively, the last being the one adopted. This story is preposterous; all Mozart's operas begin and end in the same key, and it is inconceivable that he could ever have contemplated an overture to *Don Giovanni* in any key but D. The success of the new opera was complete from everybody's point of view. Guardasoni, the stage manager, told Da Ponte that all impresarios and singers ought to bless his name and Mozart's, for as long as they lived there would never be any more bad seasons. Mozart conducted four performances in the same week, and then returned to Vienna.

Guardasoni was quite right in coupling the poet's name with the composer's in his congratulations, for although Da Ponte owes his immortality to the fortunate chance that brought him into contact with Mozart, there can be no doubt that Mozart's three masterpieces of Italian comic opera owed as much to their librettist as the last operas of Verdi did to the literary skill of Boito. It is therefore desirable to study Da Ponte's poem in detail and also to investigate the previous history of the Don Juan legend, bearing always in mind here that there are two aspects of it—the Don Juan legend as generally presented to the popular imagination, and the legend as it was treated by men of letters whose works would naturally be well known to Da Ponte, accomplished man of letters himself.

It is generally asserted that the story of Don Juan made its first literary appearance in a Spanish play called *El Burlador de Sevilla*, written by Gabriel Tellez (1571–1641), better known under the name of Tirso de Molina. It has also been asserted that Don Juan Tenorio was an historical personage and that he came of a noble family well known in Spain. There is, however, no very satisfactory evidence for this, and it is even doubtful whether *El Burlador* is really the work of the author to whom it is attributed.

The character of Don Juan falls into two clearly separable aspects, Don Juan the profligate and Don Juan the blasphemer. It is indeed only in the second case that we get a clearly defined story, and this story is in its main outline much older than the seventeenth century and by no means confined to Spain. It was a popular notion in many countries, northern as well as southern, that to insult the dead was a crime which inevitably led to the most awful punishment. The idea of statues coming to life dates back to classical times. The profligate on a grand scale is really quite a different character. There are innumerable legends of passionate and brutal rebels against all moral law, especially in Spain, where the sinner is generally related to have repented at last and to have been converted to a life of piety. Throughout the seventeenth century this story was familiar in Germany through plays of the Jesuits in which the hero is called Leontius. Leontius is almost always described as an Italian, and the play probably came to Germany from Italy, though it may have originated in Spain. But it should be noted that in the Don Juan or Leontius plays the sins committed are not so much of the flesh as of the spirit.

Tirso's play is a long, straggling series of scenes in which Don Juan makes love to various ladies and is finally taken down to Hell. His attempt on Donna Anna, followed by the duel and the death of her father, does not take place until the second act. The play opens, however, with a similar adventure, of which Isabela, the betrothed of Octavio, is the heroine. The other female characters are two peasant girls, each of whom is seduced in turn by Don Juan. Don Octavio, the respectable gentleman, the Commendatore and his statue, the peasant rival and Don Juan's comic servant are all presented in much the same form that they take in later plays. It should be noted too that after the statue has carried Don Juan off to Hell, the comic servant gives a full account of his sad end, and the play ends with the happy nuptials of the other characters.

About the middle of the seventeenth century an Italian version appeared at Naples; this was much influenced by the Comedy of Masks, and Harlequin becomes Don Juan's servant. As in the original play, there is no female character whom we could call a 'heroine'; Don Juan proceeds from seduction to seduction until the scene with the statue and the final tableau in which he is seen burning in Hell and tormented by devils. Other Italian versions succeeded this extravaganza and the play can be traced by way of Lyons (1658) to Paris (1659).

In 1665 Molière brought out *Le Festin de Pierre*, a comedy in prose which bears little resemblance to Tirso's poetic drama and presents a social and moral point of view which is entirely different. Molière's Don Juan is a Parisian aristocrat of his own time; his servant Sganarelle says of him: 'Voilà de mes esprits forts qui ne veulent rien croire.' The murder of the Commendatore does not take place on the stage; it is merely alluded to as having occurred six months before. Molière makes a very important addition to the story—Donna Elvira, whom Don Juan has abducted from a convent and then deserted. In spite of his cruelty, she preserves her devotion for Don Juan up to the end, although when she first appears she is more indignant than affectionate. But in the fourth act she says to him:

'Ce n'est plus cette done Elvire qui faisoit des vœux contre vous, et dont l'âme irritée ne jetoit que menaces, et ne respiroit que vengeance. Le ciel a banni de mon âme toutes ces indignes ardeurs que je sentois pour vous, tous ces transports tumultueux d'un attachement criminel, tous ces honteux emportements d'un amour terrestre et grossier, et il n'a laissé dans mon cœur, pour vous, qu'une flamme épurée de tout le commerce des sens, une tendresse toute sainte, un amour détaché de tout, qui n'agit point pour soi, et ne se met en peine que de votre intérêt.'

This presentation of Donna Elvira is very important, as it helps us to understand her character as it appears in Mozart's opera. There can be no doubt that Da Ponte was well acquainted with Molière's play, for there are many verbal borrowings from it in the recitatives of *Don Giovanni*. Masetto and Zerlina, too, are derived from Molière and not from Tirso. Tirso's peasants belong to a literary Arcadia; Molière's are comically realistic and even talk a peasant dialect. It should be noted that neither Donna Anna nor Don Ottavio come into Molière's play at all.

*Le Festin de Pierre* had fifteen performances and then disappeared from the stage, except in Thomas Corneille's rearrangement in verse, until 1847. It is altogether an exception among Don Juan plays, but for all that it is an historic landmark. Molière wrote it with reluctance under pressure from his actors, and was so little satisfied with it that he never printed it in his lifetime. He seems to have thought that he could put an end to the absurdities of the Italian play by transforming it into a satire on contemporary life; but he forgot that the episode of the statue was entirely inappropriate to a realistic comedy. 'Votre figure de Don Pedro baisse la tête', said a lady to Molière, 'et moi je la secoue.' The story was too extravagant to be treated seriously, and it was even considered that the play was dangerous to public morals. The Abbé Terrasson, whom we shall meet again in a later chapter, opined that:

'Rien n'est plus funeste à la morale que des pièces de théâtre telle que *Le Festin de Pierre*, où un méchant homme n'est puni qu'après avoir porté le vice et le crime à un point où personne ne veut aller, et auquel même n'arrivent que très peu de scélérats.'

In 1676 Don Juan made his appearance in England under the name of *The Libertine*, a play by Thomas Shadwell, derived, not from Molière, but from Dorimon's *Le Festin de Pierre* (1659).[1] Shadwell's preface to it shows us clearly what the general attitude of the day was to the story and to its dramatic treatment:

'The story from which I took the hint of this Play, is famous all over Spain, Italy and France: It was first put into a Spanish play (as I have been told), the Spaniards having a Tradition (which they believe) of such a vicious Spaniard, as is represented in this Play. From them the Italian Comedians took it, and from them the French took it, and four several French plays were made upon the story.

'The character of The Libertine, and consequently those of his friends, are borrowed; but all the Plot, till the latter end of the Fourth Act, is new: And all the rest is very much varied from anything which has been done upon the subject.

[1] See *The Complete Works of Thomas Shadwell* edited by the Rev. Montague Summers, London, 1927.

'I hope the Readers will excuse the Irregularities of the Play, when they consider, that the Extravagance of the subject forced me to it: And I had rather try new ways to please, than to write on in the same Road, as too many do. I hope that the severest Reader will not be offended at the Representation of those vices, on which they will see a dreadful punishment inflicted. And I have been told by a worthy gentleman, that many years ago (when first a play was made upon this story in Italy) he has seen it acted there by the name of 'Atheisto Fulminato', in Churches, on Sundays, as a part of devotion: and some, not of the least Judgment and Piety here, have thought it rather an useful moral, than an encouragement to vice.'

Shadwell's play is of interest to us now only for the fact that Purcell wrote incidental music for it. It is not likely that Da Ponte had read it, and it has no bearing on Mozart's opera. But Shadwell himself is always of interest, as he was devoted to music and a complete unbeliever in matters of religion. His audience for this play would certainly have their full money's worth of murder, blasphemy, and rape, with the pleasing horrors of a fine spectacular effect at the end, heightened by Purcell's very dramatic music. What is noteworthy is that even in England, and as early as 1676, the subject was considered extravagant, and in spite of the success of the piece the same view was held nearly a century later.

'The Incidents are so cramm'd together in it, without any consideration of Time or Place, as to make it highly unnatural. The villainy of Don John's Character is worked up to such an Height, as to exceed even the Limits of Possibility, and the Catastrophe is so very horrid, as to render it little less than Impiety to represent it on the Stage.'[1]

In 1736 Goldoni, who was then not quite thirty, produced a play in verse called *Don Giovanni Tenorio o sia Il Dissoluto*. He tells us in his *Mémoires* that he wrote the play with a definite purpose—to revenge himself on Signora Passalacqua, an actress with whom he had had a *liaison* which ended in her making a fool of him. His plan was to write a Don Juan play in which everybody would recognize under the characters of Don Giovanni, Carino (a shepherd), and Elisa (a shepherdess) his own rival Vitalba,

---

[1] David Erskine Baker, *The Companion to the Playhouse*, London, 1764.

himself, and the lady. It is highly probable that Da Ponte had read this play. The plot is as complicated as any opera-book of Metastasio. The scene is laid in Castile, but Don Giovanni, like most of Goldoni's bad characters, is a Neapolitan, and behaves curiously like the Neapolitans who come into his Venetian comedies, for he has a Harlequin-like readiness in making up an entirely untrue story on the spur of the moment. More important for us than the play itself is Goldoni's own criticism of it:

'Everyone knows that wretched Spanish tragicomedy which the Italians call *Il Convitato di Pietra* and the French *Le Festin de Pierre*. I have always regarded it with horror in Italy, and I could never understand why this farce should have maintained itself so long, attracting crowds of spectators and being regarded as the delight of a cultivated nation. Italian actors held the same opinion, and either in jest or in ignorance, some said that the author had made a bargain with the Devil to have it kept on the stage. I never thought that I should have worked on the subject myself; but having learned enough French to read it, and seeing that Molière and Thomas Corneille had treated it, I undertook to present the subject to my own country in order that the Devil's bargain should be kept with a little more decency. I could not give the play the same title, because in my play the statue of the Commendatore does not speak or walk or go out to dinner. I thought I ought not to suppress the thunderbolt which strikes Don Giovanni, because a wicked man ought to be punished; but I managed this event in such a way that it might be considered both as the immediate effect of God's anger, and as the result of a combination of secondary causes.'

In Goldoni's play Anna is betrothed to Ottavio much against her will and his too. Ottavio is nephew of the King and his immediate heir, the King being a bachelor. The reason is that the Commendatore has just returned from suppressing a plot in Sicily and the King is anxious to reward him; he has already refused money, and the King has already erected an equestrian statue to him. Anna, as an Italian critic has pointed out,[1] is a strangely complicated character; Goldoni himself seems not quite to know what to do with her, and the same is the case with Elisa, though we can trace her vagaries to Guarini's *Il Pastor Fido*. Anna is very young, and she is censured in the play as *leggera*, though she

---

[1] Mario Apollonio, *L'Opera di Carlo Goldoni*, Milano, 1932.

apparently has hitherto had no love affairs. She is resolutely determined not to marry Don Ottavio, whom she definitely detests. In Act II we meet Don Giovanni who has been attacked by robbers and is cared for by Elisa, to whom he at once makes love. There is a distinct anticipation here of *Là ci darem la mano* which is worth quoting:

'*D. Gio.*    Siate pietosa, o bella;
Io trarrovvi dal bosco. In nobil tetto
Posso guidarvi a comandare altrui:
Le rozze lane cangerete in oro,
E di gemme fornita, ogni piacere
Sarà in vostra balia.

*Eli.*    Se non temessi
Rimanere delusa . . .

*D. Gio.*    Io non saprei
Come meglio accertarvi; ecco la mano.

*Eli.*    Fra noi s'usa giurare, e sono i Dei
Mallevadori della fè.

*D. Gio.*    (Si giuri
Per posseder questa beltà novella.)
Giuro al Nume, che al cielo, e al mondo impera,
Voi sarete mia sposa.

*Eli.*    E se mancate?

*D. Gio.*    Cada un fulmin dal cielo, e l'alma infida
Precipiti agli abissi.'

Instead of Elvira, we have Donna Isabella, a deserted flame of Don Giovanni's, who is pursuing him in male attire. Shadwell also has a lady-love of Don John's who pursues him in male attire throughout his play. The amusing thing about Isabella is that her costume deceives nobody, but it is dramatically useful, for Don Giovanni, although he recognizes her at once, pretends not to do so, and indeed flatly denies that she is Isabella even when other characters acknowledge her; he persistently asserts that 'she' is a madman. Here again the situations are very like those in Mozart's opera. In Act III Don Giovanni meets the Commendatore, who receives him with the greatest cordiality and invites him to dinner; in Act IV we see them at this meal, with

Anna too. The Commendatore has to go downstairs for a moment
to receive Don Alfonso, the King's prime minister, who plays a
considerable part in the drama, and Don Giovanni seizes the
occasion to make violent love to Anna, threatening to murder her
if she will not yield at once to his desires. She resists rape, but she
is undoubtedly very much fascinated by his charms. The Commendatore returns, fights with Don Giovanni, and is killed; as in
Mozart, Don Giovanni at first refuses to fight with an old man,
but the Commendatore insists. After killing the Commendatore,
Don Giovanni runs away; Alfonso and Ottavio enter. Alfonso
orders Ottavio to 'arrest the felon' and hand him over to the
police. Anna begs Alfonso to release her from her engagement to
Ottavio, as he is now her guardian. Alfonso's words reappear
almost exactly in the duet of Ottavio and Anna in the opera:

'Voi se un padre perdeste, in me l'avrete.'

Ottavio returns to say that Don Giovanni has taken refuge in
the *atrio* surrounding the statue of the Commendatore, and that
they cannot arrest him, as the King has declared this *atrio* a sort
of sanctuary, although there is no suggestion that it is a church-
yard. The Italian critic already quoted points out that this
business of the statue erected some time before, and the right of
sanctuary around it, put too much strain on the credulity of the
audience if the play is to be considered realistic, as Goldoni
certainly intended it to be. The act ends with a soliloquy of Anna;
she will not commit herself to being still in love with Don Giovanni
but she admits that she was in danger of yielding and is thankful
to have escaped. Her last lines are a prayer to Heaven to protect
her against temptation. This last Act shows us the *atrio* and the
statue. Elisa enters, still in love with Don Giovanni, and tells him
that she can get the custodians to let him escape if he will return
to her embraces; he very naturally swears eternal fidelity. Isabella enters, still in male attire; she overhears the conversation
and interferes, like Donna Elvira, but as Don Giovanni still
pretends that she is a man he can attack her sword in hand. The
duel is interrupted by Don Alfonso. Don Giovanni addresses him
in a very lengthy speech; he admits most of his crimes, but says
he was drunk when he assaulted Donna Anna. With very Neapolitan effrontery and practicality, he puts it to Don Alfonso that
if he is executed it will be no real relief to the *figlia egra e dolente*,

the sick and grieving girl; he proposes to marry her instead, if the King will concede the usual 'clemency'. Alfonso, whose conceptions of 'honour' are as Spanish as Giovanni's are Italian, accepts his word. Enter Donna Anna, furious and insisting on the punishment of Don Giovanni. Don Alfonso explains that if she will herself ask for it, the King will probably grant pardon to Don Giovanni in order that he may marry her. She is at first indignant, but Don Giovanni, in the course of a longish scene (Don Alfonso always present), makes her change her mind. She will not go so far as to say 'Yes' definitely, but Alfonso at any rate tacitly assumes her consent and gives Don Giovanni some hope of respite. A page brings a letter to Don Alfonso stating the whole case of Isabella; Don Giovanni says it is untrue, but Alfonso this time tells him he is a liar. He orders the guard round the *atrio* to be doubled and goes away. Don Giovanni makes an appeal for mercy to Anna; she indignantly refuses, points to the statue and says that it will demand the vengeance of Heaven. Enter Carino, the shepherd, who urges Don Giovanni to repent and pray; he replies that he has long lost the habit of talking to the gods—he will rather invoke the furies of Avernus. He becomes violently rhetorical, curses everybody and everything, and finally challenges Heaven to destroy him by a thunderbolt. Heaven promptly does so; the earth opens and he sinks below. The others return to the stage; Carino describes what has happened. Alfonso tells Isabella that she can now go back to her own country; she thinks she has not been adequately compensated, so Ottavio makes a rather half-hearted offer of marriage, which she accepts with equal indifference. The main point of the play, of course, is Don Alfonso's severe reprimand to Elisa, the wanton shepherdess who represents Goldoni's faithless flame.

I have summarized this last scene rather fully in order to show its construction, which is more or less that of an operatic finale; the reader who has studied Da Ponte's libretto will also recognize many details of resemblance. But there is another play of Goldoni in which the Don Juan story makes its appearance. This is *Il Teatro Comico*, performed at Venice in 1760. The characters are the manager, poet, and actors of a theatre; the problem of the play is the conflict between the old comedy of masks and the new comedy of manners. At the end of the first act there is a speech which is of interest to us. Lelio, the poet, whose scenes of tenderness, he says, will make not only the audience but the very chairs

weep, and whose scenes of force will cause the boxes themselves
to clap their hands ('he must be a poet of the seventeenth century',
remarks one of the actors)—Lelio has read them his new play,
written in three-quarters of an hour, a mere skeleton plot for the
usual buffoonery of Pantaloon, Harlequin, and the rest—and has
been told by the leading lady that he is a lunatic:

'Is this the way they treat a man of my parts? I swear to heaven
I'll have revenge. They shall see who I am. I will have my
comedies acted in spite of them, if it is only by a troupe of strolling
players at a village fair. Who are these people who are going to
reform the theatre? Do they think that by producing two or three
new plays they have killed all the old ones? Never! and with
all their novelties they will never make as much money as was
made for so many years with *Il Gran Convitato di Pietra*.'

Here again we see that the Don Juan play is the play which
everybody knows, which everybody laughs at as silly and old-
fashioned, and which everybody always goes to see. There was a
similar play in Germany, as Jahn tells us; at Vienna up to 1783, if
not later, an improvised *Steinernes Gastmahl* was regularly given
during the octave of All Souls—'a proof that Don Juan's dissolute
life was contemplated with pleasure, and that morality was
abundantly vindicated by his being carried off by the Devil
after a long penitential speech'.[1]

Antonio Eximeno, himself a Spanish Jesuit, author of a history
of music (Rome, 1774), in a chapter on the Italian theatre speaks
with great contempt of the *Commedia dell' Arte* and the vulgar
taste of the Italians for enjoying it; he praises Goldoni's attempts
at reform. His remarks on the *Don Juan* play are therefore typical
of a man of cultivated taste at that time.

'Above all things, as regards machinery and magic one sees
things in the Italian theatre which are astonishing when one
considers the taste of the nation in other matters. In the sacred
comedies of Spain there appeared one devil at most; but in the
Italian theatre they come by legions sometimes. Not long ago
I saw in a theatre at Rome a play which opened with a committee

---

[1] A play of this type, *Dom* (sic) *Juan oder Der steinerne Gast*, adapted from
Molière by Marinelli for his Theatre in Leopoldstadt, with plenty of absurdities
for the Viennese Harlequin Kaspar, has been reprinted in the series *Deutsche
Literatur, Reihe Barock*, Band 2, *Die Romantisch-komischen Volksmärchen*, ed. O.
Rommel, Leipzig, 1936.

of devils which discussed the assistance to be given to a sorceress. The common people still flock to see *Il Convitato di Pietra*, which is a Spanish comedy full of machines and devils, no longer acted in Spain. And it is no excuse that educated persons are well aware of the improprieties of such comedies, which please only the ignorant lower classes; for in the theatre the taste of the common people upheld (*secondato*) by the educated classes is the national taste. If the devil were to appear nowadays on the French or English stage he would be stoned by the people.'

This is hardly true for England, as Byron's *Don Juan* was suggested by one of the various adaptations of *Don Giovanni* produced in London in 1817—either *The Libertine*, 'an operetta in two acts', words by Isaac Pocock, adapted from Shadwell (Covent Garden), or *Don Giovanni, or a Spectre on Horseback!* words by P. J. Dibdin (Royal Circus).

In 1775 Giovanni Bertati, a well-known librettist of that day who eventually wrote *Il Matrimonio Segreto* for Cimarosa, produced at Venice an opera consisting of two plays, the first a prologue to the second—*La Novità* and *L'Italiano a Parigi*; the music seems to have been by Alessandri. In February 1787 Bertati used the first play again, but this time (with slight alterations) for a second act consisting of *Don Giovanni Tenorio o sia Il Convitato di Pietra*, of which the music was by Giuseppe Gazzaniga. The music to the prologue was probably by Valentini. The opera was so successful that a rival opera on the same subject was brought out as soon as possible at another Venetian theatre with music by Francesco Gardi; this was itself in two acts and filled the evening without a prologue. The name of the librettist is not known. Gazzaniga's opera was very popular in Italy; it had a success in Paris and Lisbon as well, and in 1794, when Da Ponte was in London, as poet to the King's Theatre, he got an altered version of it produced there with music by various composers, including probably Leporello's catalogue song from Mozart's opera. As far as is known, Gazzaniga's opera was never performed in Vienna or at any German theatre; but, as we shall see, both the libretto and the music must have reached Vienna early in 1787 and there can be no doubt that both were carefully studied by Da Ponte and by Mozart too.

The first act of Bertati's opera deals with the troubles of a travelling Italian opera company in Germany—there were many of them, notably the Mingotti company with which Gluck was for a time associated. Policastro the manager complains that he is losing money; the company does not please. The singers are indignant, of course, all the more so as they are of a pretty humble class; the tenor boasts of the sonnets written in praise of him at Legnano and Lugo.[1]

'Yes, you are all magnificent', says Policastro; 'the dramas are splendid, the music is lovely—but it does not please the public.' 'That's the public's fault', says the *prima donna*. 'Well, we've got to content them and change our bill. In this place they have never yet seen that opera in one act that we performed in Provence. You all know it; we will just have a run through and give it this evening.' The singers hesitate and look anxious.

'Very well,' says Policastro. 'I'll have the bills posted at once.'

'Stop', says Ninetta. 'This opera is *Don Giovanni*?' 'Yes, *The Stone Guest*.' They shrug their shoulders. 'Well, of course, you never know what German taste may like, but——' 'You think it's rash?' 'Very—the action is improbable, the libretto is contrary to all the regular rules. I don't know what the music is, but I'm sure we shall be going from bad to worse.' 'Do you think the public cares about rules?' asks the manager. 'They care about what pleases them, and you will make more money out of rubbish than out of well-written serious plays.' Cavalier Tempesta, *alias* Baron von Sturm, the protector of the *prima donna*, tells them plainly that their opera is *una bella e stupenda porcheria*, only stuff for village fairs. Policastro cites Tirso de Molina and Molière, but there is a general complaint of sore throat from the singers which is relieved only by Policastro's threat to stop payment. They become docile at once, and the rehearsal of the opera forms the second act of the extravaganza.

The plot is based partly on Tirso, partly on Molière, but it differs from both in many important respects. The scene is laid in Villena, a town of Aragon. Pasquariello, Don Giovanni's servant, is keeping watch outside the house of Donna Anna, which his master has entered. Suddenly Don Giovanni and Donna Anna come out, Anna trying to unmask her assailant. She calls for help; her father, the Commendatore, enters, and she retires. A duel ensues, in which Don Giovanni kills the Commendatore;

[1] It was a common custom in Italy for sonnets to be written in praise of singers; they were then printed and dropped in showers from the gallery. These must have been some particular joke about Lugo (was it the Italian Wigan?) as the *prima donna* in Marcello's *Il Teatro alla Moda* boasts of her success and her sonnets there.

after a short dialogue Don Giovanni and Pasquariello leave the stage. Anna returns with Ottavio (here called Il Duca Ottavio, as in Tirso), followed by servants, who carry the corpse into the house by Ottavio's direction. Anna relates to Ottavio how Don Giovanni entered her house and assaulted her. Ottavio attempts to console her with the prospect of marriage; she refuses to think of it, and says she will go into a convent until her father's murder is avenged. Ottavio in an aria deplores the postponement of his marriage.

Scene 2. The country outside Villena, with rustic cottages and a noble mansion. Pasquariello reproaches Don Giovanni for his evil life. Don Giovanni explains that he has come to the country to pursue Donna Ximena. A lady gets out of a carriage; it is Donna Elvira, in search of her promised husband, Don Giovanni. They meet unexpectedly; Don Giovanni makes his escape, leaving Pasquariello to explain his character to Donna Elvira and show her the list of his conquests. She goes out, determined to assert her rights. A scene follows between Don Giovanni and Donna Ximena, from which it is clear that he intends to desert her also. A chorus of peasants now enters to celebrate the wedding of Biagio and Maturina. Pasquariello makes advances to Maturina and excites the jealousy of Biagio. The chorus goes out and Don Giovanni enters; he at once makes love to Maturina and drives Biagio away with blows. Maturina takes Don Giovanni into her own cottage. Donna Ximena returns, suspicious of Don Giovanni's intentions. Pasquariello and his master reassure her, but the situation is complicated by the entrance of Elvira and Maturina. Don Giovanni escapes in his usual adroit manner, leaving Elvira and Maturina together. He has told each of them that the other is mad, and a comic scene of mutual recrimination follows.

Scene 3. A cemetery, with the equestrian monument of the Commendatore. Don Ottavio enters with a stone-mason and directs him to carve on the base of the statue an inscription which he has written out. Don Giovanni and Pasquariello enter and read the inscription; Don Giovanni orders Pasquariello to invite the statue to supper; it nods repeatedly. Don Giovanni repeats the invitation himself and receives a verbal acceptance from the statue.

Scene 4. A room in Don Giovanni's house. Lanterna, another servant, is preparing supper. Elvira enters; Don Giovanni comes in and finds her. As in Molière's play, she tells him that she has repented of her passion and intends to take the veil after seizing this last opportunity of adjuring him to reform his life. He politely asks her to stay the night; she declines, saying that her carriage waits, and after singing an aria she takes her departure. Don Giovanni then proceeds to eat his supper, waited on by Lanterna and Pasquariello to the accompaniment of music on the stage. There is a good deal of comic business. Don Giovanni and Pasquariello propose the toast of the city where they have found the most adorable ladies, the city in this case being naturally Venice. In the manuscript score the word *Venezia* is crossed out and *Ferrara* substituted, showing that the opera was performed there also.

In the middle of the festivities the statue arrives, seizes Don Giovanni by the hand and bids him repent. The back scene changes to Hell, where Don Giovanni is tormented by furies while singing an aria. The wings nearest the audience remain, as Pasquariello is taking refuge there. At the end of the aria Hell disappears and the room is seen as before. Lanterna, who left the stage on the arrival of the statue, returns with Maturina, Elvira, Ximena, and Ottavio. Pasquariello relates what has happened; the others are duly shocked and decide to cheer their spirits with music and dancing.

Here are the concluding lines: they hardly need translation:

| | |
|---|---|
| *'Gli altri.* | Misero! Resto estatico (a) . . . |
| | Ma è meglio di tacer. |
| *Tutti.* | Più non facciasi parola |
| | Del terribile successo; |
| | Ma pensiamo in vece adesso |
| | Di poterci rallegrar . . . |
| | Che potressimo mai far? |
| *Donne.* | A a a, io vò cantare: |
| | Io vò mettermi a saltar. |
| *Duca Ott.* | La Chitarra io vò suonare. |
| *Lanterna.* | Io suonar vò il Contrabasso. |
| *Pasquar.* | Ancor io per far del chiasso |
| | Il fagotto vò suonar. |
| *Duca Ott.* | Tren, tren, trinchete trinchete trè. |
| *Lanterna.* | Flon, flon, flon, flon, flon, flon. |
| *Pasquar.* | Pu, pu, pu, pu, pu, pu, pu, pu. |
| *Tutti.* | Che bellissima pazzia! |
| | Che stranissima armonia! |
| | Cosi allegri si va a star.' |

The reader who is already familiar with Mozart's opera will have seen at once that Da Ponte incorporated practically the whole of Bertati's libretto, although he entirely rewrote the play in more elegant language. We may now summarize Da Ponte's libretto, indicating at the same time the sources to which he was indebted.

Act I. Leporello, Don Giovanni's servant, is keeping watch outside the house of the Commendatore. Don Giovanni and Anna enter from within, he trying to escape, she trying to unmask him. She calls for help; the Commendatore appears, fights with Don Giovanni, and is killed. Don Giovanni and Leporello make their escape. Anna returns with Ottavio (so far taken directly from Bertati). Anna makes Ottavio swear solemnly to avenge her father's murder (Da Ponte). Elvira arrives, in search of Don Giovanni; they meet unexpectedly. Don Giovanni makes off, leaving Leporello to explain matters and show Elvira the catalogue of his conquests. The peasants enter with song and dance, the happy couple being here called Masetto and Zerlina. Don Giovanni makes love to Zerlina and excites the jealousy of Masetto. (Bertati, following Tirso, makes the peasant girl take Don Giovanni into her own house; Da Ponte makes him lead her towards his. From this point Da Ponte diverges from his predecessors.) Elvira suddenly enters and takes Zerlina under her protection. Anna enters with Ottavio; they ask Don Giovanni's help in obtaining vengeance, neither of them being aware that he is himself the object of it. Elvira returns and accuses Don Giovanni of deserting her; he tells the others that she is mad, and leads her away as if to protect her. Anna suddenly realizes that Don Giovanni and her assailant of the previous night are one and the same. She relates the story in detail to Ottavio and again demands vengeance. Ottavio can hardly believe that her suspicions are correct, and says he will take steps to discover the truth, and either avenge her or undeceive her. (The suggestion that Elvira is mad goes back to Tirso (Isabella), but the ingenious management of the whole situation is entirely Da Ponte's.)

(From here to the end of Act I Da Ponte is drawing entirely on his own invention.) A dialogue follows between Leporello and Don Giovanni. Leporello has made the peasants drunk, propitiated Masetto as best he could, and managed to get rid of Elvira. Don Giovanni decides to entertain the peasants with a feast and dance, and hopes thereby to add at least ten more names to his list by the next morning. The scene changes to a garden.

Zerlina makes her peace with Masetto; Don Giovanni enters and Masetto hides in an arbour, in which he is discovered by Don Giovanni just as he is inviting Zerlina to come into it. Don Giovanni saves the situation by taking them both into the house for the dance. Anna, Elvira, and Ottavio enter masked; Leporello and Don Giovanni, seeing them from a window, invite them to join the festivity.

The scene changes to the ballroom, where the peasants have just finished a dance. The three masks enter and are politely welcomed; the dancing continues. A scream is heard from Zerlina; Ottavio and the others hasten to her assistance. Don Giovanni tries to accuse Leporello of being the offender, but the three avengers take off their masks, and Ottavio threatens Don Giovanni with a pistol. This is followed by an ensemble of some length, on which the curtain falls.

Act II opens with a dialogue between Don Giovanni and Leporello, who reproves his master, but is persuaded to remain in his service by a gift of money (Tirso and Molière). Don Giovanni is in pursuit of Elvira's maid, and takes Leporello's cloak as a disguise. (The changing of cloaks is taken from Tirso.) Elvira appears at the window and Don Giovanni persuades her to come down. He then makes off, leaving Leporello in his master's cloak to take her out of the way so that he may return and serenade the maid. No sooner has he finished his song than Masetto enters with some armed peasants in search of him. Passing himself off as Leporello, he offers to help them; he then sends the peasants in different directions, and, being left alone with Masetto, takes away his weapons and gives him a good beating. Zerlina enters, finds Masetto groaning, and consoles him.

The next scene is described as a dark courtyard in Donna Anna's house. Leporello enters with Elvira, from whom he vainly tries to escape in the darkness. Ottavio and Anna enter with lights, followed by Masetto and Zerlina. Leporello is discovered, and reveals his identity, to the confusion of all present. After he has escaped, Ottavio announces that he has now definitely come to the conclusion that there can be no doubt that the murderer of the Commendatore was Don Giovanni. He requests the others to stay and console Donna Anna, while he himself goes, not to fight with Don Giovanni, but to inform the police. (Modern opera-goers have often expected that Ottavio should avenge the Commendatore's death by a duel with Don Giovanni; but in

Tirso's play there is never any question of duels—Mota, when he is taken for the murderer on account of his red cloak, is simply handed over to normal justice.)

The next scene is the cemetery; Don Giovanni meets Leporello there and hears the story of his adventure with Elvira. Don Giovanni laughs, and is startled by the voice of the Statue warning him of his approaching end. It is only then that Don Giovanni discovers the monument of the Commendatore and its inscription. He directs Leporello to invite the Statue to supper, and repeats the invitation himself. The Statue first nods, and then replies with an audible 'Yes'. (Da Ponte omits the episode of Don Ottavio and the stone-mason, and he inserts himself the story of the episode with Elvira; the invitation to the Statue is more or less as in Bertati. Tirso's Statue neither speaks nor nods in this scene.)

Next follows a short scene for Ottavio and Anna; Ottavio presses for immediate marriage, but Anna protests that, although she loves him, the world would not approve. The scene changes to a room in Don Giovanni's house. Don Giovanni sups, waited on by Leporello and entertained by the music of wind instruments; Elvira makes a last attempt to induce him to repent. The Statue enters, and Don Giovanni is taken down to Hell, after which the other characters come in and are informed by Leporello of what has taken place. The survivors, being unable to hand over Don Giovanni to local justice, make the usual operatic arrangement for their own futures and conclude the opera with three lines of moral sung to the audience. (Tirso, Shadwell, and others show us the return of Don Giovanni's invitation; he goes to supper with the Statue at a church or charnel-house and is taken thence to Hell. But it should be noted that in practically all versions of the play the comic servant survives to give the other characters an account of his master's end, and there is a conventional pairing-off of some sort. In Shadwell's play the servant is the only survivor, and speaks an epilogue to the audience.)

It is important to understand exactly how Da Ponte's libretto is descended from Tirso through Molière, Goldoni, and Bertati, and to note how each of these authors made their own modifications to the story in order to meet the requirements of their own times and their own theatres.

In the course of centuries Don Juan, like Hamlet and Faust, has acquired a curious 'unearned increment' of personality. All three of these are said to have been men who really existed on earth; but the historical evidence for Hamlet and Faust is very scanty, and for Don Juan we have really no evidence at all. Yet the modern public, and especially the well-educated section of it, has gradually come to regard these three characters as if they had a real and immortal existence apart from the plays written about them. Don Juan was created by Tirso de Molina, and up to the days of Goldoni Tirso may have enjoyed the main credit for his invention; but for the present day, at any rate outside Spain and perhaps Italy, Don Juan has become Don Giovanni and his creator is Mozart. Mozart's opera has never yet been performed in Spanish, and has only had a very few performances in Italian in Spain; it is scarcely more familiar in Italy. Tirso's play is equally unfamiliar to northern readers, let alone playgoers, but it has been studied by scholars, and a good deal has been written about the Don Juan legend as a whole. Since it is perfectly impossible to translate music into words, everyone who listens to Mozart interprets him according to his own temperament, and there is a general tendency among those who are susceptible to music to interpret all music as being serious unless it is so obviously humorous as to be quite vulgar and trivial. Hence we may note a constant tendency among writers and talkers on Mozart to try to divorce him altogether from Da Ponte, as if Da Ponte were beneath contempt as a poet or dramatist, and as if Mozart were to be admired only in so far as he entirely disregarded his suggestions. But we cannot remove Da Ponte and marry Mozart's music to the original drama of Tirso, not even by the expedient of translating the libretto or rewriting it in a language that is neither Spanish nor Italian. Tirso's drama, as a modern English writer points out,[1] was in the main just one among many of the Spanish 'cape and sword' romantic plays; what is unusual about it as a drama is the episode of the statue. Otherwise Don Juan is by no means the only profligate of the theatre:

'We [i.e. we English] fail to understand the character of the Spanish hero, who pursues so seriously a life of crime, and who, believing profoundly in the powers of the supernatural, defies them so arrogantly. It is this gravity of demeanour in the Spanish Don Juan, the almost inhuman logic of his behaviour throughout the play, which repels and bewilders us, and compels us to seek, as Shadwell and Shaw have sought, to explain him philosophically.'

[1] John Austen, *The Story of Don Juan*, London, 1932.

It is certainly difficult for us northerners to take Don Juan so seriously. For most people in the northern countries profligacy is shocking and disgusting, and for a minority it is amusing; in this respect we may consider France as a northern country, though perhaps there the relations of majority and minority would be reversed. But to whichever group we belong, we cannot see anything heroic or grandiose about it, as the Spaniards apparently do and as the Italians do too if D'Annunzio is a true representative of them. There is the same difficulty as regards Don Juan's atheism or blasphemy, whichever it may be; the very devout would probably think it altogether too horrible for the stage, and the large majority would view it with complete indifference.

Much more important, however, is the purely theatrical aspect of the contrast between Tirso and Da Ponte. Tirso's play is extremely complicated, far more so even than the libretto of a Handel opera, and the constant presence of Don Juan's father and uncle, as well as of other 'grave and reverend signors' puts Don Juan himself into a position very different from that of the opera, where he is more like Macheath or Parsifal, surrounded by his lady friends with nobody very much to keep him in order. The plain reason for Da Ponte's removal of so many characters is that he had to write for a given company of singers. Bertati had to do the same, and in his case seven people had to represent ten characters. And just as in *Figaro* Michael Kelly had to double the parts of Basilio and Curzio, so at Prague Giuseppe Lolli had to sing both the Commendatore and Masetto. This was perhaps the chief reason why Don Giovanni remains on the stage for so long after the Commendatore has sunk through the trap—in order that Lolli might have time to change his clothes before returning as Masetto in the final sextet. There were only six singers available for seven parts. Bertati, although he has only one act to write, crowds in as many characters as he can—four female victims for Don Giovanni and two servants. Da Ponte, with fewer singers, has to spread his opera over a whole evening; he limits the ladies to three, but he has more scope for developing their characters.

*Don Giovanni*, as I have already pointed out, was completely misunderstood in the nineteenth century. It came to be regarded as something absolutely unique in operatic history. At the time of its first production it was planned by both Da Ponte and Mozart as an ordinary theatrical commission. The success of *Figaro* led Bondini to order another opera from Mozart, and it is obvious that what Bondini wanted was a second *Figaro*; it is equally obvious that that is what both Da Ponte and Mozart set out to supply. If we compare *Figaro* with other comic operas of the period, we shall see at once that its great merit (a merit which still helps it to hold the stage) is the abundance of incident, and especially of active incident—so many things happen in visible action. It is the same with *Don Giovanni*, and it is extremely probable that *Don Giovanni*, like *Figaro*, was originally planned in four acts. Act I would end after Anna's aria, *Or sai chi l'onore*, just as Act I of *Figaro* ends with a solo aria; Act II at the end of what is now Act I. Act III must end after the sextet, *Sola, sola*. This division into four acts suggests a certain grouping of the characters as regards their prominence in the story: Act I shows us Don Giovanni with Donna Anna, Act II with Zerlina, Act III with Donna Elvira, and Act IV with the Statue. At the same time Da Ponte has been very skilful in keeping all his characters before us up to the end. Bertati's Anna disappears altogether at quite an early stage, because the singer has to become another character, obviously Maturina. It seems pretty clear that in almost every one of Mozart's operas there was some sort of trouble during the rehearsals which necessitated a rearrangement of the score. This is most of all noticeable in *Don Giovanni*, but there is the same sort of confusion in the others, always about two-thirds of the way through or later.

As in *Figaro*, the tenor part is almost negligible, and the baritone is made into a sort of hero, although he is really more of a villain. There are also three female parts of equal importance. The lay-out of both operas was dictated by the singers available, and we know that Mozart was always singularly considerate of his singers and ready to write his music for them rather than expect them to accommodate themselves to his music. The singers in fact, for whom he wrote *Don Giovanni* were the same as those who sang in *Figaro*; he was conducting performances of *Figaro* at Prague during the rehearsals of *Don Giovanni*. There was nothing heroic about them; they were just an ordinary small Italian comic opera troupe; very little is known about them, beyond the fact that Luigi Bassi, who sang the Count in *Figaro* and Don Giovanni in the next opera, was only twenty-two, but a good actor and strikingly handsome. These qualities have seldom if ever been thus combined in any of his successors in that part.

A comparison of the two librettos will reveal many other

resemblances. The opening scene, which Gounod called 'la plus belle exposition de drame lyrique que je connaisse', is taken straight from Bertati, whose libretto is, as we have seen, a comic opera deliberately presented as an absurdity. Leporello's catalogue song[1] is in much the same style as *Non più andrai*, a conventional, chattering *buffo* aria. The chorus of peasants in 6/8 at once reminds us of the two choruses of peasants in *Figaro*. Masetto's aria is rather like Doctor Bartolo's without the quick patter. The duet *Là ci darem la mano* is paralleled by that for the Count and Susanna in Act III of *Figaro*, and Elvira's aria, *Ah, fuggi il traditor*, has a slight suggestion of the aria for Marcellina which was discarded for the duet with Susanna. The metre of *Fin ch'han dal vino* recalls the quick 2/4 section of *Se vuol ballare*, and the words of both songs bring in allusions to dancing the minuet.

*Batti, batti* must have called up other memories to Da Ponte. In the year 1775, on the morning of 16 August, a certain Doctor Giuseppe Mussolo, resident in Venice, having some cause of quarrel—the exact nature of it is not clear—with a young lady called Matilde Cassinis, daughter of a gentleman of noble family at Padua, decoyed her, as she was coming away from confession and communion at the church of San Biagio, at the far end of the Riva degli Schiavoni, into a side street, and when they reached the Fondamenta della Tana, the quay running along the canal just behind the church, he threw her down, pulled up her petticoats (women in those days wore no drawers) and spanked her soundly on her bare behind (*l'afferrò per il Collo gettandola a Terra, e levategli le vesti, la battè a Carni Nude con le mani nelle parti deretane*). And while he spanked her he sang the song which

---

[1] Mr. Lawrence Haward has pointed out that there is a parallel to Leporello's catalogue song in a poem by Abraham Cowley, *The Account*, one of his *Anacreontiques*:

> An hundred loves at Athens score,
> At Corinth write an hundred more.
> Write me at Lesbos ninety down,
> Full ninety loves and half a one.
> Three hundred more at Rhodes and Crete,
> Three hundred 'tis, I'm sure, complete.

Cowley's poem, which runs to forty-two lines, is an expansion of one of the poems called *Anacreontea* (i.e. wrongly ascribed to Anacreon) and is to be found in Bergk's *Greek Lyric Poets*, 1843. Da Ponte was not likely to have read Cowley, but he is pretty certain to have read Anacreon, if only in an Italian translation, of which there were many.

was sung by all the apothecaries' apprentices in Venice as they pounded brimstone in a mortar to make *triaca*:[1]

> 'Batti, batti, pesta sodo,
> La triaca qua se fa.'

Matilde and her family made a complaint to the authorities, and Mussolo was banished; he fled to Constantinople, where he practised very successfully for twelve years, after which he was pardoned, returned with much wealth to Venice and died there.[2] This affair naturally caused a great scandal, and the usual sonnets were circulated. Da Ponte at this time was living in Treviso, but he can hardly have failed to hear the story, and it may well have recurred to his mind when he visualized the peasant Masetto as a wife-beater, which he probably would have been in real life.

The finale to Act I is on a colossal scale, but based on the stock conventions of comic opera. For the duet at the beginning of Act II we might find a parallel in the duet between Susanna and Cherubino; there is a still closer parallel in the laughing trio of *Così fan Tutte* (Act I). Don Giovanni and his servant are here on absolutely equal terms—a situation quite inconceivable in a serious opera. The most remarkable parallel is that of the serenade *Deh vieni* with Susanna's *Deh vieni* in Act IV of *Figaro*; the opening words are the same, the metre is the same, and Mozart has set them to similar rhythms. The words *Discendi, o gioja bella* in the preceding trio are similar, and the repetition brings them into the same metre too.

The next aria (it is very curious, by the way, that Don Giovanni should have two arias in immediate succession) reminds us in metre and style of that which Susanna sings while she is dressing up Cherubino. It is all broken up into short sentences, and like Susanna's it is a series of peremptory instructions to another character. *Vedrai carino* is another aria that finds its successor in

---

[1] *Triaca*, from the Greek θηριακόν, is the origin of our word *treacle*; it was an electuary compounded of various ingredients, viscous in substance, brownish-yellow in colour and very malodorous. The word was commonly used in various other senses. (Notes to G. M. Buini, *L'Dsgrazi d'Bertuldin dalla Zena*, Bologna, 1736.)

[2] I have myself verified the documents in the Venetian archives. Mozart must have known something about this too, for in a letter of 20 February 1771, written from Venice, he tells his sister how seven German girls tried to throw him down to submit to the *attacco*, 'that is, have his bottom spanked when he is lying on the ground, so that he may become a true Venetian'. *Letters of Mozart and his family*, translated by Emily Anderson, London, 1938.

*Così fan Tutte* (Act II), both in its 3/8 metre and in its imitation of a beating heart. The sextet, as I have already pointed out, is obviously designed to end an act; it has the conventional form, with repeated sections and a hurried *stretta* in quicker *tempo*, which we find in all Mozart's Italian finales. It seems clear that something went wrong at this point during rehearsals.

Da Ponte can give us no information on this. He had to be in Vienna on 1 October for the first night of Martin's *L'Arbore di Diana*; he left the next day for Prague, but could only stay a week to direct rehearsals, as Salieri summoned him back to Vienna in all haste for the production of *Axur*. Evidence has recently been discovered which makes it pretty certain that alterations in the libretto were made by no less a person than Casanova. It is known that Casanova was in Prague on 25 October; how long before or after that date he was in the city has not been ascertained. But among his papers, now at Hirschberg, a sheet has been found with the following words in his handwriting:

|  | ((Literal translation) |
| --- | --- |
| Il solo Don Giovanni | Don Giovanni alone |
| M'astrinse a mascherarmi, | forced me to disguise myself, |
| Egli di tanti affanni | he of so many disasters |
| È l'unica cagion. | is the only cause. |
| Io merito perdon, | I deserve pardon, |
| Colpevole non son. . . . | I am not blameworthy. |
|  |  |
| Ei prese i panni miei | He took my clothes |
| Per bastonar Masetto, | to beat Masetto, |
| Con Donna Elvira io fei | with Donna Elvira I did |
| Il solo mio dover. | my duty and no more. |
| Fu tale il suo voler. . . . | That was his wish. . . . |

More lines follow, which unfortunately have not been communicated; they end with the words 'Lasciatemi scappar (fugge)'. On another page is written:

| Leporello: |  |
| --- | --- |
| Incerto, confuso, | Uncertain, confused, |
| Scoperto, deluso, | discovered, deluded, |
| Difendermi non so, | I cannot defend myself, |
| Perdon vi chiederò. | I will ask your forgiveness. |

Donna Elvira
Don Ottavio    Perdonarsi non si può. (He cannot be
Zerlina                                              pardoned.)
Masetto

More follows (not communicated) ending:

Leporello: Il palpitante cuor (fugge).

The transcriber of these pages says that they show cancellations and corrections, so they are evidently a first draft, not a fair copy.

It will be noted at once that no word of the above is to be found in Mozart's score except the stage direction *fugge* (he escapes); but it is obvious that these lines belong to the situation following the sextet. I should imagine that at some moment during rehearsals three at least of the singers begin to complain that they have been scurvily treated as regards solo arias. Mozart then decides to put in a scene after the sextet in order to satisfy Ponziani (Leporello) and Baglioni (Ottavio) and asks Casanova to write words for it. Teresa Saporiti (Anna) is provided with the entirely unnecessary aria *Non mi dir* later on. Casanova first sketches the aria for Leporello printed above, followed by an ensemble for all the characters except Donna Anna, who has left the stage at the end of the sextet. Mozart then probably points out that the audience already knows everything that Leporello says in this aria, and that another ensemble would be an anti-climax. Casanova rewrites the scene under Mozart's direction, making it much less formal and far more amusing and dramatic. As Mozart has taken away the sheet with the revised words, it is naturally lost; Casanova puts the rejected draft in his own pocket, and accident has preserved it. This reconstruction of what may have happened is purely conjectural.[1]

If the opera had been played in four acts, obviously the cemetery scene is the right opening for Act IV. All three of these Italian comic operas are very long; each of them in its entirety would take about four hours, allowing for short intervals. It was surely a wise idea to plan *Figaro* in four acts; but from about 1775 onwards there is an increasing tendency for Italian comic operas to be in two acts instead of three, and the manager at Prague may have insisted on giving *Don Giovanni* in two. When *Don Giovanni* was performed at Vienna in 1788

[1] See Paul Nettl, *Da Ponte, Casanova und Böhmen*, in *Alt-Prager Almanach*, Prague, 1927.

(7 May) Mozart had to make various alterations, and most of them occur at this point, between the sextet and the cemetery scene. First, the tenor was unable to sing *Il mio tesoro*, which in the Prague version comes after the sextet and after Leporello's aria. But the new song substituted for it, *Dalla sua pace*, was inserted not in the same place, but in the first act, just after that aria of Anna which probably ought to have ended the first act of four. Ottavio is left very awkwardly on the stage alone, just as Ferrando is in *Così fan Tutte* to sing the famous *Un' aura amorosa*; both songs hold up the action and are like concert songs. Madame Cavalieri demanded a *scena* for Elvira, so Mozart wrote her one— *In quali eccessi* and *Mi tradì*. This had to go in after the sextet and it was preceded by a *buffo* duet which is now never performed anywhere—*Per queste due manine* (Leporello and Zerlina). The situation is ludicrously silly, judged even by comic opera stand- ards, and the duet is an admirable piece of music, Mozart at his best in that particular style; it is really a great pity that we never hear it. These additions made the opera longer still, and Mozart drastically cut the whole of the final sextet, where the survivors rush in after Don Giovanni's disappearance.

The nineteenth-century custom was to follow Vienna and end the opera at this point, without bringing on the survivors at all; this was considered more dignified and tragic. But we have already seen that the entrance of the survivors is an integral feature of all Don Juan plays, from Tirso onwards; and Mozart evidently thought so too, for having cut the sextet he directed them to enter and sing a combined shriek on the notes of the chord of D major. This was found to be impossible of execution, so they came on and shrieked as they pleased. The people who maintain *Don Giovanni* to be a tragic opera point to Mozart's cut as proof that he was himself in favour of a tragic ending; but how can they reconcile this with the comic duet, also a 'second thought'? The answer is that they never hear it, and most of them do not even know of its existence, although it is printed even in Novello's edition.

The cemetery scene naturally has no parallel in *Figaro*; but the aria for Donna Anna, *Non mi dir*, is dragged in superfluously, just as *Dove sono* is in *Figaro*, to please a *prima donna*. The final sextet is pure comic opera.

## 9

## DON GIOVANNI—II

BETWEEN the first performances of *Figaro* at Vienna and *Don Giovanni* at Prague little more than a year elapsed; but it was an important year for Mozart, both as regards his compositions and his personal relations. As he himself kept a carefully dated catalogue of his works at this time, his progress as a composer can be followed very exactly. The first few works are mostly chamber music—the pianoforte quartet in E flat, the trio in G, the sonata for pianoforte duet in F, the clarinet trio, and a string quartet in D, all produced before the end of August 1786. These, and other chamber music of this year, were probably written for amateurs—the clarinet trio, for instance, was written for the sister of Gottfried von Jacquin—but they often show a seriousness of purpose and a depth of poetry that classes them among their composer's best works. This is very noticeable in the minuet of the clarinet trio, although one does not generally expect the minuet to be the most serious movement of a sonata. In December we come upon the noble pianoforte concerto in C major, the 'Prague' symphony in D, and the touching aria for Nancy Storace, *Ch'io mi scordi di te?* in which the pianoforte *obbligato*, played by Mozart himself, was skilfully treated as if it were a second character joining with the first in a duet.

At Prague, as we have seen, there was not much work done. Returning to Vienna in February 1787, Mozart was soon to lose three of those most dear to him within a few months of each other— first Count August Hatzfeld, then his father, and lastly Siegmund von Barisani, the son of the court physician at Salzburg, who had followed his father's profession and had been Mozart's medical adviser as well as his closest friend. How deeply he felt the loss of Hatzfeld may be seen from the fact that it was his death that inspired that well-known letter which he wrote to his father on 4 April, in which he speaks of death from the Masonic point of view.[1] Hatzfeld, who was the same age as Mozart, was a remarkably good violinist; he had often played in Mozart's quartets, and

---

[1] This letter will be considered more fully in a later chapter.

Mozart is said to have preferred his interpretation of them to all others. It is therefore possible that the two great string quintets, composed in April and May of this year, may have been to some extent connected with his death in the composer's mind. We must, however, beware of jumping to such conclusions as a matter of course, otherwise we may be tempted to suppose that the death of Leopold Mozart on 28 May was the direct inspiration of the *Musical Joke* dated 14 June.

Other works of this period are the Sonata in C for pianoforte duet, the beautiful song *Abendempfindung*, the *Kleine Nachtmusik*, and the violin sonata in A (K. 526). To say that all the compositions of this date are of a tragic or even serious character is manifestly untrue; but there are certainly cases, notably the G minor quintet and *Abendempfindung*, in which we may recall Vincent d'Indy's criticism on the 'second period' of Beethoven— 'jusqu' alors il n'a écrit que de la musique, maintenant il écrit de la vie'. We must take into consideration also the peculiar circumstances under which the new opera was being composed. *Figaro* had been planned with a view to attracting attention; Italian comic opera was fashionable in Vienna, and Mozart was determined to show that he could write a better Italian opera than the Italians themselves. *Don Giovanni* was written for a different audience. I do not know what authority there is for a statement ascribed to Mozart that he wrote *Don Giovanni* a little for Prague, not at all for Vienna, and mostly for himself; but it seems no unreasonable representation of the composer's attitude.[1] Vienna had crowded to *Figaro* for a few nights, and had probably regarded it mainly as a *succès de scandale*; Prague had shown a real understanding and enthusiasm for Mozart's music. Mozart may very probably have felt that whatever he wrote Prague was sure to accept, and that he need have no anxiety about giving the fullest liberty to his imagination. Da Ponte says that Mozart wished to treat the subject seriously; but we cannot suppose him to have meant that Mozart wished to treat the libretto as high tragedy with an earnest moral purpose. What he probably meant was that Mozart treated the music too much in the manner of *opera seria*: too many arias on the grand scale, and too much study of harmony and orchestration instead of attractive tunes that

[1] Vienna in Mozart's day seems to have had the same utter superficiality of musical taste that it had in our own, despite its perpetual boast of being the most musical city in Europe. Prague, both then as now, showed a far more passionate, serious and universal devotion to the art.

anybody could remember. But as a matter of fact *Don Giovanni* is by no means overburdened with grand arias; its melodies constantly verge on the trivial and are redeemed only by that elaboration of harmony which frightened not only Da Ponte but most of the Viennese as well.

There are three factors which contribute to make *Don Giovanni* an opera of a very unusual type. The first is that the composer allowed himself a free hand to try experiments in expression and push every technical device to its furthest limits; the second is that, owing to external circumstances, he happened at that time to be in a mental condition favourable to a certain emotional expansiveness; the third is that the libretto dealt with a subject utterly incapable of regular and formal treatment (such as we find in *Così fan Tutte*), and therefore sought to produce an illusion of regularity by disconnected conventionalities which are often a mere hindrance to the progress of the story. Putting these three things together, we are led to expect a work containing moments of overwhelming beauty and the greatest dramatic power, along with curious lapses into the mannerisms of an old-fashioned style, the whole being to some extent marred by a general vagueness and confusion of plan.

Concerning Da Ponte's indebtedness to Bertati, there can be no doubt whatever. Mozart's relation to Gazzaniga is less clear; it seems clear from the introduction that he was acquainted with Gazzaniga's score, but he never adopted his style as he did that of Sarti in *Figaro* and Gluck in *Idomeneo*. Giuseppe Gazzaniga (1743–1819), a native of Verona, but educated at Naples, was a voluminous composer, but left no great mark on the music of his day. His *Don Giovanni*, although far inferior to Mozart's, is nevertheless quite interesting, and it is curious to see how genuinely dramatic he can be with very limited resources, in spite of the fact that his opera required a whole act of apology to precede it. The best example to quote here is the introduction, since it is in this that Bertati's and Da Ponte's librettos are most alike. The first part of it, as far as the entrance of the Commendatore, is printed by Jahn in an appendix; the extract on pp. 147–54 continues from that point to the Commendatore's death.

If we judge Gazzaniga's treatment of the scene by the standard of the average Italian comic opera style of the period, we notice a very strong dramatic sense, and a considerable power of sustaining the musical interest through a long continuous scene. The

Ex. 23.

NOTE.—The stage directions are in the original.

(*Enter* COMMENDATORE *with a light, which* DON G. *strikes out with his sword.*)

de - gno! sot - trar - ti in va - no spe - ri da me.
*trai - tor! In vain you hope my wrath to e - vade.*

*f* Tutti.

DON GIOV.

*(They fight.)*

Vec - chio, ri - ti - ra - ti,
*Back, ere too late it be!*

*p*

ch'io non mi de - gno del po - co san - gue che scor - re in
*Do - tard, I scorn you, your fee - ble arm's no match for my*

*p*     *sfp*    *sfp*    *sfp*

te, Del po - co san - gue che scor - re in te.
*blade, your fee - ble arm's no match for my blade.*

*f* Tutti.

Pasq.

Ah! che ci sia - mo!
*Now there'll be fight - ing!*

Il Comm.

Non fug-gi-
*You shall not*

ra - i.
*fly!...*

Don Giov.

Ch'io da vil fug - ga non sper-ar ma - i, non sper-ar
*Thus you'd in - sult me? no cow-ard I!...... no cow-ard*

Il Comm.

ma - i. Un' al-ma no - bi-le in te non v'è.
*I!...... None that was brave such a deed could have done.*

Pasq.

Per do-ve
*Where can I*

fug-ga-si? non so più af-fè, per do-ve fug - ga-si non so più af-
*hide me now? where shall I run? where can I hide me now? where shall I*

IL COMM.

Ahi!.......... ahi!..........
*Ah!.......... ah!..........*

PASQ.

Io tre - mo
*I'm all a -*

tut - to, son...... quà di ge - lo.
*- trem - ble, fro - zen with ter - ror.*

IL COMM.

Sen - to man - car - mi di già la
*All strength has left me, life is de -*

vi - ta. (*staggers and falls.*)
*- part - ing.*

PASQ.

Io tre - mo
*I'm all a -*

d'u - - dir mi par, d'u - - dir mi par.
*nou but his groans, nought but his groans.*

Il Comm.

Sen fug - ge
*Now my last*

l'a - ni - ma, gia vò a spi - rar, sen fug - ge
*hour is come, now I must die. Now my last*

(*dies.*) Pasq.

l'an - i - ma, gia vò a spi - rar. Più non si
*hour is come, now I must die. Dark - ness has*

orchestra employed is small, the treatment of the instruments
old-fashioned and wanting in sonority, especially as compared with
Mozart's orchestration. As usual, the violas play with the basses,
and the violins are often in unison, the harpsichord being left to
fill up the void. But there is a continuous attempt, despite a rather
paltry invention, to make the instruments express some emotional
idea; when the Commendatore is wounded, the oboes take up the
theme of his groans, and later on, after he has fallen, their thin
voices repeat the theme and suggest what he can no longer express
audibly. Gazzaniga's music is certainly dramatic, and it is also
reasonable—there are no places where the succession of harmonies
does not make sense. But from beginning to end there is not a
single theme of any real musical significance. Every figure, vocal
or instrumental, is a stock pattern, a dummy with neither life
nor originality. Compared with Mozart's, it suggests a rehearsal
at which the actors walk through their parts in their ordinary

clothes, on an empty stage in daylight. And the music moves slowly too; each character enters at regular distances, speaks at the same pace and in much the same rhythms; if it were a play, we should say that the actors are very slow at taking up their cues. Mozart, on the other hand, starts with themes which mean something, and even where he employs stock patterns he develops them and makes his voices enter more closely on one another's heels; thus he obtains an effect of overwhelming energy which almost disguises the regularity of the construction.

Yet there is no note of tragedy; it is all planned from the standpoint of *opera buffa*. This is a very difficult thing for a modern audience to realize, because neither *opera buffa* nor even *opera seria*, as Mozart knew them, are now familiar conventions. That is why it is urgent to keep in mind perpetually the style of *Idomeneo*, or at least that of Gluck, to give us some sort of a tragic standard. Could anyone imagine Leporello's chattering repeated quavers in the background of a duet between Armida and Rinaldo? Leporello has always been instanced as a wonderful example of Mozart's power of character-drawing; but in reality Leporello is as little individualized as Bartolo or any other *buffo* part. The patter of reiterated notes runs through every *buffo* part ever composed from Alessandro Scarlatti onwards to Sullivan; it is absurd to say that it expresses fear. The words may express fear in some places, but they may express dozens of other emotions, though the patter goes on just the same. Leporello gets his best chance of asserting himself in his opening *arietta*; the brilliant effectiveness of the catalogue aria expresses not so much Leporello himself as his view of his master. I suspect that the aria for him after the sextet in the second act was put in at his own request. Bassi, the singer of Don Giovanni, is known to have complained to Mozart that he never got a chance of a really big aria throughout the opera, and Leporello comes off a good deal worse; he never gets the sort of chances that Figaro had. It is clear that Mozart, after his experience with the all too leisurely style of *Die Entführung*, began to see that comic opera required a general quickening up of the pace all the way through; and after *Figaro*, which no one could call 'leisurely', he still felt that the whole *tempo* had to be accelerated. There must be shorter and fewer instrumental introductions, for one thing; the actual arias must be quicker in pace and shorter as well. There is in fact only one place in the whole opera where Mozart spreads himself instrumentally—the mandoline solo which precedes the serenade; and as Don Giovanni is supposed to be playing it himself on the stage, it is not a mere instrumental introduction but a piece of stage business.

The interest of Leporello is that he is almost constantly on the stage, like Don Giovanni's shadow. It is only rarely that his own emotions come into prominence, as they do just before the duel, when he is really afraid that his own life is in danger:

The importance of this theme is shown by the fact that it is played by the orchestra in unison, the voice strengthened by the bassoons. German critics often insist on the supposed cowardice of Leporello; the reason is that they have been accustomed to derive his name from *lepus*, a hare, and the German word *Hasen-fuss* (hare-foot) happens to mean a coward. As the name Leporello is the invention of Da Ponte and does not occur in any previous version of the play, there seems more likelihood that it was an Italianization of the German *Lipperl* (Austrian diminutive of *Philipp*), a name sometimes given to that comic figure more generally known as *Kasperl* or *Käsperle*, the German Harlequin.[1]

In Gazzaniga's opera the *recitativo secco* starts directly after the extract that I have quoted; Mozart draws all three voices into a terzetto as the Commendatore expires. He emphasizes the emotional situation with an ensemble, but it sacrifices something of the dramatic effect, for one inevitably gets the impression that all three characters are in close proximity, instead of being dispersed in the darkness. The dialogue that follows is apt to sound more than usually absurd; but its very absurdity makes an effective contrast and brings us back to the world of *opera buffa*. The terzetto is one of those curious movements so characteristic of this opera, in which Mozart seems to have forgotten the whole play for a moment in a complete self-absorption into his musical

[1] I do not know who first suggested this derivation; it is mentioned by Jahn and other German writers.

idea. And there is a curious commentary on this terzetto in Beethoven's pianoforte sonata in C sharp minor, the conscious derivation of which from this source is indicated pretty clearly by the existence of a leaf on which Beethoven has hastily scribbled down the voice-parts of the terzetto, but with no accompaniment except one bar of the violin figure in triplets.[1]

Donna Anna and Don Ottavio, who now come on to the stage, were evidently intended by Da Ponte to be the pair of more or less serious lovers customary in most Italian comic operas. *Figaro* had none, but *Figaro* is in every way unconventional. Mozart, as we have seen before, almost always tends to lay his colours on too thick for the style; but this duet is peculiarly interesting, because while Anna is obviously very much overwrought, Ottavio is perfectly self-possessed. Her ravings and his consolations are expressed with perfect truth, almost with exaggeration, yet the music flows on continuously, and the sense of musical form is maintained throughout the whole movement, despite its being much broken up by patches of recitative.

With the return of Don Giovanni and Leporello we revert to *opera buffa* again. Here we come upon a new example of Mozart's delightful ingenuity. Donna Elvira soliloquizes in a formal aria, but the two men, standing in the background and unable to see her face, make their brief comments in what would normally be the *ritornelli* of the orchestra. It is an admirable stage picture, and we seem to learn more about Don Giovanni and Leporello in these short remarks than we do about Elvira in the whole aria. Also, the play is definitely carried on during the *ritornelli* which are a musical necessity but dramatically a nuisance; and what is most important, these comments make sure of the comic atmosphere—we know at once that we are not going to be allowed to take Elvira seriously for a moment. *Don Giovanni* and *Figaro* present a curious contrast of method, for although the proportion of arias to ensembles is the same in each, it is mainly the arias, rather than the ensembles, in *Don Giovanni* which give it its peculiar character, whereas in *Figaro* the reverse is the case. But on the other hand it must be noticed that all the arias in *Don Giovanni* are much shorter and more concise than those of *Figaro*[2] and that in every case the singer of an aria is directly addressing

---

[1] This was pointed out to me by the late Professor Max Friedlaender, who was the owner of the leaf.

[2] Except for *Il mio tesoro* (Ottavio, in Act II).

someone else on the stage. There are no soliloquies at all, except this one of Elvira's which is made ridiculous by being overheard and commented on. And whereas in *Figaro* all the characters are well mixed up together, so that practically every one of them has occasion to talk to every other, in *Don Giovanni* it is only Don Giovanni himself who comes into contact with everybody else. Anna and Ottavio make practically no contact with Zerlina and Masetto, and Leporello has no direct conversation with the first couple either, except in the sextet, where Anna's obvious and very natural desire is to get away from everybody as quickly as possible. Nor has Elvira any meeting with the Commendatore; he is dead before she first appears, and at the end she just sees the Statue and runs away.

Elvira is by far the most interesting of the characters, after Don Giovanni himself. Anna has been made into a tragic figure by later interpreters, but it may be doubted whether she is really anything more than self-absorbed and aloof. In so far as she comes into the earlier plays, she is not tragic at all; she is simply young and very foolish, almost as inexperienced, though nowhere near so lovable, as Tatiana in Tchaikovsky's *Eugene Onegin*. She has a narrow escape, and may be thankful that at the end of Tirso's play Don Juan, with his dying breath, states definitely that she is *virgo intacta*, which cannot be said of any of the other females in it. But in Da Ponte's libretto the whole situation is changed by the fact that Don Giovanni, unlike Don Juan, has no practical success with any of his so-called victims; he gets the worst of it with all three, even with Elvira, although we must pretty certainly admit that she was definitely seduced at Burgos.

Anna treats even Don Ottavio in so distant a manner that we cannot expect her to reveal her true self in any duet or trio. She seems to have been brought up from childhood always to conceal her real feelings and never acknowledge to herself any motive but duty and family pride. If she had been Italian and not Spanish, she might have been Fiordiligi in *Così fan Tutte*, and there seems every probability that she will eventually become first lady-in-waiting to the Queen of Night. She is in fact a thoroughly unpleasant young lady. Elvira, on the other hand, knows no restraints. We know from Molière, who created her, that she is an escaped nun, but that hardly justified Baudelaire in calling her *la chaste et maigre Elvire*, and the second epithet seems peculiarly inappropriate to any reader who has seen the opera in Germany.

Don Giovanni is probably the first man in whom she has ever taken an interest, and whether she is in love with him or in a rage with him, he is always uppermost in her thoughts. She is really the central female figure of the opera; she is always in the thick oi the plot. She almost deserves the tragic aria *Mi tradì* which was written for Mme. Cavalieri at Vienna, but dramatically there is nowhere to place it, and it is really quite superfluous, for it tells us nothing about her that we do not know already. If we give her a moment's serious consideration, she is as tragic a personality as Gluck's Armida or Verdi's Amelia, but by the exigencies of that very character which Da Ponte has given her she is forced to conform to the general *opera buffa* standard set by Don Giovanni himself throughout the opera, and which is an absolute necessity, because a really serious treatment of the whole story would have been too utterly repulsive for stage presentation. It is only by accepting a generally frivolous standpoint to the whole opera that we can tolerate the dialogue between her and Don Giovanni, or the scene with Leporello that follows, culminating in the famous catalogue-aria.

The atmosphere of frivolity is kept up for several scenes, notably, of course, in the duet *Là ci darem la mano*, in which, as in the *Figaro* duets, there is a wonderfully delicate sense of characterization shown in the different ways in which the tune is divided between the two voices, and in those tiny variations of melody which make so enormous a difference to the poetic significance of the phrases. Elvira's air which follows is a deliberate imitation of the Handelian style; Jahn supposed that it was intended as the musical equivalent of a sermon. Elvira here seems to pose as a lady abbess, in which character it is difficult to take her seriously. But in any case it is a fine piece of music and has its dramatic value.

The next scene does great credit to Da Ponte's powers of invention. No more delightfully humorous situation could have been imagined than for Don Ottavio and Donna Anna to invite the co-operation of Don Giovanni in their plan of vengeance on the murderer of the Commendatore. The very promptness with which Elvira reappears makes her entrance all the more comical, and the quartet, in spite of the momentary seriousness of Anna and Ottavio, still maintains the *buffo* style. This movement has often been regarded as tragic in the extreme; but I can only tell those who take this view to turn back to the quartet in the third act of *Idomeneo* for a standard of style in musical tragedy. Most ingenious is the use of the little phrase—

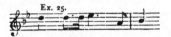

which is first sung by Elvira to the words *Te vuol tradir ancor*, and then repeated by violins, clarinet and flute successively in various places. It comes in with comic effect when Don Giovanni interposes and apologizes for Elvira's eccentric behaviour by saying that she is mad. She may well seem mad to them, with her wild outburst that mixes the styles of 'patter' and *coloratura* so strangely:

Further on such little dignity as she had breaks down completely.

With Donna Anna's long recitative and aria (*Or sai chi l'onore*) we return to tragedy for a moment. It is on this occasion above all others that we feel the utter inadequacy of Don Ottavio. We had hoped on his first appearance that his character would be developed as the opera went on; but instead of that he becomes steadily less and less interesting. Mozart seems to have been unfortunate in his Italian tenors. Kelly must have been pretty competent, but he was evidently a *tenore buffo* by temperament, to judge from his own memoirs; the sort of part that he enjoyed was the comic old prime minister in Paisiello's *Re Teodoro in Venezia*, or the poet in Righini's *Demogorgone*, where he openly caricatured the airs and graces of Da Ponte himself. The tenor Morella, who sang Don Ottavio in Vienna, was unequal to the difficulties of *Il mio tesoro*, and Mozart composed the other tenor aria for him—*Dalla sua pace*. Ottavio's inadequacy is in fact the weak point of the whole opera. It is all the more apparent in this scene with Donna Anna, for she appears here as a regular virago—more like Electra than Ilia in *Idomeneo*. The result is that in practice Ottavio's little interjections of anxiety and relief during the long story of her encounter with Don Giovanni and his

attempted rape of her become positively comical, and it is noticeable that a modern English audience almost invariably receives
them with ribald laughter, however earnestly he may try to
ejaculate them. *Dalla sua pace*, beautiful as it is, falls very flat
after the energetic outburst of Anna's exit aria.

Don Giovanni and Leporello restore us to the normal comic
atmosphere. The aria *Fin ch'han dal vino* is in Germany always
called the 'champagne aria', and it is a standing tradition of the
German stage that Don Giovanni must wave a champagne glass
while singing it. As there is nothing whatever in the words to
suggest that Don Giovanni himself is drinking at this moment, it
looks as if German singers had always found the song rather long
and difficult to make effective without some subsidiary business to
hold the audience's attention. It is followed by a scene for
Zerlina and Masetto in which Zerlina soothes Masetto's jealousy
with the all too famous *Batti, batti*.[1] The tune is trivial enough to
have been written by Paisiello, but what gives it its undeniable
charm and its delicate suggestion of what Weber would have
marked *lusingando* is the orchestral treatment and especially the
violoncello solo, which continues throughout the song with curious
persistence—a regular *perpetuo moto*.

The first finale is a masterpiece of construction on the part of
Da Ponte. He and Goldoni, from whom he must have learned the
technique, deserve a good deal more gratitude than most librettists
are ever conceded by musical critics, for when we look at a finale
on this scale, as composed by Mozart, we see that the finale is
really the foundation of all continuous opera technique. The
modern opera, *durchkomponiert* as the Germans would call it, i.e.
continuous music all the time, with the minimum of absolute
recitative, is simply a finale extended backwards to the beginning.
The first episode, with Masetto hiding in the arbour, recalls the
episode of Cherubino hiding in the armchair. Masetto is a more
interesting character than audiences generally realize. His
previous aria—the last number of the opera that was written, an
afterthought during rehearsals at Prague—ought never to be
omitted. It has more than a touch of that indignation and

---

[1] The almost religious devotion with which Victorian connoisseurs used to
speak of this aria is probably due to the memory of Adelina Patti. Her performance of Zerlina was once described to me by Mme Jean de Reszke: 'Elle ne
chantait pas Zerlina, elle l'était; c'était adorable! Mais, comme elle était bête!'
But there was one subject on which Patti was anything but *bête*, and that was
money—see *The Mapleson Memoirs*.

revolutionary feeling which appears in Figaro's arias and is, of course, the social background of that whole opera. Da Ponte and Mozart were men of their own time, and we must not forget that *Don Giovanni* has no less 'social significance' than *Figaro*; that is indeed the sole purpose of Masetto and Zerlina in the dramatic scheme. An amusing feature in this section is the little chorus of footmen; this must have been entirely Mozart's own idea, because the words which they sing are absurdly inappropriate, being borrowed from Don Giovanni's previous invitation to the peasants. But it is just conceivable that Mozart has made a mistake in his stage directions, and that the chorus of men ought indeed to be sung by the peasants and not by the footmen, although it is marked *Servi*.

After Don Giovanni has led Masetto and Zerlina into the ballroom, Don Ottavio, Donna Anna, and Donna Elvira enter masked. It is the energetic Elvira who takes the lead; Ottavio follows any lead that is offered him, and Anna can hardly be persuaded to take any action at all. A window in the palace is opened by Leporello, and we catch the last notes of a minuet played inside. As the dance is repeated Leporello sees the three masks and draws Don Giovanni's attention to them; he tells Leporello to invite them in, and they accept. The dance ends and Leporello shuts the window again. Here follows the trio *Protegga il giusto cielo*, one of those ensembles such as I have described before, in which no action takes place, but there is a moment of lyrical contemplation which provides a point of repose and also prepares the audience for the importance of the action to follow immediately. All who have seen the opera will remember its startling impressiveness and the strangely beautiful effect of the wind instruments (without strings) which accompany it.

The scene now changes to the ballroom, where the country folk have just finished a dance; Leporello and the other servants are handing refreshments. In spite of Don Giovanni's previous injunctions, this entertainment seems to anticipate the austerity of Miss Cons at the Old Vic, for we hear only of coffee, chocolate, lemonade, and biscuits. No wonder Masetto implores Zerlina to be careful! The three maskers are ushered in by Leporello and are received by Don Giovanni with all stateliness. A minuet is played, and is danced by Donna Anna and Don Ottavio alone. This has often been misunderstood; it was customary in Mozart's day for a single couple to take the floor alone on occasions, and

Da Ponte wants here to make Anna as conspicuous as possible. The others force her to dance against her will simply in order to keep up appearances; we hear their *sotto voce* encouragements.[1] There are three orchestras on the stage, playing three different dances simultaneously. The first consists of strings, two oboes and two horns; this one plays the well-known minuet. As the last half of the minuet is repeated we hear (or ought to hear) the second orchestra tuning; it has only violins (in unison) and bass, and plays a *contre-danse* in 2/4 time. Later on the third orchestra (also violins and bass) begins tuning and then plays an old-fashioned German waltz in 3/8. Leporello makes Masetto dance the waltz with him, much against his will, in order to get him out of the way into another room, while Don Giovanni invites Zerlina to dance the *contre-danse* in order to lead her into the room on the opposite side of the stage. This arrangement of three orchestras on the stage was apparently Mozart's own idea, suggested by the excellent instrumentalists available at Prague. It is very seldom that they are made effective on the stage in modern performance, even if the players are actually there, which is not always the case.

As it is impossible to make the three dances clear in a pianoforte arrangement, it may interest some readers to see how they are contrived to fit. Note that the first three bars of the waltz are purely introductory; the dance starts at the fourth bar.

Ex. 27.

WALTZ.

CONTRE-DANSE.

MINUET.

<hr />

[1] We may compare (and contrast) this scene with the dance of Calantha in John Ford's *The Broken Heart* (Act v, sc. 2).

The wind instruments are very ingeniously used to support all three orchestras at different moments and bring into prominence whichever is dramatically important.

The idea of the three dances and three orchestras was derived from the public balls at Vienna, for which Mozart himself wrote large quantities of dance music. But there, of course, the three orchestras would be in different rooms, though near enough, no doubt, for a sensitive ear like Mozart's to hear all three together sometimes, suggesting the possibility of combining them in a *quodlibet*. The three dances represent three social strata— minuet for the aristocracy, *contre-danse* for the *bourgeoisie*, and the waltz for the proletariat.

Suddenly Zerlina is heard screaming for help. The musicians break off and go away, as there is a general confusion. The door of some secret chamber is supposed to be forced; Zerlina comes out, followed by Don Giovanni, who pretends to throw the blame on Leporello. The three conspirators are not deceived by this; they unmask and accuse Don Giovanni to his face, while Ottavio threatens him with a pistol. What happens on the stage after this is not indicated either in the libretto or the score. A long and very conventional movement of the finale type begins at this point; it is longer than the finales of either *Figaro* or even *Così fan Tutte*, but much less interesting. It is just Da Ponte's *lo strepitoso, l'arcistrepitoso, lo strepitosissimo*, and might almost have been written by Sarti. The only difference between Sarti's formula (quoted in Ex. 15) and Mozart's is that Sarti takes the scale down and Mozart takes it up. It sounds really like a long and more than usually aggressive assertion of the chord of C major such as we might find at the end of any extended piece of classical music.

In Act II Da Ponte is thrown mainly on his own invention; he has plenty of ideas for farcical situations, but there is no dramatic construction, and the confusion of plot is redeemed only by the fascination of Mozart's music. The first scene is the street before the inn where Elvira is staying.

Da Ponte's original idea had been to begin with dialogue between Don Giovanni and Leporello, but Mozart put in the little duet which precedes the conversation. It is to us nowadays a most curious thing that in *opera buffa*, and indeed in *opera seria* too, an act will quite often start with nothing more than a chord on the harpsichord and a stretch of ordinary recitative. The modern ear demands at least a few bars of orchestral music 'to take up the curtain'. But in the earlier part of the eighteenth century the curtain did not as a rule fall between the acts of either operas or plays, and it is still a matter of uncertainty when exactly the act drop came into regular use, in operas or in plays, and in the different countries. As far as the Continent is concerned, I should imagine that France set the example for plays, and Italian comic opera for opera, all over Europe.

The little duet is amusing and perfectly conventional; Leporello has played this game over and over again. He is always pretending to be shocked at his master's evil life and threatening to leave him, because he knows he will always be bribed to stay on. And there is no differentiation of character in the music; master and man are on absolutely equal terms. Don Giovanni is intent on pursuing Elvira's maid, whom he has already marked down; to this end he changes hats and cloaks with Leporello. Elvira appears on the balcony and starts the trio *Ah taci, ingiusto cuore,* which is perhaps the most beautiful number of the whole opera. The dramatic situation is the most repulsive; it is endurable only if one takes a completely frivolous view of the whole play, and even then one feels that it would be more appropriate to a puppet-play than to one in which real human beings appear. Elvira has shifted round again from indignation to desire. She contemplates her own emotions with deliberate romance; Don Giovanni perceives at once that she is in that frame of mind when the prospect of an adventure of any kind will make her throw discretion to the winds. He pushes Leporello forward (dressed in his master's hat and cloak) and addresses her in tones of exaggerated pathos. The trick succeeds; in the gathering darkness she takes Leporello for Don Giovanni, and we watch her gradually yielding to temptation, as his voice grows more and more insistent, adjuring, cajoling, threatening suicide—he has done it so often that he almost believes in his own words—while Leporello watches the game in fits of suppressed laughter.

The music of this trio recalls the trio in *Zaide* quoted in an earlier chapter (Ex. 12); Italian as it is in melodic detail, its composition as a whole is more German than Italian. As soon as the three voices unite to repeat Elvira's opening phrase their individualities become merged in Mozart's; they cease to be persons—they are merely representatives of musical themes. It is not drama, but when used with judgement by a composer who whenever he wishes is a complete master of drama, it has an emotional and poetical value, as we have already seen in *Idomeneo*.

Elvira leaves the window and Don Giovanni reveals his plan: Leporello is to take charge of the lady in the character of his master and manage somehow to get her out of the way, so that Don Giovanni may pay his attentions to the maid. Elvira falls into the trap without a moment's hesitation and proceeds to lavish caresses on Leporello, who enjoys the situation extremely. Don Giovanni pretends to attack them as a robber, and they fly, leaving the stage clear for the serenade. Taken seriously, Elvira's degradation is horrible; after being insulted to her face first by Don Giovanni and then by Leporello in Act I, she is now subjected to a cruel practical joke and then discarded again by the 'gentleman's gentleman'. Donna Anna, of course, would say that it was all her own fault and serve her right, as she was 'that sort of person'.

The serenade is notable for its mandoline *obbligato*, in most theatres played by a violin pizzicato,[1] which is not at all the same thing. The use of this instrument in the orchestra was nothing new, as we have seen in the case of Paisiello's *Barbiere*; moreover Martín had employed it in *Una Cosa Rara*. This last example is worth quoting as the style of the melody is sufficiently like Don Giovanni's serenade to make it probable that Mozart had noted the effect and meant to show how much better he could do it[2] (see p. 167).

Martín's innocent melody no doubt pleased Vienna better than Mozart's, and the syncopations would be regarded as Spanish local colour. Mozart borrowed a *fandango* from Gluck for *Figaro*, but otherwise he makes no attempt to be Spanish in either of these operas, and Da Ponte, as far as I can judge, seems to have visualized the Don Juan story in some Venetian town of his own time.

No sooner has Don Giovanni finished his serenade than he is interrupted by the arrival of Masetto, who takes him for Leporello. The aria in which Don Giovanni directs the peasants to right and left in search of his supposed self, keeping Masetto behind for a good beating, is very amusing; it has often been pointed out how he begins by imitating the musical style of his servant, and as he proceeds forgets his part and unwittingly expands into the expression of his own character. Masetto, left groaning on the

---

[1] If an English orchestral violinist played it on the mandoline, he would probably have to be paid double fees.

[2] Mozart had himself composed two songs with mandoline accompaniment in 1780 for a horn-player at Munich called Lang.

ground, is consoled by Zerlina in a graceful little song which recalls the favourite 'heart-beat' effect of Pergolesi and Logros-cino. We meet it again in *Così fan Tutte*.

We now come to the great sextet, which is one of the finest numbers in the opera. It is a long and complicated series of movements, in the course of which various things take place on the stage; it is also remarkably full of striking musical ideas, both comic and serious. Leporello and Elvira, wandering about the town, have taken refuge in the courtyard of a palace to avoid a party of people with lights, since Elvira has not yet discovered her mistake and Leporello does not want to expose himself. Indeed, he does his best to make his escape under cover of the complete darkness, but is defeated, since he cannot find the way out. It so happens that the palace is that of Donna Anna, and the lights which Leporello has seen are those of the torch-bearers escorting her home, in the company of the inevitable Don Ottavio. They enter the courtyard, but do not at first notice the other two, who both take advantage of the light to make for the doorway, but run straight into Masetto and Zerlina, who enter from the street. There is no apparent reason why they should be there at this moment, unless they perhaps thought that the dark entry offered a convenient place for endearments. They naturally take Leporello for his master; he casts off his cloak to save himself. Donna Elvira is thrown into confusion, while Donna Anna, gravely scandalized, retires upstairs, leaving Ottavio on the doorstep. The situation is most amusing, but totally unnecessary to the drama, unless it is to lead up to Ottavio's curiously illogical deduction that all this misunderstanding proves Don Giovanni to have been the murderer of the Commendatore, and, following on this deduction, his courageous determination to inform the police. But there is one reason of indisputable cogency for the presence of all these characters on the stage together—they are there to sing a sextet built up on the conventional scheme of the operatic finale. If the evidence is hardly adequate proof of Don Giovanni's crime, it is irrefutable proof that this was intended to be the end of an act, for at no other point could such a movement possibly be introduced; and if it is not to end an act there is no conceivable reason for introducing it, or its characters, at all. Nothing but a curtain can follow it. Leporello's explanatory aria is an anti-climax, and any way it tells us nothing that we do not know already. Ottavio's aria, lovely as it is, is a still worse anticlimax, and dramatically impossible, all the more so because it is the most formal and elaborate solo of the whole opera and the nearest approach that Mozart ever makes in it to the style and constructive method of *opera seria*. It takes a great singer to execute it, and if we once begin to fear that the singer may not be equal to his task, it is agonizingly embarrassing to sit through it. If Ottavio is merely a voice and nothing more, it is a glorious opportunity; if we are to think of him as a character in a drama, it is simply his ruin, at any rate, in that particular scene. The additional numbers written for Vienna, masterly as they are, only add to the confusion.

The cemetery scene was originally intended to begin at once with the duet, but the recitative connects it with the previous scenes, and gives Don Giovanni time to notice the Statue and its inscription. Apart from the idea of the inscription, all this introduction is Da Ponte's invention, and it may be doubted whether the isolated remarks of the Statue, accompanied by trombones, are dramatically advantageous. In practice it is always very difficult to bring them in exactly right and to secure the proper balance of musical colour, not only in the chords themselves, but in their relation to what precedes them. At rehearsal Mozart himself had trouble with the trombone-players, and hastily added the parts for oboes and bassoons to safeguard them in case they went wrong. It must be borne in mind that the trombones in this opera, the parts for which have given rise to much textual criticism,[1] are treated as if they were played on the stage, or even under the stage, like Purcell's in *The Libertine*.[2] They are as foreign to the normal orchestra as the organ is in *Robert le Diable*, *Lohengrin*, or *Meistersinger*. In all operatic church scenes the indispensable organ is a stage property, not part of the orchestra, and the trombones in Mozart's day belonged normally to the church and not to the theatre at all. Gluck had employed them in the same way for the oracle scene in *Alceste*, and Mozart did the same thing in *Idomeneo*. The trombones here belong exclusively to the Statue and the devils who are associated with it; they do not come into the overture, although that opens with a foretaste of the Statue's music. If the Statue is not present in marble, their sounds cannot be heard.

[1] The textual problems of the trombones have now been settled once for all by Dr. Alfred Einstein and the correct text established in the miniature full score edited by him and published by Eulenburg of Leipzig in 1930. (See p. 170).

[2] The music is printed on the next page.

Ex. 29.

Trombones.

First Devil. Pre-pare, pre - pare, pre-pare, pre - pare, new guests draw

near, And on the brink of......... Hell ap - pear.  Chorus. Pre-pare, pre -

Instruments.  Chorus.  Instr.

- pare.  Pre-pare, pre - pare.

Dramatically the voice of the Statue has at least the function of letting us contrast the different reactions to it of Leporello and Don Giovanni; the former always superstitious and credulous, the latter sceptical to the last. There is a delightful touch about his recognition of the monument; he is a modern critic of sculpture

and hails it with the words 'O vecchio buffonissimo!' We may be
quite sure that the equestrian statue of the Commendatore would
have been as orthodox, for its own period, as any of those in our
London streets. The duet in which the invitation to supper is
given, first by Leporello and then by Don Giovanni, is a fine study
of the two characters—Leporello trembling with fear,[1] Don
Giovanni fearing nothing, because he believes in nothing. There is
even a faint touch of almost Weberish romanticism about the
duet; Don Giovanni seems to have got into the wrong century by
mistake, and to be himself half-conscious of it, as he says, 'bizarra
è in ver la scena'.

The scene which follows has no reason whatever for its existence,
except to give Donna Anna the opportunity of singing a set aria.
*Non mi dir* has always been famous, and it is certainly beautiful,
though singularly cold and unemotional. German critics have
censured the *coloratura* of the latter half of it, but Mozart without
*coloratura* is only a very mutilated Mozart; and here it is a welcome
contrast and relief after the rather over-declamatory style of
Anna's earlier utterances.

The concluding finale begins with the next scene, which opens
with a brilliant introduction making great use of trumpets and
drums, as is the first finale at the moments when Don Giovanni
comes into the park with his footmen to invite the peasants into
the palace, and again when he welcomes the three maskers.
Trumpets and drums always suggest noble hospitality; Ferrando
(in *Così fan Tutte*) intends to engage them (but actually does not)
to entertain his bride at their wedding.[2] The musicians are
supposed to be on the stage, though it is clear from the autograph
score that they are not—in that very small theatre at Prague there
probably was not room for so many. Don Giovanni, like any fine
gentleman of Prague, has his own domestic orchestra, and they
play the popular tunes of the moment. Our modern listener has
probably never heard of Martín's *Una Cosa Rara* or Sarti's *I due
Litiganti*, and is so much accustomed to regard Mozart as a
classic that he cannot conceive of a time when *Non più andrai*
was the latest accomplishment of every whistling street-boy.
All this finale was composed in Prague during rehearsals, and

[1] Leporello is not cowardly by nature; he is frightened only because he is
ignorant and superstitious.

[2] In medieval Germany it was only a bride of noble birth who was allowed to
have trumpets and drums; those of the middle classes had to be content with
shawms.

no doubt the presence of such excellent wind-players as were available there gave Mozart the idea of inserting this *servizio di tavola*, as it would have been called at Salzburg. Whether Mozart's keenly satirical mind had any malicious intention in making the band play these particular tunes I do not know; it is curious that with all the legends current about *Don Giovanni* there appear to be none relating to this episode. The first piece is from the finale to Act I of *Una Cosa Rara*; the second is the scoffing song, *Come un agnello*, from *I due Litiganti*. Neither of these choices seems to have any particular significance; they were probably chosen merely because they were popular. The third tune is *Non più andrai*, from Mozart's own *Figaro*; it shows at any rate, for us moderns, how much inferior the music of Martín and Sarti was to his.

The little concert is interrupted by the sudden entrance of Elvira. In Bertati's libretto her entrance precedes the supper-music (Bertati too specifies wind instruments); Da Ponte was wise to change the order, as the festive music provides a good contrast to Elvira's passionate appeal and gives her entry more importance. The hurrying violins give an impression of breathless haste; Donna Elvira is so much excited that she does not make herself very clear, and it is not unreasonable that Don Giovanni should treat her outburst with mocking courtesy. She is supposed to have undergone another emotional reaction and to have decided to go back to her convent; but from all that she actually says, Don Giovanni might quite well imagine that she was merely asking him to give up his pleasures in order to settle down to marriage and respectability with herself. Mozart has given us a wonderful expression of Don Giovanni's character in this scene, if actors were equal to realizing it. There is a delightful exuberance about his shouts of—

> 'Vivan le femmine!
> Viva il buon vino,
> Sostegno e gloria
> D'umanità!'

Elvira rushes out, and as she reaches the door gives a shriek that upsets even Don Giovanni's equanimity for a moment. He sends Leporello to see what is the matter, and Leporello, with a cry almost as startling as Elvira's, returns in a condition of grotesque terror. From this point onwards the finale is a strange mixture of tragedy and farce. Such a mixture is based on a fundamental truth of human nature, and it is in evidence throughout the Italian opera of the seventeenth century, in which the comic servant, especially the elderly female, scatters her absurd remarks in the most unexpected places. But in the reign of Metastasio the comic servant was no longer tolerated in *opera seria*, and these relics of the comedy of masks could only find a home in *opera buffa*. Leporello's description of the Statue's arrival is frankly comic and the comic atmosphere is maintained quite unmistakably up to the moment when Don Giovanni accepts the Statue's invitation to supper and takes its hand. It must be clearly understood that the figure of the Commendatore is not an intangible ghost, but the actual solid marble statue (minus his horse) out of the cemetery; Leporello leaves us in no doubt about that, and we hear its heavy steps on the floor.

The solemnity of the scene is provided by the trombones, and there is a further good reason for their employment; the old gentleman has a great deal to say, and like most people of his age is very slow in delivery, so that in practice his supernatural impressiveness is very liable to break down before he has come to the end of his part, with the result that the audience finds him as much of a bore as Don Giovanni obviously does. The awe-inspiring voices of the trombones (if the players are efficient and do not get out of breath in their very fatiguing parts) form a useful background to enable him to sustain the dignity of his position. As in the previous scene, Leporello always presents a comic aspect, chattering and shivering with fright under the table; and even Don Giovanni, who is a very reasonable man, begins to get a trifle impatient at the Statue's relentless prolixity. But from the moment when Don Giovanni accepts its invitation and takes the hand of the Statue Mozart quickens the pace and rouses the orchestra to effects of horror that must indeed have seemed frightening to audiences of those days. The sudden alternations of loud and soft disconcert the nerves like the pitching of a ship in a storm. An invisible chorus of devils calls to Don Giovanni through the rising flames and rolling thunder to descend to eternal torment. The devils rise from the depths; they seize him, they drag him down as he utters his last cry of agony, while Leporello crouches under the table watching his master's struggles.

The orchestra settles down to the chord of D minor; flames and devils have disappeared. Into the half-darkened room there burst in

Elvira, Zerlina, Ottavio, and Masetto, accompanied by the police, to seize Don Giovanni and hand him over to the arm of the law. Donna Anna has come with them, but stands apart, always conscious of her social position; she will not be content until she sees Don Giovanni in chains. Leporello, with grim humour, tells them that his master is well out of their reach, and gives a comic description of his end. There is a momentary shiver, as Elvira and the others too recall the mysterious spectral figure that they have all seen on the road;[1] then the ever-tactful Don Ottavio, seeing that Don Giovanni has been disposed of by a higher authority, leads the way, like the chairman of a committee, in a general settlement of affairs, as befits a *dramma giocoso*, by expressing the hope that Donna Anna will now permit him to lead her to the altar; to which she replies, with that characteristic propriety for which Mozart's elegant *coloratura* seems precisely the correct expression, that after the decent interval of a year's mourning, she will in all probability condescend to bestow her hand upon him. Elvira, with less ceremony and with a certain bitter tone of disillusionment, announces that she intends to resume the veil, while Zerlina and Masetto, transferring her phrase from minor to major, prepare to trot home to their interrupted rustic wedding feast. Leporello, who has become a cheery optimist again, will go to the tavern to find a better master. And so, after the united exclamation of—

'Resti dunque quel birbon
Tra Proserpina e Pluton.'

—a grotesque mixture of plain language and classical dignity—they bring the opera to an end with a copy-book maxim starting off as if it was going to be an elaborate fugue, but turning almost at once into a proper Italian finale, with just a few pretences at counterpoint thrown in—who could have done anything so ingeniously effective but a master contrapuntist like Mozart?—so that the audience may disperse to their supper-parties edified, but not so much as to forget that they have been thoroughly well amused.

[1] Elvira met the Statue at the door; but where did the others see it? Did it come up again out of the basement and walk back to the cemetery by the same road that the others took?

P RAGUE had accepted *Don Giovanni* with enthusiasm; Vienna was less appreciative. Salieri did his best to prevent the opera being represented at all, since he had just completed his revision of his French *Tarare* under the name of *Axur, Re d'Ormuz*, which came out in January 1788 and deservedly aroused great interest, for it is a work of remarkable originality from all points of view, literary, dramatic, and musical, although to-day we can only regard it as a museum piece. It was not until May that *Don Giovanni* was presented to a Viennese audience, and then only at the express command of the Emperor Joseph II, who, in spite of his limited intelligence for music, was always ready to give Mozart a certain amount of encouragement. There were various troubles with the singers, and as has already been said, many alterations had to be made in the music. Considered individually, the cast could hardly have been bettered. Leporello was Benucci, who had created the part of Figaro; Madame Cavalieri sang Elvira and Anna was taken by Aloysia Lange. About the singer of the title-part we know little. It was not Mandini, the original Count Almaviva, as has often been stated, but Francesco Albertarelli, who had only recently come to Vienna. Mozart wrote for him, shortly afterwards, a lively air, *Un bacio di mano*, to sing in an opera of Anfossi's; it is clear from this that he was a *buffo* singer of the usual type. The first performance met with small success; further repetitions taught the public to understand it a little better, but, as the Emperor himself observed, it was no music for the Viennese. After fifteen performances between May and December it disappeared from the repertory altogether, and apart from a single performance in German, organized probably by Schikaneder, in 1792, it was not heard again in Vienna for another ten years. The Viennese public on the whole preferred its operas in Italian, with a company of Italian singers, or Austrians like the Cavalieri singing in Italian, and the ordinary Italian comic repertory of Anfossi, Paisiello, Cimarosa, and the rest. *Don Giovanni* could not become popular in Germany until it had been translated into German.

The first translations were definitely comic in style. Mainz was the first town outside Prague and Vienna to perform the opera; this was in March 1789, the translation being by H. G. Schmieder. Schmieder's translation was also used at Frankfurt in May of the same year.[1] At Mannheim (September 1789) and Bonn (October) the version by C. G. Neefe was used, and there was yet a third, by F. L. Schröder, sung at Hamburg (October 1789) and Berlin (December 1790). The style of Neefe's translation, which seems to have been the favourite one during these early years, may be judged from his list of characters: Don Giovanni becomes Herr von Schwänkerich; Don Ottavio, Herr von Fischblut; and Leporello, Fickfack.

The criticism of the *Chronik von Berlin* was written (even in 1790) in that style of contemptuous condescension which was characteristic of Berlin musical criticism down to our own day. The writer considered the opera to have been much overrated and to be deficient in sincere feeling. Grétry, Monsigny, and Philidor were the composers whom he held up as an ideal; the romantic movement had not yet taught German critics to believe that music is the exclusive property of the German people. Mozart, he thought, was too much bent on astonishing his audience.[2] That the opera drew crowded houses was incontestable; but that was due to the attraction of a ghost in armour and a chorus of fire-breathing furies. Another critic considered *Don Giovanni* to be 'a very suitable opera for Saturday night'.[3] A third admitted Mozart to be a musical genius, but thought him wanting in general culture and uneducated in taste. This may not have been very far from the truth, if we judge Mozart by the standard of literary education which we expect from our own composers at the present day; but we must remember that the early German translations of Mozart did little justice to the elegant wit of Da Ponte. A fourth critic said: 'In this opera the eye is feasted and the ear enchanted, but reason is offended and morality insulted, while vice is allowed to trample on virtue and sensibility.' In Munich

[1] These dates have been established by Dr. Alfred Loewenberg (*Annals of Opera*); previously it had been supposed that the first German performance was that of Mannheim.

[2] Thompson, the famous Master of Trinity College, Cambridge, remarked of Stanford's organ-playing in the 1870's: 'Mr. Stanford sometimes pleases us and sometimes astonishes us; and I may say that the less he astonishes us, the more he pleases us.'

[3] I once saw *The Bohemian Girl* described in these identical terms in the preliminary prospectus of a performance at the Cambridge Theatre.

the opera was at first forbidden by the censor, and was only performed at the special command of the Elector. Beethoven, as is well known, had a passionate admiration for the music, but said that he could never bring himself to write an opera on a subject so immoral as those of *Figaro* and *Don Giovanni*. We may note that *Fidelio* contains various reminiscences of *Die Zauberflöte*, but none of Mozart's Italian operas.

The romantic conception of *Don Giovanni* in Germany begins with Rochlitz's translation (1801), which held the stage for half a century and is not even now completely superseded, for its phrases have impressed themselves so deeply on the popular memory in Germany that no subsequent translator has dared to abandon them altogether. And in considering this romantic outlook on Mozart's opera we must remember that it coincided with that gigantic theatrical revolution which is associated for most of us with the names of Schiller and Goethe. In that revolution, considered as a whole, the plays of Schiller and Goethe themselves, great as they are, stand for perhaps less than those of Shakespeare alone do in the history of our own Elizabethan and Jacobean stage. But we may note that Mannheim, one of the very first German theatres to produce *Don Giovanni*, had already, a year and a half earlier, seen the production of Schiller's Spanish tragedy, *Don Carlos*. The German romantic theatre absorbed not only Shakespeare from abroad but the Spanish dramatists too, as well as the two Italian playwrights who were almost contemporary with it, Goldoni and Gozzi. It is curious to read at the present day (1944) how the educational theatre in the remoter centres of Soviet Russia is constantly producing plays by Goldoni and Calderon as well as by Shakespeare; it looks as if Schlegel's famous lectures on the drama, first delivered in Vienna in 1808, were still taken as the basis of the theatrical curriculum there. In England the Spanish and Italian dramatists are known only to research students. But Germany, in those days, was still closely in touch with France; French taste had dominated German literature far more than it ever did our own. No Englishman cared much what Voltaire might say about Shakespeare, and few Englishmen had ever heard of the 'dramatic unities'; even now most English critics imagine 'that they are an obsolete pedantry invented by some obscure Frenchman in the days of Louis XIV. To the German romantics the release from the unities was a really serious matter; it was the victory of the allied forces of Germany,

Spain, and England over the tyranny of France. A north German intellectual of 1800 or later would therefore approach the story of Don Juan in a spirit totally different from that of Da Ponte. The *Burlador de Sevilla* links up Seville and Naples, it is true; but we have already seen that Da Ponte's acquaintance with the story must be traced back through Goldoni and the Jesuit plays to Molière, and through Molière to Tirso, if indeed Da Ponte ever actually read Tirso in Spanish.[1] The disciple of Lessing and Schlegel would go straight to the Spaniards themselves, even if only in a German translation, and he would at once note their affinities to Shakespeare, more affinities perhaps than our own Shakespeare scholars would readily admit. Further, there is the whole moral outlook on the theatre to consider. In the Italianate south, at that moment—I mean during the last quarter of the eighteenth century—the theatre had signified first dynastic opera, Metastasio and Hasse, followed by the trivial comic operas of Galuppi, Anfossi, and their like, and in the spoken drama, the Comedy of Masks, whether in Italian or in German, and at best, Goldoni and Gozzi whose plays we can regard only as commercial entertainment, for their own day, however respectfully we may read them now. In north Germany the theatre had suddenly become a religion; it was no longer an amusement, it was a morally uplifting force, deliberately planned as such by those who directed it and as such willingly and gratefully accepted by a devout and enthusiastic audience. By the time we reach 1813—and here I must beg the reader to pause for a moment and reflect on all the events, political, social, as well as cultural, that had taken place in Europe between 1787 and 1813—we are confronted with two commentaries on *Don Giovanni*, which, as Samuel Butler would have said, throw perhaps more light on the commentators than on the original author. One of these is musical, the other literary; they are complementary to each other. The musical commentary, if I may so call it, is Spohr's opera, *Faust*, composed in 1813, but not produced until 1816. Spohr at that time was conductor of the Theater an der Wien in Vienna, the theatre which Schikaneder had built out of the profits of *Die Zauberflöte*; on the top of the pediment which surmounted the façade he had placed a statue of himself in the character of Papageno. *Faust* came out first at Prague in 1816; Vienna saw it in 1818 and it held the stage until

---

[1] Da Ponte was a remarkably well-read man, and it is quite conceivable that he had some knowledge of the Spanish theatre in the original.

about 1860. As late as 1852 it was given at Covent Garden by the urgent desire of Queen Victoria; for this production, which of course was in Italian, Spohr composed recitatives and indeed considerably revised the whole opera. These facts deserve mention because Spohr's *Faust* is now completely forgotten. It is really the first German romantic opera, for it precedes both Weber's *Freischütz* and Hoffmann's *Undine* by a few years. Its indebtedness to *Don Giovanni* is conspicuous, and what is important to note is that the features of *Don Giovanni* which Spohr has so obviously imitated are the ensembles and finales, although in the opera, as in his quartets and violin concertos, Spohr has based his entire musical style fundamentally on Mozart. But between 1787 and 1813 there had grown up the whole German conception of the symphony orchestra—not merely the technique of instrumentation and symphonic composition, but the moral idea of orchestral music—and therefore of the symphony, as the only existing non-theatrical form—as the most uplifting and edifying type of musical art. 'Beethoven's music is edifying. . . . Beethoven's sense of duty is to preach.'[1] Spohr's *Faust* is probably the first attempt made, though perhaps in this case unconsciously, to amalgamate the personality of Don Juan with that of Faust; and ever since Goethe the Germans have perpetually tended to translate Don Juan into terms of Faust.[2]

The other commentary of 1813 is the fantastic story of E. T. A. Hoffmann, *Don Juan, eine fabelhaftige Begebenheit*. Hoffmann (1776–1822), whose name is probably known to many English readers only through Offenbach's comic opera, was not only a prose-writer of distinction—he is indeed one of the most fascinating authors in the whole history of German literature—but a musician as well. He was no mere talkative amateur like Robert Browning, but the composer of eleven operas, one of which (*Undine*) was revived in recent years in Germany, and the leader of that school of literary musicians and musical men of letters which included Schumann and Weber, Heine and Berlioz. Whether he was acquainted with Tirso's play I do not know; he is pretty certain to have had some knowledge of Spanish drama, if only at second hand. He wrote vividly about life in Italy and

---

[1] D. F. Tovey, *Beethoven*, London, 1944.

[2] Many modern German writers, e.g. Oswald Spengler, seem to use the adjective *faustisch* as equivalent to *deutsch*, when speaking of matters intellectual and temperamental.

other countries, but his own life was spent entirely between
Königsberg, where he was born, and Bamberg, where he conducted opera, his other places of residence being Warsaw, Posen,
and Berlin.

The most characteristic feature of Hoffmann's romanticism is
his delight in making perfectly commonplace people of his own
day come unexpectedly into contact with the supernatural. It is
a literary device very familiar to English readers of the last fifty
years or so; Anstey's *The Brass Bottle* was an early example, and
David Garnett's *Lady into Fox* a more recent one. W. S. Gilbert
exhibits the same sort of thing in *The Sorcerer* and *Iolanthe*, with
this difference, however—that his ordinary people are quite unreal
and fantastic, while his supernaturals are uncomfortably realistic;
his fairies and wizards come not from fairyland, but from the flies
and traps of contemporary English pantomime. It is an inverted
romanticism which Hoffmann perhaps would hardly have understood, though perhaps Tieck might have appreciated it.

The 'travelling enthusiast' who is supposed to be the author of
Hoffmann's story stays a night at a town between Germany and
Italy, and finds that Mozart's opera is being performed in Italian.
He also finds that the theatre adjoins his hotel and that he can
walk out of his bedroom straight into a box.[1] In the course of the
first act he becomes aware that there is a lady with him in the box
too. He does not look at her until the act is over and then finds
that it is Donna Anna herself. They discuss the opera together,
and after the interval she leaves him. He goes back to his
room, eats his supper, and retires; finding the room stuffy, he
anticipates Miss Baylis at the Old Vic and transfers his writing-
table to the box (which one would imagine would have been
stuffier still). Here he sits down to enjoy a jorum of punch and
write a long letter to his friend Theodor. The story is, of course,
an excuse for an analysis and explanation of 'the opera of all
operas'.[2]

For Hoffmann, Don Giovanni is what is now called a superman,

[1] German writers always say that this was the case at Bamberg. But as late
as about 1910 there existed a famous hotel—the *Kaiserkrone*—at Bozen in the
Tyrol, with a wooden theatre built into its courtyard. The theatre had at that
time been already condemned as unsafe and was to be demolished. Schikaneder's
theatre in Vienna, at which *Die Zauberflöte* was first performed, must have been
much the same sort of building. Hoffmann's introduction is therefore quite
plausible. But Hoffmann never visited either Bozen or Vienna himself, as far as
I can ascertain.

[2] This phrase is Hoffmann's own; it has sometimes been ascribed to Wagner.

and Anna comes very near being a superwoman. She is the woman destined for him by Heaven; but he meets her too late. All he could do was to violate her; and from that moment she is consumed by an unearthly passion for him. She requires at the same time both the destruction of Don Giovanni and the satisfaction of her own desire. She spurs on her 'ice-cold' bridegroom Ottavio to revenge, but when Don Giovanni has disappeared she cannot think of marrying him. When at the end she tells him that he must wait a year, she knows that she will never live that year out—'Don Ottavio will never clasp in his arms the woman who has been saved only by her inborn piety from becoming the elect bride of Satan'. The author sits writing in the box from midnight until two in the morning; the next day he hears at the *table d'hôte* that the *prima donna* was suddenly taken ill and died from over-exertion, at two o'clock precisely.

Hoffmann stands a good deal nearer to the eighteenth century than our modern 'travelling enthusiasts'; he is quite ready to enjoy a realistic representation of Hell in the second act, with a stage full of smoke and a legion of live devils, and after that he is quite definitely relieved when they disappear and the other characters make their entrance for the final sextet. But the essentials of romanticism are there; Hoffmann is disgusted at the whole idea of Don Giovanni unless he can read an allegory into him, and he cannot conceive how Mozart could have written such beautiful music unless he had had the same interpretation at the back of his mind.

What really was at the back of Mozart's mind we shall never know, unless further letters of his are discovered. As far as Mozart's mind is concerned we have the score and nothing else to guide us. Tirso's original play will not help us in the least, though a study of that and of the other Don Juan plays will help us to account for some of Da Ponte's inventions. Tirso's play stands halfway between the *comedias de capa y espada*, the characters of which are mostly kings and gentlemen, set in some country rather like Spain, and the *comedias devotas*, in which the most abominable scenes of crime could be represented as long as the play ended with the penitence and conversion of the sinner. In many ways it is more like an opera than a play; there is in fact a certain amount of incidental music, and the spoken parts are in formal rhyme or assonance, full of rhetoric and poetical phraseology for their own sakes. Mozart's music (or anybody's) may be regarded as the equivalent for all that in another currency. But as regards the individual characters and their relations one to another, apart from Don Juan himself and his relations to women in general, Tirso, Da Ponte, and Hoffmann are just irreconcilable.

The first scene of Tirso's play is laid at Naples, in the royal palace. The Duchess Isabela receives Don Juan (who is masked) in the dark, believing him to be the Duke Octavio, and apparently ready herself to go to all lengths. She suddenly discovers her mistake and calls for help. The King of Naples enters with lights; she covers her face and exclaims that her honour is lost. Enter Don Pedro Tenorio, who is Don Juan's uncle; he is a lord in waiting to the King, who tells him to deal with the case, but secretly, to avoid scandal. Don Pedro sends Isabela away in charge of the guard; Don Juan then reveals himself as Don Pedro's nephew. Don Pedro professes to be gravely shocked at Don Juan's conduct, especially in view of the lady's high rank; but he admits to having been young himself, and suggests that Don Juan should jump down from the balcony. He does so; his uncle, having been told by him that he had pretended to be Octavio, tells the King an entirely untrue story—that the mysterious aggressor had overpowered his guards, jumped out of the window, and even when found again below had succeeded in escaping altogether. He also says that Isabela told him that the man was Octavio, though she never mentioned his name. Don Pedro then calls on Octavio, whom he finds in bed, although the morning is well advanced, and proposes to send him to prison. Octavio is naturally bewildered, and is concerned only about the honour of Isabela, to whom he is betrothed. Don Pedro arranges for him to escape to Spain, like Don Juan. Octavio, we see, has nothing to do with Ana at all. The next scene is the coast of Tarragona, where Juan meets the fisher-maiden Tisbea. All this episode with Tisbea is very long in proportion to the rest, and it is further balanced later in the play by similar scenes with Aminta, a shepherdess. These scenes are exaggeratedly poetical and seem to belong to the same sort of dramatic type as Tasso's *Aminta*, Guarini's *Pastor Fido*, and Fletcher's *Faithful Shepherdess*.

We now meet the King of Spain, who is supposed to be Alfonso XI (*d.* 1350), and Don Gonzalo de Ulloa, the Comendador, father of Ana. The King suggests that Ana should marry Don Juan; all marriages in these illustrious circles are naturally arranged by the parents. But Don Diego Tenorio, Don Juan's father, tells the King that his son has been caught in the act with Isabela, on which the King decides to banish Juan to Lebrija, not very far from Seville, and to marry Ana to Octavio by way of compensating him for the loss of Isabela. Juan meets Octavio, but Octavio has no idea that Juan has dishonoured his fair lady, and they are the best of friends, very much pleased to meet each other again in Seville. The Marquis de la Mota then enters, evidently just as much of a gay dog as Juan himself. Mota for the moment is in love with Ana, and quite sure of her favour, but her father keeps her shut up because she has already been betrothed by the King to someone else. Ana, like Rosina in *The Barber of Seville*, writes a letter to Mota, inviting him to visit her at eleven that evening; the door will be open and he is to wear a red cloak as a sign to the *dueñas* to let him pass. But as her maid throws the letter out of the window, it is picked up and read by Don Juan, who immediately seizes his opportunity. He gives the message by word of mouth to Mota, but tells him that the hour agreed on is twelve. Mota brings a band of musicians with him, and while they are singing Don Juan borrows his red cloak and keeps the appointment with Ana himself. The same sort of thing happens as in the first scene; Ana discovers that her visitor is not Mota; she screams and her father comes to the rescue. Don Juan kills him and then escapes with his servant. He restores the cloak to Mota in the street; torches are seen approaching, and Mota is arrested by Don Juan's father. The curious parallelism of the Isabela-Tisbea scenes and those of Ana and Aminta suggest the first and second subjects of sonata form.

The rest of the play is taken up with the episode of the statue, the gradual assembling in Seville of all the four deluded females, and their final appearance together before the King to demand justice. Catalinon, Don Juan's servant, enters and describes his end, adding what is most important from the Spanish point of view, that Don Juan, just before his disappearance, has assured him of Ana's virginity. Octavio pairs off with Isabela and Ana is handed over to Mota.

It is characteristic of the Spanish theatre that married women do not appear in it at all. Not even in comic plays can there be a mother-in-law.[1] Once safely married, a woman was regarded as something too sacred to be exposed to stage presentment. But before marriage, Spanish heroines seem to be allowed a

[1] Pedro Muñoz Peña, *El Teatro del Maestro Tirso de Molina*, Valladolid, 1889.

surprising amount of liberty; indeed, even Spanish critics have accused Tirso of making his female characters *demasiado sensuales y libidinosas*. Tirso's Ana, like Goldoni's, is obviously a very young girl, but she goes to much further lengths than Beaumarchais's Rosina; that 'saintly purity' with which German and English critics have credited her on the strength of Mozart's arias is the last quality that is hers. She is, however, the one female in the play whose physical integrity is guaranteed by all the playwrights who bring her on, so that Hoffmann's view of her condition has no justification whatever. It is entirely his own invention, and its only value is to illustrate the German romantic mind. In Tirso's play both Isabela and Ana are quite small parts; they have next to nothing to say on the stage, whereas the parts of Tisbea and Aminta are very long, and far more literary than dramatic. Apart from the pastoral scenes, it is the male characters who have the most to say in the drama. The literary form of *El Burlador* is very evidently determined by fixed conventions of the Spanish theatre; Da Ponte's libretto is shaped not so much by the standard conventions of Italian *opera buffa* as by the actual membership of Bondini's company at Prague. The shortage of male singers made it necessary to eliminate half the *dramatis personae* of Tirso's play, and just those which give it its peculiarly Spanish character. By the mere fact of being set to music the females become more prominent, and as the three *prime donne* have to be more or less equalized in value, Zerlina, the substitute for both Tisbea and Aminta, is reduced to about a quarter of their joint length, and the other two females are expanded. This gives the operatic females importance enough to make the modern spectator think that they ought to dominate the drama still more; he is accustomed to heroines of the size of Wagner's or of Verdi's and Puccini's, forgetting that their operas were composed for companies assembled on quite different principles—all too often on that of *ma femme et cinq poupées*, as the husband of Madame Catalani used to say. That is why modern audiences tend to regard either Anna or Zerlina as the 'heroine' (or, rather, as the *prima donna*), according to taste; Elvira gets comparatively few votes. And when we think of Manrico or Tristan, we naturally find Ottavio a poor sort of tenor, not realizing that in Tirso he is quite a subordinate character and an absurd one at that. The delicate question of exactly how far Don Giovanni succeeds with any of his attempts on female virtue is hard to answer, and really need not be seriously pursued; the important thing is the character of Don Giovanni himself and the visible results of his efforts on the stage. Tirso called him the *burlador*, the 'deceiver' of Seville; his servant actually gives him the title in the course of the play, and he accepts it as a compliment. It is by systematic deceit indeed rather than by irresistible charm that he seems to secure his results. To his seniors in the play, concerned as Spanish grandees with 'honour' and female honour above all things, he is the man who brings ruin on all women, and therefore a criminal. Modern moralists might take a quite different view; Busoni used to say that Don Giovanni was the man who gave every woman the supreme experience of happiness. In any case, Da Ponte's Don Giovanni does not do that, for if his adventures within the limited period of the opera are a fair sample, he has no success at all and is placed in a completely ridiculous situation every time. There is really no need whatever for Heaven to intervene. And when Heaven does intervene, as in Tirso, it is made quite clear that the Statue is taking a personal revenge. Don Juan protests that he did not violate his daughter; 'that does not matter', says the Statue; 'you meant to do so'. And Don Juan asks for a priest, that he may confess and receive absolution before dying; the Statue refuses, saying that it is too late. Da Ponte's Don Giovanni owes more to Molière; however ignoble his behaviour in life may have been, he has at least the courage to go down to Hell unrepentant. Writers on Mozart have made the most of Don Giovanni's sacrilege, blasphemy, and all the rest of it in the cemetery. Tirso makes Don Juan pull the Statue's beard, but the Statue does not seem to mind that in the least. Don Giovanni never goes as far as beard-pulling, if only for the simple reason that, as the Statue is on horseback, his beard would be out of reach.[1]

Dr. Alfred Einstein, who prepared the Eulenburg miniature full score of the opera in 1930—a work of most accurate and careful scholarship—prefaces it with some wise words which I take the liberty of translating here:

'This present edition makes a claim that is both modest and gigantic. It sets out to present the work in as faithful and unadulterated a form as is possible for dead print in comparison with live handwriting. The attempt thus made must surely lead to a

[1] Beard-pulling was a form of insult well known in medieval Spain, e.g. in the time of the Cid, who died in 1099, and it was punishable under the law of the land.

new intellectual conception of the opera. Or rather it should be a symbol and a challenge to envisage the work once more in its nakedness, free from all the romantic and unromantic mystifications of the nineteenth century which began with those of E. T. A. Hoffmann; free from moralizing, all ethical or philosophical valuations, free from all searching for Wagnerian *leitmotiv*, and above all without discussion of "questions of style", whether it is an *opera buffa* or a mixture of *buffa* and *seria*. This question of style has never had any relevance for a work which is absolutely *sui generis*.'

The reader's first reaction to this will be to laugh at me for quoting it after a discussion of the *seria* and *buffa* styles which may already have bored him to distraction. Dr. Einstein writes as a German for Germans, professional musicians, newspaper critics and professed musicologists; he knows his readers and what *their* mental background is likely to be. But if German readers probably know too much, English ones know too little. Dr. Einstein is perfectly right in stressing the quality of uniqueness which characterizes *Don Giovanni*, but we cannot understand the nature of that uniqueness properly until we can see the opera against the background of its own century. Hoffmann and his successors were determined to make *Don Giovanni* into a romantic opera. They were like Hoffmann in the first act of Offenbach's opera; they had put on a magic pair of spectacles which made them see the whole universe in a romantic light. Like Spohr, they wanted to write definitely romantic operas, and as Mozart's were obviously the finest that they knew and the most modern as well, they naturally took Mozart as their technical model. Hoffmann's *Undine* shows perpetual indebtedness to Mozart and Cherubini, but he does actually carry romanticism a good deal further than either—further, in fact, than Spohr does. He invents a technique of romantic music, which is a different thing from merely trying to express a spirit of romance. Spohr wants to be romantic all the time, but is so obsessed with the Mozartian classical technique that he hardly ever achieves a really romantic result. Whether Mozart is inwardly romantic or not every listener will decide for himself; it is a matter of personal temperament rather than of hard fact; but it is difficult to find in Mozart any traces of a consciously romantic technique. He knows all depths of human emotion, but he is always Italian and strictly realistic; his music is often complex in the extreme, but invariably clear. He has no mystifications and no sense of symbolism, apart from certain conventions of religious music which might by a stretch be called symbolic.

And *Don Giovanni* forces us to ask ourselves what we really mean by the word 'romantic', as applied to music. That again is a temperamental question. For some listeners, to-day as well as a hundred years ago, all music is of its very essence romantic. But it must be obvious that our modern attitude to romanticism cannot be the same as that of the creators of romanticism; nor can we take their view of the classical art against which they reacted. Hoffmann thoroughly enjoyed old Italian music; he was a pioneer in the appreciation of Beethoven, but he seems to have found that quite compatible with a delight in *opera buffa.* In one of his books he says that he wants the characters in *opera buffa* (he uses the Italian term) to be so life-like as to be recognizable as people we know, but the 'fantastic' element is to dominate them, in place of the 'romantic', and then *das Abenteuerliche* will begin and turn normal life into a crazy fairy-tale. One could apply that criticism to *Don Giovanni*; could we apply it to *Figaro* or to the comic operas of Anfossi and Cimarosa? I think one can, not in the sense of introducing a recognizably supernatural element, but recognizing that the mere fact of musical setting gives these otherwise ordinary people a delicious absurdity—an absurdity that we sometimes do recognize in actual life when we say of some of our friends that they go through the whole of life as if it was an opera. And that leads us directly to our next chapter and *Così fan Tutte.*

## 11

## COSÌ FAN TUTTE

THE performance of *Don Giovanni* at Vienna brought Mozart neither fame nor money. He had received the appointment of court composer on the death of Gluck in the autumn of 1787, but the stipend seems to have been very inadequate to his needs as the father of a family, and he was still more hurt by the fact that the Emperor gave him hardly any opportunity of earning it by new compositions of a serious type. All that was required of him was a supply of dance music for the public masked balls given during the carnival season. He had a few pupils, but not enough to support his wants; in the summer of 1788 he wrote his three great symphonies, but the subscription concerts for which they were intended had to be postponed, and it is thought that they never took place at all.

In the spring of 1789 a welcome diversion presented itself in the shape of an invitation from Prince Carl Lichnowsky to join him on a visit to Berlin. The King of Prussia, Frederick William II, was an enthusiastic lover of music; he maintained a first-rate band, and was himself a very good violoncello player, so that Mozart had some hopes of turning his talent to good account at the northern court. On the way to Berlin he visited Leipzig, where he made friends with Doles, a pupil of J. S. Bach, whom he had succeeded as Cantor of the Thomasschule. He gave an organ recital in the Thomaskirche, extemporizing on a chorale in such a way as to make Doles say that his old teacher had come to life again. By way of return, Doles made the choir sing to him Bach's eight-part motet, *Singet dem Herrn*—a work now in the repertory of most English choral societies; he was quite taken by surprise at the imposing effect of it and cried out, 'That's music that one can learn something from!' Learn something from it he did, for he made Doles fetch out Bach's other motets; there was no score in existence, and he had to read them from the parts spread out on a table before him.[1]

[1] It has sometimes been stated that he had to spread them out on the floor and read them on hands and knees.

At Berlin his criticisms were a little too outspoken to meet with the approval of the local musicians, but the King showed a marked appreciation of his music and offered him the post of Kapellmeister. He declined the invitation, not wishing to abandon Joseph II, although the Emperor's recognition of his abilities had been none too cordial. Joseph had a vigorous appetite for music, but was not very discriminating. Mozart's devotion to him was probably based not so much on his artistic interests as on the nobility and liberality of his character. Moreover, it is only natural to suppose that to a man of Mozart's temperament there would be little temptation to exchange the cheerful and easy-going life of Vienna for the severer atmosphere of Berlin.

He returned home at the beginning of June and set to work at once to write the series of six quartets that had been commissioned by the King of Prussia, as well as six pianoforte sonatas for his daughter, Princess Frederica. Only one of each set, however, was completed at this date, and the Princess seems never to have received her remaining sonatas; of the King's quartets two more were written at a later time. The only other important work of this year is the clarinet quintet composed for Anton Stadler.

At the end of August *Figaro* was revived again, and its success was so definite that the Emperor decided to commission another opera from Mozart. He was not allowed to choose his libretto this time; but he was at any rate given his old friend Da Ponte as a collaborator. This new opera was *Così fan Tutte, ossia La Scuola degli Amanti*; it has been said that the subject was based on events that had actually taken place in Vienna shortly before, and that the Emperor had given a special command to Da Ponte to work the story into his libretto. The opera seems to have been written in great haste; the autograph score is very full of abbreviations, a proceeding not at all usual with Mozart. It has sometimes been alleged that Mozart disliked the subject and composed the music very much against his will; but there seems to be no authority for this tradition, and it is certainly the last deduction that one could possibly draw from a study of the music itself. The work was first performed on 26 January 1790.

The plot of the opera is simplicity itself. Ferrando and Guglielmo are two young Neapolitan officers engaged to be married to two young ladies, Fiordiligi and her sister Dorabella. A cynical old bachelor, Don Alfonso by name, persuades the young men to put their mistresses' constancy to the test. They pretend to be called away from Naples on duty, but return that same afternoon disguised as Albanian noblemen. Don Alfonso, with the help of Despina, the ladies' maid, persuades the two sisters to receive them. The strangers make violent love to them, and after some hesitation each succeeds in winning the heart of his friend's betrothed. The affair proceeds with such rapidity that a notary is called in that very evening to draw up a marriage contract for their signature. Suddenly Don Alfonso announces the return of the soldiers; the Albanians vanish, and the terrified ladies are obliged to confess everything to their original lovers. Needless to say, all ends happily.

This libretto was denounced throughout the nineteenth century as being intolerably stupid, if not positively disgusting, and various attempts were made in Germany and elsewhere to 'improve' it, or even to substitute an entirely fresh libretto on a totally different subject. In 1863 the authors of the libretto of Gounod's *Faust* adapted it to a French version of *Love's Labour's Lost*; early in the present century a singer at the Dresden Opera adapted it to a Spanish comedy. There is not the least necessity for such a proceeding. *Così fan Tutte* is the best of all Da Ponte's librettos and the most exquisite work of art among Mozart's operas. It is as perfect a libretto as any composer could desire, though no composer but Mozart could ever do it justice. Those who know the opera only by vague recollections of some clumsy German translation, or by the summary printed in those hand-books which are sold for the benefit of lazy opera-goers, may well think it stupid, for they will only see the skeleton; to appreciate the delicate filigree of Da Ponte's comedy, one must read every word of the Italian original and sing it through, recitatives and all, to Mozart's music.

What Da Ponte did was to take an extremely simple idea as a foundation, an idea in itself absurd enough, but hardly more absurd than many old-fashioned Italian opera plots, and possessing the advantage of a certain stiff and conventional symmetry. There are three men and three women; one pair of philosophers, two pairs of lovers, the one sentimental, the other practical—six pieces of humanity which the poet can arrange in as many patterns as he pleases. On the basis of this simple plot, he builds up a most elaborate artificial comedy. *Così fan Tutte* is very different from either of the two operas which preceded it, and they are both extremely different from the conventional *opera buffa* of their time. Da Ponte, like Mozart, was always ready to learn from his contemporaries and rivals; the construction of *Così fan Tutte* is clearly modelled on that of *La Grotta di Trofonio*, the libretto which Casti wrote for Salieri in 1785. In Casti's play there are also two pairs of lovers, whose characters are completely changed by passing through the mysterious grotto and restored again after they have passed through it once more in the reverse direction. Trofonio, the magician who manages the grotto, is the obvious model for Don Alfonso. The old-fashioned *opera buffa* presented stock types of singers, who sang stock types of songs. *Figaro* and *Don Giovanni*, as we have seen, present real individual characters whose personality was faithfully reflected in the music. *Figaro* had the advantage of being taken from one of the most brilliant comedies ever written, so that it has a far better plot than almost any opera ever composed. *Don Giovanni* falls far short of *Figaro* in construction of plot; its plot, indeed, is rather its weak point —its originality lies in its fantastic imagination, in its exciting rapidity of movement, and in its fascinating studies of feminine frailty. I have already drawn particular attention to its rapidity of movement; it may be pointed out here that in all three operas Da Ponte quite clearly intended to observe the dramatic unities of time and place. He was under no obligation to do so; from the seventeenth century it had been understood even in France itself that opera was not subject to these laws. But Beaumarchais, as a French dramatist, observed them as a matter of course, and he called his play *La Folle Journée* as its original first title. Da Ponte observed the unities too by the mere fact of following the French comedy exactly, and indeed shortening it. And as it is quite clear that in writing *Don Giovanni* he was first of all concerned to produce another opera as like *Figaro* as possible in its externals, *Don Giovanni* also obeys the law of the unities, and the action takes place within a period of twenty-four hours. Some English critics have refused to accept this, and have asked how the statue could have been erected in the time, or how Donna Anna and Don Ottavio could have had their mourning clothes made. The problem of the erection of the statue had to be faced by various playwrights before Da Ponte, and each solved it in his own way. For the purposes of the opera, I cannot see that such realistic details are of any importance; we can pretend, if we like, that the first scene takes place on Monday, the second on Tuesday, the third on Wednesday, and so on, but that will not alter the fact that the hour or the scenes proceeds uninterruptedly from about midnight to midnight. *Così fan Tutte* takes rather less time; it is actually a very long opera, especially as it is in two acts only, and probably designed in two acts, the first of which takes a good hour and a half, but the supposed action starts about an Italian breakfast time and ends with a late supper. To the realistic mind, this will no doubt make the opera still more absurd; 'we might possibly imagine the ladies changing their affections in the course of a month or so, but not within a single day'. From the musical point of view, *Così fan Tutte* is much more leisurely than either *Don Giovanni* or *Figaro*, though still not nearly so leisurely as *Die Entführung*; yet a great deal happens on the stage, enough to keep the spectator always entertained and amused. The concentration into one day is an immense advantage in all three operas. Modern productions, at any rate in England, have taken every care that each new scene should follow its predecessor without a break; we owe this technique, not to the cinema, as some people fondly imagine, but to the Shakespeare producers of about thirty years ago or more, who reacted violently against the over-elaborate staging of Irving and Tree. In those days, and probably in some countries still, operas with many different scenes were set realistically, so that for every change of scene there had to be an interval of at least five minutes and often of many more; this completely destroyed the vitality of the opera and made it unendurably tedious.

*Così fan Tutte* can be put on the stage realistically or artificially, but in any case it is an opera for a sophisticated audience. It is artificial comedy of the best, and the unity of time helps to heighten the artificiality which makes its charm. Don Alfonso is a real person, and far more real than Doctor Bartolo or the Commendatore; Despina too has a certain reality, although she is obviously the conventional operatic *soubrette*. But the four lovers are utterly unreal; they are more like marionettes than human beings. Yet, as the opera develops, we see them express an amazingly wide range of emotions; indeed, it is only because they are marionettes that they are capable of such emotions, for they are themselves playing parts all the time. *Così fan Tutte* is the apotheosis of insincerity—the only moment when anybody speaks the truth is when Don Alfonso utters the statement which forms the title of the opera. For this reason the opera is to some auditors bewildering and almost embarrassing. German chivalry in the last century was shocked at seeing women made ridiculous; the present age, at any rate in England, is merely amused. If the realists maintain that the story is an insult to human nature, let them read the reports of the Divorce Court during the period of a war. Such embarrassment as modern listeners sometimes do feel is due to the sheer beauty of the music itself; they cannot bear to think that it is the deliberate expression of sham feeling and sometimes of comically exaggerated passion. It finds its parallel in Goethe's play, *The Triumph of Sensibility*, which belongs to about the same period. The opera introduces us into a curious world in which even the most ardent musician may find himself rather a stranger at first; for Don Alfonso, who is the only person consistently honest with himself, has no emotions, and the four lovers, who are all emotions, are never quite clear how far their emotion is genuine and how far fictitious.

The overture starts with a slow introduction which gives us two characteristic ideas at once. The first is the theme given out by the oboes; the theme is of no great importance in itself, but we shall always find that the nasal tone of the oboe is generally associated with cynical old Don Alfonso. The second point is the motto of the whole opera:

Ex. 30.

This leads at once to the *allegro*, a lively chattering movement, full of strong contrasts between quick and giggling solos for various instruments and vigorous syncopated chords which may stand for the young men's chivalrous protestations. The themes are deliberately empty and commonplace; they must be so deliberately, for Mozart never wrote commonplaces by accident. Towards the end we hear the *così fan tutte*[1] theme again.

The curtain rises on a café, at which the two officers are breakfasting with Don Alfonso. He has evidently been saying something rather naughty about their young ladies, since each of them

[1] *Così fan tutte* means 'all women behave like that'. If an English title for the opera is wanted, the alternative title ought to be translated—*The School for Lovers*.

asserts in turn with great firmness that his particular bride is utterly incapable of falsehood. Don Alfonso wants to finish his breakfast in peace; but they tell him he must either prove his assertions or draw and defend himself. He is not going to be disturbed; he sits quietly smiling, while they start up, thump the table and make the spoons rattle in the saucers. He hums an old song to them, flute and bassoon joining in with mocking laughter:

'Woman's faith is like the Phoenix
In remote Arabia dwelling;
Travellers oft such tales are telling—
Have they seen it? No, not they!'

'What proof have you', he asks, 'of their fidelity?' 'Their promises, their vows, their protestations.' 'Ah yes! their tears and sighs, their embraces, and their swoons—forgive me if I laugh at you!' He will undertake to prove to them that their ladies are no better than any other and stakes a hundred guineas on it, so long as they promise to keep the wager a secret from the ladies, and to carry out all his instructions obediently for the next twenty-four hours. They give their word, and begin to think how they will spend their winnings, for about these they have no doubt. Trumpets and drums ring out a couple of bars of introduction, and Ferrando the romantic sings confidently that he will spend his share on a serenade for Dorabella. Guglielmo is more of a realist; he means to give a dinner-party. 'And shall I be invited?' asks Don Alfonso. 'Certainly, sir, since you will have the bill to pay.' Off they go, the young men in high spirits, Don Alfonso chuckling to himself. He finds this sort of thing very rejuvenating.

The scene changes to a garden leading down to the sea. In the background is the bay, with Vesuvius in the distance. The clarinets in thirds, hypocritical and voluptuous, tell us that the ladies are here. Fiordiligi and Dorabella are certainly no romantic *deutsche Mädchen*. The symmetry of the plot suggests that Da Ponte was acquainted with the Spanish comedy of manners; but in any case that Spanish comedy had influenced Italian opera a hundred years before, and the tradition of it may well have continued in Italy down to the days of Da Ponte. It would be too much to say that our heroines are *sensuales y libidinosas*, but they are both of them at least as ready for an adventure as Rossini's Rosina. Each is contemplating a medallion portrait—did anyone ever look so dashing as Ferrando, so distinguished as Guglielmo? The sentimental slow movement quickens up to an *allegro* of vows and protestations, interrupted only when the word *amore* makes them both collapse into the exquisite rapture of a slow, simultaneous *cadenza*. It is a fine morning, and both of them feel rather inclined for some new excitement—but who comes here? Don Alfonso? Yes, but alone, and evidently in a state of great perturbation. What is the matter? 'Ferrando——' 'Guglielmo——' 'Oh, 'tis too dreadful', answers Don Alfonso, recitative gliding insensibly into aria, and his broken phrases becoming almost melody against the background of sobbing violins and sighing violas. The ladies are in the last agonies of fear—and curiosity, for Don Alfonso continues to tell them to bear up and prepare for the worst, without letting out too soon what the horrible news is. He breaks it to them at last, and the officers come in themselves, accoutred for their voyage to the seat of war.

Here Mozart, as might be expected, sums up the situation in a quintet. This is, in fact, the opera of ensembles, more of them than in any other, quite possibly more than in any opera ever written, and all of them ravishing. The gentlemen approach with dignified hesitation, and Don Alfonso extols their manliness and courage. The ladies are more agitated, and desire their lovers instantly to draw their swords and run them through, since they cannot bear to live without them. Ferrando and Guglielmo dig Don Alfonso in the ribs. 'Wait and see', he remarks, unmoved; and at that moment the two ladies, having done their duty by their emotions, settle down to one of Mozart's enchanting *sotto voce* ensembles, in which the others join, to contemplate the cruelty of Fate and the vanity of human hopes. Once more the ladies protest, once more the young men nudge each other and laugh at Don Alfonso, smiling and enigmatic as before, once more they repeat their adorable platitudes—for in this world the whole of life proceeds in sonata form.

A few more tears, a last embrace, consolation in a comical double recitative—Mozart had already discovered in *Figaro* the delightful absurdity of treating recitative as ensemble—followed by a little duet, deliberately rather dry; if the young officers are not very emotional, it shows how well disciplined they are. A drum is heard in the distance; Don Alfonso sees the boat approaching. The ladies prepare to faint, while the regiment crosses the stage to a swaggering march, followed by a crowd of villagers—we are at Posillipo, a village just outside Naples—singing 'Oh, a soldier's life for me!' The boat is waiting, but it will have to wait a long time yet, for the ladies know no end to their farewells, which culminate in another quintet of the most exquisite beauty and humour, the four lovers embracing to long-drawn rapturous phrases, while Don Alfonso is shaking with laughter in the background. The swooning ecstasies of this scene reappear amusingly to the words *in mortis examine* in the well-known motet, *Ave verum Corpus*, composed in June of the following year.

The march is repeated, and the officers embark; the ladies and Don Alfonso wave a last good-bye, singing a little trio to the accompaniment of rippling violins as the boat recedes into the distance. The ladies retire, and Don Alfonso, left alone, pours out his contempt for women in an accompanied recitative that has the concentrated fury of Figaro's in the garden on the night of his wedding. 'What grimaces! what silly nonsense! Was it for these women that they wagered a hundred guineas?' The two conventional chords of the orchestra are the only possible comment.

The next scene is the ladies' boudoir. Despina, the maid, has brought their chocolate, and thinks she may as well taste it before they come in. Here they are—'Chocolate! No! Give me poison!' 'Shut the windows! Pull down the blinds! I hate the light, I hate everything—oh, go away and leave me alone!' It is Dorabella who leads off like this—she is the more temperamental of the two—in an accompanied recitative of the most absurdly tragic order, followed by an aria in which she declares that she intends to go mad for the rest of her life and teach the Eumenides themselves how to scream. She does in fact give them a specimen of her abilities, starting on a high G flat and slowly descending the chord of the diminished seventh—the chord of all romantic horrors —while the fiddles, who have been supporting her with energetic agitation all the way through, stop in horror until she reaches the perfectly conventional closing phrase.

All through the opera we shall meet these parodies of the grand tragic manner, both in aria and in accompanied recitative; it was the perfection of ingenuity on the part of Da Ponte and Mozart together (for they cannot have planned such a thing independently or against each other's wishes) to invent these opportunities for enhancing the absurdity of the dramatic situation and at the same time giving the singers the most glorious opportunities for showing off their voices.

Despina is quite accustomed to tantrums and asks what is the matter this time. 'Our lovers have left Naples!' says agonized Fiordiligi. 'Is that all?' laughs Despina. 'They'll come back.' 'But they've gone to the front!' sobs Dorabella. 'So much the better for them; they'll cover themselves with glory.' 'But perhaps they'll be killed!' shrieks Fiordiligi. 'So much the better for *you*, then; you can find new ones—no shortage of nice young men in this world.' The ladies are furious. 'Oh, they're all alike', says Despina. 'You love one man now, you'll love another presently; one's as good as another, because none of them are any good at all. I dare say they'll come back; still, as long as they *are* away, why waste your time crying? See if you can't—amuse yourselves.' This is really quite shocking. 'Nonsense!' says Despina. 'Aren't you out of the nursery yet? Do you suppose that Signor Ferrando and Signor Guglielmo aren't doing just the same thing? Aren't they men? And soldiers?' She goes off into a fit of giggles, as the ladies gather up their skirts and leave the room. Despina is evidently Zerlina in domestic service.

Enter Don Alfonso to pay a call of condolence. 'No one at home? Ah, there's Despina; h'm, maids are such mischief-makers. Well, a guinea will go a long way.' Don Alfonso has brought with him two Albanian noblemen who desire to pay their respects to the ladies; Despina is quite ready to have a look at them. Their clothes and beards are rather odd, but then all these Orientals are as rich as Croesus.[1] The ladies have heard laughter and call Despina with angry voices. She pays no attention, and they enter in a fine state of temper at being disturbed during their midday *siesta*. 'Strangers in the house? You shameless hussy, send them away this minute, or we shall give you notice on the spot.' The Albanians fall on their knees and crave pardon with Oriental compliments. Don Alfonso is watching behind the door. The ladies are at first indignant, then a little frightened, but they gradually find that this Eastern imagery has a certain charm about it. As the sextet ends, Don Alfonso comes forward as if he had only just entered the room. What is all this noise? Do the ladies wish to rouse the whole neighbourhood? 'Look! *Men* in the house!' 'Well, and why not?' He looks round. 'Heavens, am I dreaming? My dear friends, my very dearest friends, however

---

[1] Those who take opera realistically can be assured that at Venice, Trieste, or Naples in those days there would have been nothing odd about the appearance of magnates from the Balkans.

did *you* come here? This is too delightful! (Come, act up to me!)'
They are presented formally and continue their extravagant
compliments. Dorabella is almost inclined to be agreeable; but
Fiordiligi is an elder sister who always does the correct thing. She
has had the advantage of a sound, old-fashioned education, and
knows that when strange men misbehave in this manner, a well-
bred operatic heroine always sings an aria about rocks and
tempests, with a pompous introduction, wide leaps from high
notes to low and back, plenty of *coloratura*, and a long shake at the
cadence. It is all superbly done, for was not Fiordiligi acted by
Madame Ferrarese del Bene, with a compass to be envied by any
soprano and by any contralto as well? And was not the Reverend
Abate Da Ponte violently in love with her and enjoying all her
favours? She deserved some return, and he repaid her generously.

In vain Don Alfonso begs her to be kind, in vain Guglielmo
tries to laugh it all off cheerfully; she evidently thinks that not at
all in good taste, and takes Dorabella and herself off at once. The
young men burst into loud guffaws; Don Alfonso tells them not
to make so much noise—he who laughs last laughs longest. This
laughing trio is one of the most amusing numbers in the opera.
Would Don Alfonso like to strike a bargain, and be let off with
five-and-twenty guineas and an apology? He reminds them that
the time is not up yet, and that they have promised to obey him
for twenty-four hours. After a beautiful and quite superfluous
song (*Un' aura amorosa*) from sentimental Ferrando, they leave
the stage to Don Alfonso, who has another interview with Despina.
She is still unaware (or pretends to be) of the identity of the
bewhiskered strangers, but as long as they are rich she is ready to
help them. In fact, she has made her plan already, though she
does not tell either Don Alfonso or the audience what it is. Don
Alfonso too keeps his secret. She understands how to manage
her ladies. Love, indeed! what's love? 'Pleasure, amusement,
pastime, diversion, merriment; if it becomes tiresome, it's not love
any longer!' We are a long way from *Fidelio, oder die eheliche Liebe*.

The ladies have gone into the garden to take the air and pour
out their woes to the midges, as Despina says. Very prettily
indeed they pour them out, while flutes and bassoons echo each
other with delicate runs in thirds. Suddenly there are two
simultaneous cries of agony; the strangers rush on in a great state
of excitement, with Don Alfonso panting behind. Each carries
a small bottle, and before the philosopher can catch them up, each

has drunk his fatal dose. 'Have they really poisoned themselves?' ask the ladies. Yes, they really have, Don Alfonso tells them, and apparently there is nothing to do but go on singing a quintet until the poison takes effect. How can we suggest a cure until we have observed the symptoms? Gradually the sense of horror deepens—a triplet figure for the violins recalls the death of the Commendatore; a hard harmony reminds us of Donna Anna. The phrases become more broken, and finally Ferrando and Guglielmo fall writhing on the grass. 'Won't you be kind to them even now?' asks Don Alfonso. The ladies' only answer is a shriek for Despina, who very practically tells them to look after the suicides while she and Don Alfonso go for a doctor. The ladies dare not approach at first, and the two officers seize the opportunity to express their amusement in a quiet aside. But the poison must take its course; it is about time for a good groan. This brings off its effect. The sisters look at one another and hesitate. Fiordiligi, always correct, considers that it would be really wrong to leave them at such a moment. Dorabella thinks they are very good-looking. And so they draw nearer and nearer, while Mozart develops his two characteristic themes through various keys. They even feel the patients' pulses and realize, as the music mounts to a cry, that the case is serious unless help comes soon. The men remark *sotto voce* that the ladies are becoming a little more tame at last, and the ladies, also *sotto voce*, acknowledge that the occasion is quite a suitable one for a few tears.

Don Alfonso interrupts the quartet briskly by introducing the doctor—a pompous old gentleman in the largest of spectacles and the most voluminous of white wigs. Donna Elvira, said Leporello, talked like a printed book; this personage talks like a prescription. But the patients think they have heard that squeaky little voice before, and control their laughter as best they can. The doctor makes elaborate inquiries of the ladies, and reassures them in the best professional manner; finally, he draws from beneath his flowing robes (did we catch a glimpse of Despina's apron?) a magnet, for he is a disciple of the great Doctor Mesmer himself.[1] He strokes the patients with it, and we hear the mysterious fluid pass along their bodies in the prolonged shakes of flutes, oboes and bassoons. They begin to twitch, and in order to guard

---

[1] It will be remembered that Dr. Mesmer had been an intimate friend of the Mozart family: it was in his garden that *Bastien und Bastienne* was first performed.

against possible convulsions the doctor directs the ladies to hold
their heads. They look round, they recover strength—ah! this
is something like a doctor!

Slowly they rise to their feet. 'Are these the Elysian fields?
Pallas and Cytherea, that we see before us?' They recognize the
ladies and seize their hands with fervour. The ladies must not be
frightened, says the doctor: these are only the after-effects of the
poison. The virtues of animal magnetism will restore them to
complete health in an hour or two. The 'after-effects', however,
are still potent, and the gentlemen positively and in so many
words demand a kiss. 'Heavens! a kiss!' This was premature,
and the ladies' feelings are outraged. People must behave properly
even if they have been poisoned, says Fiordiligi. Whether the kiss
is given or not, Da Ponte does not tell us; but the mixture of
indignation and amusement provides Mozart with an excellent
*strepitoso, arcistrepitoso, strepitosissimo* on which to bring down
the curtain.

It is a long first act, but no one could ever feel tired of listening
to it. Cimarosa seems to have been Mozart's model on this
occasion; not the *Matrimonio Segreto*, which did not appear until
after Mozart was dead, but *Giannina e Bernardone*, produced
originally at Venice in 1781 and performed at Vienna in 1784.[1]
Mozart, as usual, has infinitely surpassed his model both in melody
and in instrumentation, although *Così fan Tutte* is written in a
much simpler vein than either *Figaro* or *Don Giovanni*. At the
same time the style of the music, in spite of being less complex, is
very definitely later in its essential qualities. What is very striking
is the almost total absence of the conventional *buffo* element.
Benucci, who created the part of Figaro and sang Leporello in the
Vienna performances, took the part of Guglielmo in this opera;
Bussani, who had sung Doctor Bartolo and later on Masetto,
doubling with the Commendatore, was Don Alfonso. But there is
only one aria, that in the second act, in which Guglielmo ap-
proaches the old-fashioned *buffo* style; it is lively and humorous,
but one could never call it a 'patter-song'; its melodic outlines
have more affinity to the song of Monostatos in the second act of
*Die Zauberflöte*. One is tempted to think that Bussani must have
been an excellent actor, but not much of a singer; after all, no

---

[1] This was pointed out to me by the late Professor Max Friedlaender. *Giannina
e Bernardone* had a great success in its own day and was revived at Florence in
1870; further revivals took place at Naples (1882 and 1895), Rome (1905) and
Turin (1932).

*basso buffo* was expected to be what we should now call a singer—
the conventional Italian terminology definitely differentiates him
from the *basso cantante,* the 'singing bass', who hardly appears in
Italian opera until much later. None the less, there is no trace of
the conventional *buffo* in the part of Don Alfonso. He takes part
in almost all the ensembles, but in the course of this very long
opera he has only two quite short arias and one accompanied
recitative; both the arias too are more talking than singing. If
we were to judge the importance of an operatic part by the
singer's standards—how many arias have *I* got?—we should find
Don Alfonso almost as dumb as Pasha Selim; yet anyone who has
seen the opera cannot have failed to notice that Don Alfonso
dominates it from beginning to end. He may have next to nothing
to 'sing', but he certainly has the most important part in the
drama. The other striking feature is the immense development
of the ensembles. In this opera there are eleven arias, six duets,
five trios, one quartet, two quintets, one sextet, and two huge
finales, each of which includes every possible combination of
voices. It is in these ensembles especially that we are reminded
not so much of Mozart as of the young Beethoven, especially in
the pseudo-tragic episodes, which often recall the septet or the
early pianoforte sonatas and trios. It is interesting and amusing
to note that while Beethoven was taking Mozart seriously and
putting his whole heart into his subconscious imitations of him,
Mozart himself was laughing at his own emotionalism.

The second act opens in the ladies' boudoir. They are still
rather indignant, Fiordiligi especially, but Despina patiently
continues her lesson in philosophy. Some day, she says, they will
thank her for her good advice. When she is out of the room the
sisters discuss the matter from a more practical standpoint.
Fiordiligi hesitates to take any responsibility, but Dorabella, who
has begun to feel very much bored with all this rigid propriety,
induces her to give way, and in a little duet they agree to receive
the attentions of the foreign noblemen. Dorabella will take the
dark one, who is more gay and amusing, Fiordiligi the fair one,
whose sentimental style appeals to her taste. (Ferrando, all
through, is much more like the German romantic tenor than the
mere *tenore buffo* of Michael Kelly.) As they discuss the possibilities of the affair, they grow more lively; by the end of the duet
they have not only recovered their former spirits, but are quite
prepared for adventures. We note that in this duet they are

accompanied, not by the sentimental clarinets, but by Don Alfonso's oboes.

Here is Don Alfonso himself in great excitement; the ladies must come into the garden at once to listen to the music. The scene changes to the garden; at the back there is a boat gaily dressed with flowers, and in the boat are Ferrando and Guglielmo with a band of musicians. Not the trumpets and drums which he contemplated in the first scene; those are reserved for the very end of the opera. The serenade he has ordered will be quite expensive enough; but the bill has not yet been sent in, and, anyway, Don Alfonso will have to pay it. The soft warm notes are heard of clarinets,[1] horns, and bassoons; Ferrando and Guglielmo join in, and as the song is taken up by the chorus they step ashore and present themselves to the ladies, wearing chains of flowers. The ladies are quite overcome; the gentlemen seem to be equally embarrassed. Don Alfonso explains—it is their apology for this morning's indiscretion. 'Let us have no more old-fashioned airs and graces', he says. 'Shake hands, and let us all be good friends.' Despina gives the ladies' answer: the gentlemen are to break their flowery fetters and offer their arms to the two sisters. They do so, not without awkwardness and bashfulness on both sides, while Despina and Don Alfonso run away laughing.

The two couples begin—they positively might be English—with polite remarks about the weather and the garden. Fiordiligi suggests a walk in one of the avenues, and Ferrando is only too delighted to oblige. Guglielmo seizes the opportunity to press his suit on Dorabella, who requires little persuasion to accept from him a tiny golden heart, which he hangs round her neck, at the same time taking possession of Ferrando's portrait. They sing their duet and make room for the other couple. Ferrando has not been so successful; Fiordiligi rushes back from the avenue in a great state of perturbation. It is only a passing storm; Ferrando's ardent speeches can make her turn and look at him, can even draw a sigh from her. But he is too chivalrous to press her; he only gives vent to his ardour in a rapturous aria (need I say that the clarinets are prominent?) and leaves her to think it over. Fiordiligi is tormented by a conscience. She admits to herself in recitative that she is in love with the stranger, but duty reminds her of her absent lover. She apostrophizes him in an aria:

---

[1] This is no doubt one reason why only oboes were employed in the previous duet.

'Oh forgive, dear heart, forgive me!
Far astray my thoughts have errèd;
Here for ever in shadow buried,
Leaf and flow'r my fault shall hide.'

The aria is a rondo of great beauty, scored with inimitable
grace. There are very elaborate parts for two horns, perhaps
intended by Mozart as a joke in the same sense as the well-known
flourish of horns at the end of Figaro's aria, *Aprite un po' quegli
occhi.*

A very amusing dialogue follows between Ferrando and
Guglielmo. Ferrando is overjoyed at being able to show that
Fiordiligi is constancy itself to her Guglielmo; but Guglielmo finds
it a little inconvenient to tell Ferrando how much progress he has
already made with Ferrando's Dorabella. Ferrando is distracted,
but he bears Guglielmo no ill-will—this is a charming trait of
character—and, indeed, asks his advice. Guglielmo is already
half-converted to Don Alfonso's philosophy, as Dorabella is to
Despina's. Women are charming creatures, but they must not be
surprised if their lovers complain of the liberality with which they
distribute their favours—this is the burden of his cheerful song.
Ferrando takes his case more seriously. He is still genuinely in
love with Dorabella, in spite of the way she has treated him. This
is one of the airs which remind us of early Beethoven.[1] Mozart
has for once in a way employed both clarinets and oboes together
in the accompaniment, so that neither pair of instruments seems
here to have any special dramatic significance. The aria is very
neatly constructed on two short but markedly contrasted subjects;
the first is in C minor, the second (with clarinets) appearing for
the first time in E flat, after which it reappears in C major accompanied by the oboes with the most delicious effect, the whole
orchestra joining in afterwards for a coda.

Once more we are admitted to the ladies' apartments. Fiordiligi is in great distress. She confesses frankly that she is in love
with her Albanian, but is shocked at Dorabella's matter-of-fact
acceptance of her confession. A last effort must be made to
conquer her passion. 'My dear,' says Dorabella, 'you had much
better give way to it'; and she expounds her philosophy in a
charming aria, which naturally resembles Despina's to some

---

[1] Compare the beautiful tenor aria for Jesus (also in C minor and major) in
*The Mount of Olives.*

extent, but has a warmth of feeling and an aristocratic distinction that is quite foreign to the backstairs mind of the lady's-maid.

Fiordiligi is left alone. Suddenly she makes up her mind, and sends Despina to fetch two old uniforms of Ferrando and Guglielmo. (How they come to be in the ladies' wardrobe Da Ponte does not explain.) She and Dorabella will put them on, and will go out to the front themselves; it is the only way to escape temptation. She tears off her *toupé*, little knowing that through the open door Don Alfonso, Ferrando, and Guglielmo are all watching her, and puts on her lover's hat and cloak. Ferrando, still disguised, steps in to restrain her. Has she forgotten him? She protests; he presses, until finally her determination gives way and she yields completely, in as naïve and simple a phrase as that in which Gluck's Alceste makes her great sacrifice.[1] Guglielmo is on the point of bursting in, but Don Alfonso pulls him back, though he must have hard work to hold him during the long *allegro* in which Fiordiligi and Ferrando voice their transports.

Is this really our cheery philosophical Guglielmo? Ferrando has touched him on a tender spot, and when he comes back again expecting congratulations on his conquest, he finds his friend in a very bad temper. 'Fiordiligi? *Fior di diavolo!*' They are both agreed, however, that the errant ladies must be severely punished. 'Very well,' suggests Don Alfonso, 'marry them.' Marry them? They would as soon marry the Devil's grandmother. Then will they remain celibate for life? 'Do you suppose men like us will ever want for wives?' Oh, there are plenty of women in the world, says the philosopher, but will any others be any better? It seems they are still in love with these particular ladies, in spite of their faithlessness; they had better stick to them. Don Alfonso takes the stage.

> 'Man accuses the women, but I excuse them,
> And my forgiveness never will refuse them.
> A man's love's a passion, a life's anxiety;
> To her love's only charm—variety!

> 'Let no man who has found himself deluded
> Say the lady's to blame; 'tis all his own fault.
> Be she young, old, plain or a beauty,
> Every woman's the same: *così fan tutte!*'

---

[1] *Je volerai remplir un devoir qui m'est cher*—the three bars immediately preceding *Divinités du Styx*.

And as they join with him in chorus—*Così fan tutte!*—enter Despina, as usual extremely pleased with herself, to say that the ladies are prepared to marry them at once; they have sent for a notary to come this very evening, and they will be ready to sail for Albania in three days.

The final scene shows us a saloon lit up for a party. Despina is ordering the servants about, and Don Alfonso looks in to see that all is in order. The two couples enter, with all Posillipo come to congratulate them. The quartet receive their good wishes with due acknowledgements to the valuable assistance rendered by Despina, and after the chorus have left the room they sit down to supper. They toast each other and drown the memory of the past. They are in that agreeable and convivial mood when it is obviously the right thing to sing a round, the sort of social canon that Padre Martini used to compose. Fiordiligi leads off, Ferrando follows, Dorabella makes the third entry: where is Guglielmo? The fact is that the round is too high for Guglielmo's bass voice; so Mozart very ingeniously makes him start up from the table in a rage, muttering angrily, 'Oh, I wish the wine would poison them!' But they are much too happy to notice anything. Don Alfonso introduces the notary, who, of course, is none other than the versatile Despina. The contract is read over and presented for signature. The two ladies have just appended their names when— was that a drum? And those distant voices, are they singing, 'Oh, a soldier's life for me'? Don Alfonso goes to the window—yes, the soldiers are coming back, the boat has reached the shore, the two officers are getting out! What is to be done? The Albanian bridegrooms are hastily bundled into another room, and while Don Alfonso consoles the ladies, they slip out again unobserved to reach the main door. A moment later Ferrando and Guglielmo enter in uniform; the King has just given orders for them to return at once. The ladies seem silent and uncomfortable, but perhaps that is due to excess of joy. Suddenly Guglielmo discovers the notary and demands an explanation. Despina takes off her wig and says that she has just come back from a masquerade. The ladies are still more embarrassed. Don Alfonso discreetly drops the marriage-contract where Ferrando can pick it up. Indignation boils over; wicked Don Alfonso tells the officers to look into the next room. The ladies are in agony, when their lovers re-enter wearing their Albanian costumes all awry, and recall the words and music of the previous tender episodes, with a jest at the magnetic doctor. Explanations are now superfluous, and all the ladies can do is to throw the blame on that odious Don Alfonso. Don Alfonso takes it all with his habitual serenity, puts their hands together and recommends them to make peace. The opera ends with an ensemble in which the six characters give the audience the excellent advice always to let their actions be guided by reason, and always to look at life with a sense of humour.

Whether the ladies pair off with their original lovers or their new ones is not clear from the libretto, but, as Don Alfonso says, it will not make any difference to speak of.

*Figaro*—Beaumarchais's *Figaro* at any rate—was called a pro-logue to the Revolution, and *Don Giovanni* presented the same kind of ideas at a rather different angle; it was an opera for heedless pleasure-loving aristocrats dancing on the crust of a volcano.[1] These two operas came out before the fateful year 1789. *Così fan Tutte* in January 1790 must have seemed a last jest at the departing age, to those who understood the humour of it. To a later generation, unaccustomed to look for humour of this kind in music, it must have been merely the apotheosis of the *rococo* in its most frivolous and superficial aspect.

With *Così fan Tutte* we bid farewell to Lorenzo Da Ponte as Mozart's librettist, and the reader may like to know what became of this curious and fascinating character. The death of Joseph II in February 1790 left him without a protector. His enemies were too strong for him, and the result of intrigue and calumny was that he was obliged to take flight to Trieste, glad to escape from Vienna with his life, as we learn from the verses in which he dedicates to Byron his Italian translation of *The Prophecy of Dante*. At Trieste he made the acquaintance of an English mer-chant, and fell violently in love with his daughter, whose name was Nancy. The father's name was Grahl, and he was born at Dresden, but Nancy always maintained firmly that she was an Englishwoman. She had been asked in marriage by an Italian who was in business at Vienna, but he demanded too large a dowry, and the father, furious at the idea of giving his daughter to a man who only wanted her money—Mr. Grahl must indeed have been English if he was so much surprised at the normal Italian outlook on matrimony—handed her over to Da Ponte. It has been suggested that Nancy was a Jewess, and that Da

[1] This was well pointed out by O. G. Sonneck in an article on the Mozart Festival at Munich in 1896 (*Rivista Musicale Italiana*, Turin, 1896).

Ponte married her by the Jewish rite, although he was a Catholic priest.[1]

He left Trieste with Nancy in August 1792, with the idea of seeking his fortune in Paris. Casanova, whom he met in Prague, recommended him to go to London instead, and gave him two pieces of sound advice: 'When you are in London, never set foot inside the Italian café, and never sign your name to a bill.' In London he obtained the post of poet to the Italian Opera. On 1 March 1794, Bertati's *Don Giovanni* was given there, with music put together from Gazzaniga, Sarti, and others, Mozart being represented by Leporello's catalogue aria. In 1797 Da Ponte was sent to Italy to engage singers, and seized the opportunity of visiting his old home at Ceneda. He arrived quite unexpectedly on All Souls' Eve, just as his old father, aged eighty, was drinking the health of his long-absent son, surrounded by Lorenzo's seven sisters and two brothers, with numerous other relatives. Lamartine wrote of this episode:

'Même dans les confidences de Saint-Augustin, si tendre et pieux pour sa mère, il n'y a pas beaucoup de pages en littérature intime supérieures à ce retour d'un fils aventurier dans la maison paternelle.'

He came back to London, but his inexperience seems to have been taken advantage of both by Taylor, the manager of the King's Theatre in the Haymarket, and by Messrs. Corri and Dussek, the composers and music publishers with whom he went into partnership. It need hardly be said that he disregarded both the wise counsels given him by Casanova. In 1805 he fled from his creditors and made his escape to America. He arrived first at Philadelphia, but about 1807 he settled in New York, where he taught Italian and entered into various unfortunate business ventures. The great event of his life in America was the visit of Garcia to New York in 1825 with an Italian opera company which performed *Don Giovanni*—Mozart's this time. In 1832, when he was eighty-three, he lost his Nancy. It was about this time that he entered into correspondence with the Patriarch of Venice, who had formerly been Bishop of Ceneda. He sent the Patriarch some poems, and received a kindly letter of thanks, in which the worthy prelate

---

[1] Paul Nettl, *Da Ponte, Casanova und Böhmen*, in *Alt-Prager Almanach*, 1927. Nettl points out that it was not until after Nancy's death that Da Ponte took steps to reconcile himself with the Catholic Church.

begged him to make his peace with Holy Church. He died on 17 August 1838, in his ninetieth year, having made his confession and received extreme unction. A document quoted by one of his biographers, Monsignor Bernardi, from the ecclesiastical archives of New York, says that since it was not generally known that Da Ponte was a priest, it was considered advisable not to draw attention to the fact either on the occasion of his reconciliation with the Church or on that of his funeral.[1]

[1] Jacopo Bernardi, *Memorie di Lorenzo Da Ponte*, Florence, 1871.

## 12

## LA CLEMENZA DI TITO AND DIE ZAUBERFLÖTE

THE death of Joseph II in February 1790 put an end to
Mozart's hopes as a court composer. The new Emperor,
Leopold II, cared little for music and only supported it as
a matter of duty. Besides, he had no sympathy with the ideals of
his predecessor, and anybody who had been patronized by Joseph
might be certain of Leopold's disfavour. Discarded by the
Emperor, Mozart set out on a concert tour; he still enjoyed a
considerable celebrity as a virtuoso on the pianoforte and could
be certain of appreciation in the smaller German capitals. But his
concerts brought him in no profits, and he returned to Vienna to
find matters only worse than before. His chamber music was
beyond his audiences; the number of his pupils had dwindled to
two; his wife was in chronic ill-health owing to her perpetual
pregnancies,[1] and his finances were in the most desperate condition.
The state of his own health probably accounts for the fact that
his whole output for 1790 was curiously small. The only important
compositions are two quartets for the King of Prussia, the string
quintet in D and the Fantasia for a mechanical organ which is
mostly in F major, although, like the other one, it begins in F
minor. He composed additional accompaniments to Handel's
*Alexander's Feast* and the *Ode for St. Cecilia's Day*; for the rest
there are only fragments of works begun and left unfinished after
a few bars, which tell their own melancholy tale.

He took up composition again after his tour, and in the early
months of 1791 was occupied with a number of works, most of
them small and of very miscellaneous character. It was early in
May that he received an invitation to compose what must to him
have seemed an almost more unusual type of work than the pieces
for clockwork instruments that had just been occupying his
thoughts, and one, too, still less likely to bring him adequate
remuneration. The proposal came from an actor-manager by
name Emanuel Schikaneder, whom he had first met at Salzburg

[1] After Mozart's death Constanze recovered her health completely; she had no
children by her second husband.

eleven years before. Schikaneder was an altogether extraordinary character. His life and his general behaviour were so grotesque that one could only imagine him to have been invented by a German Dickens as the German original of Mr. Crummles; at the same time he was in many ways a man of singular ability, invention, and foresight, who contributed much to the history of the German stage. Born at Regensburg in 1751 in the most miserable circumstances, he had spent his childhood as an itinerant fiddler; later he became an actor, and although devoid of education had sufficient natural talent to achieve a decided success by the time he was twenty-four. At twenty-seven he was managing a company of his own and touring South Germany and Austria with a repertory that included *King Lear*, *Hamlet*, and *Macbeth*, as well as plays by Lessing and Schiller. He was musician enough to perform Gluck's *Orpheus*, besides all sorts of patriotic pieces, ballets, spectacular entertainments, and German comic operas, some of which he composed himself. He was a capable manager, very popular with his subordinates, a passably good singer, and clever enough to see that an energetic appeal to German national sentiment was a sure road to success at a time when his countrymen were growing tired of the tyranny of French and Italian taste and preparing subconsciously for the romantic outburst of the early nineteenth century. He gave a season of German *Singspiel* (comic opera) at Vienna in the winter of 1784–5, often patronized by the Emperor; a season mainly of patriotic and spectacular pieces, interspersed with comic operas, at Regensburg in 1787. In 1789 he came back to Vienna to begin a long series of successes at the 'Theater im Starhembergischen Freihause auf der Wieden' a flimsy erection which had been run up in one of the numerous courtyards of what is still called the 'Freihaus', a huge block of low yellow buildings south of the Naschmarkt. In those days it was outside the fortifications of the city, just on the right hand of the road leading out of the Kärntnerthor. The whole position of both Schikaneder and his theatre is not unlike that of the Royal Cobourg Theatre in Lambeth a generation later.

After the collapse of German opera that followed Mozart's *Entführung*, Joseph had reinstated Italian opera at court; but the people of Vienna were only too glad to support some sort of popular musical entertainment in their own language. One Marinelli had obtained considerable success with comic operas, burlesques, fairy plays, and topical pieces during the last eight years; and Schikaneder, seeing what the public wanted, set himself to beat Marinelli at his own trade. He began with simple *Singspiel*, but soon saw that what drew the largest audiences were operas on Oriental subjects and romantic fairy tales, in both of which the local Viennese comic character 'Kasperl' or one of his tribe could be introduced. His first 'magic' opera was *Oberon*, libretto by C. L. Giesecke, music by Paul Wranitzky, produced 7 November 1789. He now came to Mozart with the offer of a similar kind of libretto.

Mozart accepted it. It is difficult to imagine what process of thought led him to do so. It was hardly dignified for a musician who had been constantly associated with court life at Vienna and elsewhere, both as composer and pianist, to undertake to collaborate in a fairy play to be acted in what was little more than a wooden barn, to an audience that cared only for trivial and vulgar melody, 'gag' and 'business' of the silliest kind, crude spectacular effects and the introduction of a whole menagerie of animals on the stage. On the other hand, he had been insultingly neglected by the new Emperor, and had practically no hope of reinstatement. For years he had been passionately desirous of writing a German opera, and this chance might well be better than none. His sister-in-law, Josefa Hofer, belonged to Schikaneder's company; Schikaneder himself was an old friend, and the type of friend who knew how to make the most of friendship. There was yet another reason: Schikaneder and Mozart were both Freemasons, and we shall eventually see that this was very probably the most cogent reason of all.

Concerning the history of the next few months there is a mass of legend and tradition, and a scarcity of well-authenticated facts. Time was pressing, and Schikaneder well knew how difficult it was to induce Mozart to write anything down. But fortune favoured him; Mozart's wife was taking the waters at Baden near Vienna during June and July, and the composer was left alone without even a servant.[1] Schikaneder provided him with a summer-house[2] in the courtyard where the theatre was erected, in which he could work with the manager's eye always upon him, and kept up his spirits at other times by encouraging him to share his own riotous

---

[1] Mozart writes to his wife on 6 June: '*J'ai congédié Léonore, et je serai tout seul à la maison, ce qui n'est pas agréable.*' Why this letter was written in French does not appear.

[2] The summer-house remained in position till the middle of the last century, when it was removed to Salzburg and re-erected on the Capuzinerberg.

and profligate life. The opera was finished in the rough in the course of July, and rehearsals for the singers had already begun.

Two new commissions interrupted the course of *Die Zauberflöte* (*The Magic Flute*), as the new opera was to be called.

It was in July that a mysterious messenger presented Mozart with an anonymous letter inviting him to compose a Requiem Mass, and to name his own price for it. He accepted the offer, as he was anxious to show the world what he could do in the ecclesiastical style, now that Leopold II had reinstated the church orchestras which Joseph had abolished. In August came a more pressing invitation. The Emperor was to be crowned King of Bohemia at Prague on 6 September, and the local authorities decided at the last moment to celebrate the occasion with an opera by Mozart. The libretto chosen was an old one of Metastasio's, remodelled for this festivity, *La Clemenza di Tito*, a pompous and frigid drama of Roman history such as had always been chosen for court festivities in the first half of the century. Mozart was obliged to set off at once for Prague, accompanied by his wife and his pupil Süssmayr, composing in the carriage and writing out his ideas with Süssmayr's help wherever they stopped for the night. The opera was finished in eighteen days, rehearsed, and finally performed with all possible magnificence after the coronation banquet. It was a complete failure, and the Empress Maria Luisa, who was a daughter of the King of Naples, called it *una porcheria tedesca*. Later on it achieved what was almost popularity. It was repeated at Prague and much applauded; it was the first opera of Mozart to be performed in London (1806). For the stage of to-day it can only be considered as a museum piece.

It is obvious that the libretto was chosen by the authorities to present the monarchy in the most favourable light. The French Revolution of 1789 had struck terror in all reactionary states, and it was urgent, first, that the principle of absolute monarchy should be reasserted, and, secondly, that it should be held up to the advocates of liberty as tempering justice with mercy. The story turns on the unfailing and therefore rather monotonous clemency of the Roman Emperor Titus. Vitellia, daughter of the late Emperor Vitellius, being offended because Titus does not desire to make her his wife, induces his intimate friend Sextus to form a conspiracy against him, Sextus being madly in love with her, and wax in her hands. Titus is at present contemplating marriage with Servilia, the sister of Sextus, but on finding that she is in love with Annius, a friend of her brother's, performs his first act of clemency by giving her up to him. He then decides to marry Vitellia after all, and sends his general Publius to inform her of his intentions. Publius arrives just too late; Vitellia has at that very moment sent Sextus off to set fire to the Capitol and murder Titus. Sextus manages to perform the first part of her instructions, but is too nervous to kill Titus himself, and comes back to Vitellia. The first act ends with the burning of the Capitol and the agitation of the principal characters, supported by the chorus.

At the opening of the second act we learn that Titus has escaped death and has discovered the whole plot. Sextus confesses his guilt to Annius, who urges him to flight; Vitellia is also anxious to get Sextus out of the way, since she knows that if Titus treats him with the inevitable clemency, he will probably confess everything and expose her. Publius comes to arrest Sextus, who is tried by the Senate and condemned to death. Titus has an interview with him, but he refuses to inculpate Vitellia, and is sent back to prison; Titus, after some hesitation, tears up the death warrant which he had just signed. Finally, however, Vitellia makes up her mind to confess her share in the plot. She does this with her usual sense of dramatic effect in the amphitheatre where Sextus and his fellow conspirators are to be thrown to the wild beasts. Needless to say, Titus performs his third act of clemency and pardons everybody so that the opera may end with general rejoicing.

The remodelling of the libretto was done by Da Ponte's old friend, Caterino Mazzolà. He removed a good many of the solo arias on which every drama of Metastasio depends, and replaced them by duets, trios, and ensembles to suit the taste of a more modern audience. The result is a rather shapeless opera, and one feels its shapelessness the more because its only *raison d'être* as a coronation opera is to be formal. Here is Mozart, definitely in his 'third period', being forced to revert to the style of his first. It was impossible. *Idomeneo* is the work of a young man at the height of his powers, anxious above all things to express his emotions and to put in everything that he could give; *La Clemenza di Tito* was written by a man in broken health, exhausted by overwork, and forced to write in haste against his will. He knew, too, what sort of an audience he had to expect; remembering Joseph II's remark, 'Too many notes, my dear Mozart!' he purposely adopted a plain and easy style with obvious melodies of old-fashioned cut, the simplest harmonies, and the thinnest orchestration. The arias, which ought to be long and stately, he cuts down to the shortest proportions; he invents a new form for them, based on Gluck's French operas, with a slow introduction and a quick movement to follow. We have met with it in Fiordiligi's aria, *Come scoglio*, and indeed in *Idomeneo*, but in both of these he could take his time. In *La Clemenza di Tito* he takes his time only in the two great arias that have now become favourite concert-pieces, partly for the opportunity given to the singer and perhaps still more for the elaborate instrumental *obbligato* parts, one for clarinet, the other for basset-horn, both played at Prague by Anton Stadler. In the opera both arias stand out as concert-pieces, just like *Martern aller Arten* (which also has elaborate instrumental *obbligati*) in *Die Entführung*. There are two charming little duets, and the second —*Ah perdona*—is one of Mozart's loveliest inspirations.[1] In the concerted numbers Mozart allows his dramatic genius more freedom, and we meet with modulations and other complexities which may well have bewildered the Empress. The finest movement of all is the finale to Act I, in which the conflicting emotions of Sextus and Vitellia, Servilia and Annius are painted against a choral background. This finale has great importance because it is the first in which Mozart has combined both solo voices and chorus too in a great ensemble. The comic operas never employ the chorus in a finale at all, except for short isolated passages (as in *Figaro*, Act III, and *Così fan Tutte*, Act II); each act of *Idomeneo* ends with a chorus on a large scale, but the soloists take no part in them. Here the chorus is a factor in the drama. We begin with the agonized perplexity of the principal characters; suddenly the cry of the terrified people, still far distant, tells us and tells them too that Rome is in flames. This idea must have been entirely Mozart's own invention, since the chorus have nothing to sing except horribly dramatic cries of 'Ah!' until the principals join together to sum up the situation in four short lines—a procedure hitherto confined to *opera buffa*—the last two of which are repeated by the chorus. But the chorus is not brought in just to make more noise. In fact, it is not brought in at all; it remains permanently *in lontananza*, though obviously it must have been

---

[1] Mr. H. Buxton Forman discovered that it was to this melody that Shelley wrote the song, 'I arise from dreams of thee' (see *The Athenaeum* of 31 August and 2 November 1907). But it cannot be said that the words go well with the tune.

drawing nearer and nearer all the time. The chorus sings anti-
phonally with the group of soloists, and it is most carefully planned
never to overpower them. But the mixture of formality and a
certain modernity produces effects which are very curious to ears
of to-day. Anyone coming across this passage[1] in ignorance of its
context might well be tempted to ascribe it to some English
organist of about 1861 than to a composer of Italian opera. But
we must train our minds to forget such disturbing associations
and try to approach Mozart's opera from the point of view of
those who heard it first performed.

Directly after the production of *La Clemenza di Tito* at Prague,
Mozart and his wife returned to Vienna. Constanze went back to
Baden to continue her cure, and Mozart was as much in need of
medical treatment as she was. He had started the year badly, and
the life he had been leading with Schikaneder now began to tell on
his constitution. At the moment of his departure for Prague, he
had experienced a severe nervous shock on the sudden reappearance
of the mysterious messenger to ask what was to happen to the
Requiem. Well or ill, the opera had to be finished at once. Besides
the instrumentation of the whole, there still remained the Chorus
of Priests in Act II (No. 18), Papageno's song (No. 20), and the
Finale (No. 21), as well as the overture and the March of the
Priests which were not written till 28 September. Two days later
the first performance took place. Schikaneder sang Papageno
and Madame Hofer the Queen of Night. The general reception of
the piece was considered disappointing, but Schikaneder had the

---

[1] It occurs near the end of this first finale; the words sung are:

'Oh nero tradimento! oh giorno di dolor!'
'Oh deed of blackest treason! Oh day of grief and pain!'

courage of his convictions. He continued to repeat the opera, and no doubt added continually to his own comic business, possibly to the stage effects as well; eventually it became a popular success of a quite exceptional kind.

The opera once started on its course, Mozart returned to the Requiem, even refusing a pupil rather than neglect it. Constanze was still at Baden and remained there for most of October. *Die Zauberflöte* was now going on well, and Mozart was pleased to find that his old rival Salieri went to see it and enjoyed it. Yet he could not rid himself of the idea that he had been poisoned, that the mysterious messenger was a visitant from the other world, and that he was composing the Requiem for his own death. After Mozart's death a legend was current that he had been poisoned by Salieri, but there is not the slightest evidence for it, and no serious student of Mozart now places the least faith in it.[1] His wife on her return called in a physician, and took the score of the Requiem away from him. A Masonic cantata to words by Schikaneder gave his thoughts a change, and he became less depressed; but on returning to work at the Requiem he relapsed, and two days after he had conducted the cantata (it was finished on 15 November and probably sung a few days later) his last illness definitely set in. He struggled to go on with the Requiem, and got a few friends to try the vocal parts through with him on 4 December. But it seems to have been the opera that gave him the happiest thoughts. In the evenings he used to follow the performances in imagination, with his watch beside him, and on the same day that his friends came to try over the Requiem 'he said to his wife, "I should like to have heard my *Zauberflöte* once more", and began to hum the bird-catcher's song in a scarcely audible voice. Kapellmeister Roser, who was sitting at his bedside, went to the pianoforte and sang the song, to Mozart's evident delight.' At one o'clock in the morning of 5 December he died; in the afternoon of 6 December he was tumbled into a pauper's grave. The Requiem was finished by Süssmayr, copied out by him (his handwriting was almost indistinguishable from Mozart's) and handed over by the widow to the messenger who had commissioned it. It is now known that this man was merely the steward of a certain Count Walsegg, an amateur musician who

[1] It forms the subject of Pushkin's little play, *Mozart and Salieri*, written in 1830 and first performed 1832; it was set to music as an opera by Rimsky-Korsakov in 1898.

wished to pass for a composer. He had, however, the good sense to recognize his own want of ability, and therefore adopted the simple expedient of giving anonymous commissions to composers of merit for quartets and other works. He paid for them liberally and had them executed under his own name. The Requiem was ordered in memory of his deceased Countess, and he himself conducted a performance of it in the church of the Cistercians at Wiener Neustadt on 14 December 1793.

## 13

## DIE ZAUBERFLÖTE—II

THE libretto of *Die Zauberflöte* has generally been considered to be one of the most absurd specimens of that form of literature in which absurdity is regarded as a matter of course. What Schikaneder wanted was a fairy-tale plot of the conventional kind—a good fairy, a wicked magician, a pair of lovers passing through various trials and ultimately united, thanks to the virtues of a musical instrument endowed with magic properties; the scene was to be laid in what is conveniently called 'the East'; there were to be startling scenic effects, with plenty of coloured fire and plenty of animals; the actor-manager himself was to have a comic part full of popular songs, with endless opportunities for talking to the audience and attracting an actor-manager's share of attention and applause. He found his material in the story of *Lulu*, one of a collection of Oriental fairy tales published in 1786 by Wieland and others under the title of *Dschinnistan*.[1] He had in fact already produced a very successful opera of the same type, *Oberon*, which had come out towards the beginning of November 1789; the music of this was by Paul Wranitzky and the words by Carl Ludwig Giesecke, a young man who had recently joined Schikaneder's company—it was his first attempt at writing for the stage. The plot of *Oberon* was also taken from Wieland, and is substantially the same as that of the English *Oberon* libretto which J. R. Planché wrote for Weber in 1826, Planché's libretto being taken largely from Wieland too. It should be superfluous to remind the English reader that in this opera Oberon sends the knight Huon of Bordeaux to rescue the Turkish maiden Rezia and bring her to the court of Charlemagne; Huon overcomes all difficulties with the help of a magic horn bestowed upon him by Oberon.

The initial idea of *Die Zauberflöte*, then, was to be more or less as follows: the hero makes the acquaintance of the fairy queen, who gives him a portrait of her daughter and sends him to rescue her from captivity in the castle of the wicked magician, which he

---

[1] *Lulu, oder die Zauberflöte* is not by Wieland, but by A. J. Liebeskind.

will be able to do by the help of the magic flute. For some reason which has never yet been satisfactorily explained, the whole plot was completely changed at this stage. The wicked magician was made the agent of good, and the fairy queen the representative of evil. Some of the music was already written, but Schikaneder was not going to have that wasted, so the join was covered up as well as could be managed. The reason generally accepted for the alteration is that on 8 June Schikaneder's rival Marinelli had brought out at his theatre a comic opera called *Der Fagottist, oder die Zauberzither*, words by Joachim Perinet, music by Wenzel Müller. An edition of this libretto printed in 1795 for the court theatre at Munich informs us that the story was taken from Wieland's *Lulu*, and that it contained so much vulgarity and indecency that it required considerable expurgation before it was fit for a court theatre. What is more difficult to explain is the fact that the new opera was transformed completely from a conventional fairy tale to a glorification of Freemasonry under a very thinly veiled allegorical disguise. The scene was transferred to ancient Egypt and an entirely new set of characters was introduced into the story—Sarastro, the high priest of Isis and Osiris, the Orator and the chorus of subordinate priests. The wicked magician of the first plot was reduced to the status of a grotesquely tyrannical servant, and the fairy queen was unmasked as a vindictive female always seeking to do injury to the priests and their followers. Probably too, at this point, the names of the original characters were changed, so as to destroy all appearance of connection with Wieland's story.

We must now consider the libretto as it stands. The first scene opens with the entrance of the hero, now called Tamino, but still by an oversight described as a 'Japanese' prince.[1] He is pursued by a huge serpent and has no arrows with which to defend himself. With a cry for help he falls to the ground unconscious, and at that moment three Ladies dressed in black and carrying spears enter and kill the serpent. They are much impressed by Tamino's good looks, but after a brief but energetic quarrel among themselves for the advantage of being left alone to watch over him, they depart together to inform their mistress, the Queen of Night, to whom they think he may be able to be of service. Tamino on awaking encounters the bird-catcher Papageno, who tells him that he has killed the serpent himself. The three Ladies reappear, and after

[1] In some editions of the opera he has been called Javanese.

locking up Papageno's mouth with a padlock as a punishment for
boasting and lying, present the Prince with the portrait of
Pamina, the Queen of Night's daughter.[1] Tamino at once falls in
love with her and is dispatched by the Queen herself to rescue her
from the clutches of Sarastro,[2] whom she describes as an evil
magician. The Ladies remove the padlock from Papageno's
mouth and bid him accompany Tamino on his journey. They
present Tamino with a magic flute and Papageno with a chime of
magic bells; the Ladies also tell them that they will be guided
safely by three boys or Genii.

In the second scene we see Pamina being ill-treated by the
blackamoor Monostatos, who even goes so far as to make love to
her. Monostatos is a servant in the employ of Sarastro, but he is
a thoroughly bad character, redeemed only by a considerable
touch of the grotesque. Papageno enters; he and the blackamoor
are each terrified at the strange appearance of the other and run
off in opposite directions. Papageno, however, returns in a
moment and informs Pamina of what has happened in the
previous scene; he persuades her to run away at once to find
Tamino. In the third scene the story begins to take a new course.
Tamino is led on by the three Genii, who counsel him gravely to
silence, patience, and perseverance. Before him stand the three
temples of Nature, Reason, and Wisdom, each of which he
attempts to enter in turn. Twice he is driven back by mysterious
voices from within, but on his third attempt he is met by a priest
(the Orator) who tells him that he has been deceived by the
Queen, and that Sarastro, so far from being a monster of cruelty,
is the chief priest of the Temple of Wisdom. Tamino presses him
for further explanations, but he refuses to say more:

'*Tam.*    When wilt thou break the bonds of silence?

*Priest.*   When friendship leads thee by the hand
           To join the temple's holy band.'

[1] It is extremely probable that the hero and heroine were originally intended
to have names identical except for the masculine or feminine termination, on the
analogy of Papageno and Papagena. The difference may have been due to a
clerical error or to a misprint in an early proof, but no doubt both author and
composer soon realized that the identity of name would be a practical inconvenience.

It should be noted that almost all the names of characters have an Italian form
and that therefore they should be pronounced as in Italian—Papageno and
Papagena with a soft *g*, although the current practice in Germany is to pronounce
the *g* hard.

[2] The name Sarastro must obviously have been suggested by Zoroaster.

The Orator re-enters the temple, and Tamino, consoled by the assurance of mysterious voices that Pamina still lives, begins to play on the magic flute, while all sorts of wild animals creep out to listen to him. Suddenly he hears an answering signal from Papageno on the panpipes which he carries as a bird-catcher, and rushes off in search of him; at that moment Papageno and Pamina, who have heard his response on the flute, run in to look for Tamino. They are intercepted by Monostatos and his slaves, but Papageno plays on the magic bells and Monostatos and the slaves start singing and dancing against their will. Sarastro now enters with his train; Pamina confesses her attempt at flight, to which he replies with characteristic gentleness. Meanwhile Monostatos has secured Tamino and brings him before Sarastro for judgement; to his great surprise, he himself is rewarded with the bastinado, while Tamino and Papageno are led into the temple with a view to their initiation.

The second act opens with a scene in which Sarastro and the priests agree to accept Tamino as a candidate. Nothing is said about Papageno, but he accompanies Tamino through some of his subsequent ordeals in order to provide comic relief. In Scene 2 Tamino and Papageno are left in darkness by the priests, and are visited by the three Ladies, who attempt to turn them from their purpose, threatening them with the Queen's anger and with eternal damnation as well. They remain steadfast, and the Ladies flee on hearing the execrations of the priests. In Scene 3 Monostatos finds Pamina asleep in Sarastro's garden, and is on the point of taking advantage of her, when he is prevented by the sudden appearance of the Queen, who gives Pamina a dagger, commands her to kill Sarastro and secure for her the 'sevenfold shield of the sun' which is in Sarastro's possession. Monostatos, who has overheard all, threatens to betray Pamina, or even to kill her, unless she yields to his desires, but his evil designs are frustrated by the entrance of Sarastro. He tells her that he must still keep her under his own care, but he is too magnanimous to revenge himself upon the Queen; revenge of any kind is contrary to the fundamental principles of the Temple of Wisdom.

Scene 4 brings the second trial of the candidates, the test of silence. Papageno cannot resist talking to an old woman who frightens him by claiming him as her lover. The three Genii appear, bringing in a table spread with food and drink, and also the flute and the bells, which had previously been taken away by the priests. They repeat their counsel of courage and silence. Pamina enters, but both Tamino and Papageno refuse to speak to her; she interprets this as a sign that Tamino no longer loves her and leaves the stage in despair. Tamino is then conducted for the first time to the assembly of the priests (Scene 5) where in the presence of Sarastro he is told to take farewell of Pamina, although Sarastro assures them that they will meet again. Papageno, left alone, has another interview with the old woman, who is finally transformed into his female counterpart, Papagena, only to be immediately removed by the Orator. A scene follows in which Pamina, convinced that Tamino has deserted her, attempts to commit suicide, but is prevented by the Genii. Tamino is now submitted to the third and final ordeal, the test of fire and water. In this Pamina is allowed to join him; they pass through the fire and water together, protected by the music of the magic flute, and are welcomed into the temple as initiates by the chorus of priests. Papageno reappears, and, like Pamina, is prevented from killing himself[1] by the Genii, who tell him to summon Papagena with the call of the magic bells; he does so and they are happily united. In the last scene the Queen, accompanied by her Ladies and led by the traitor Monostatos, makes a final despairing attempt on the temple and its votaries, but is frustrated by the rising of the sun, the opera ending with a *tableau* in which Sarastro and the lovers are hailed with joyful solemnity by the chorus.

We may consider this libretto from various points of view. On the face of it it is a mere agglomeration of absurdities; the language of the dialogue is for the most part a ludicrous mixture of theatrical commonplaces and trivial jests, while the versified portions are clumsy doggerel relieved occasionally by passages borrowed from popular Masonic songs. From Schikaneder's point of view as a manager, it contained excellent theatrical situations, all opportunities for spectacular effect, and a very conspicuous part for himself, although it is said that after the first performance he remarked: 'Yes, it has been a success, but it would have been far more of a success if Mozart had not ruined so much of it!'[2] But it is clear that whatever may have been the opinion of Schikaneder's own audiences (and they were none too favourable

[1] Mrs. L. G. Marcus (Girton College, Cambridge) informs me that this scene, in all its details, was a traditional monologue for Harlequin in the *Commedia dell' Arte*. Truffaldino appears as a bird-catcher in Gozzi's play *Il Re Cervo*.

[2] C. F. Wittmann, in the introduction to the Reclam edition of the libretto. I do not know what authority he had for this statement.

at first) the opera can appeal to later generations only in a symbolical sense. About its Masonic significance there is not the least shadow of doubt. Jahn mentions a Masonic interpretation published as early as 1794. In 1838 the opera was performed in London in a translation by Planché; in his autobiography he speaks very well of the whole performance and production, and resolutely defends the libretto and its symbolism of good and evil. He rightly condemns the current Italian translation by G. de Gamerra. Whether he realized the Masonic sense of the story is not clear. The most important Masonic commentary on the opera is an anonymous pamphlet published at Leipzig in 1866; it is now known to have been written by Moritz Alexander Zille (1814–72), a well-known theologian and teacher in Leipzig. He was an ardent Freemason and a man of unusually wide religious views in the Leipzig of the fifties and sixties—half mystic, half rationalist, with a great sympathy for the old pietists. According to Zille, Tamino represented Joseph II, Pamina the Austrian people, Sarastro Ignaz von Born, a Freemason and a scientist of great eminence; the Queen of Night was the Empress Maria Theresa and Monostatos the clergy, especially the Jesuits and the religious orders. It is also suggested that Monostatos stood for one Leopold Aloys Hoffmann, a traitorous Freemason who in 1792 persuaded the new Emperor Francis II that the Freemasons were organizing a revolution in Austria; but we cannot be certain that his machinations were known at the time of the first appearance of *Die Zauberflöte*. The moral sentiments with which the opera abounds were drawn largely from Masonic teaching. The reader will at once notice the importance assigned to manliness and friendship, to the secrecy of the mystic rites and to the subordination of the female sex. The second act contains, besides many things intelligible at once to the initiated, plenty of lines which any reader can recognize as characteristic of the ethical and political tendencies of the period. Whether it was true or not that the Viennese lodges were organizing a revolution, it is plain that the writer of this libretto was saturated with the ideals of liberty, equality, and fraternity. Thus in Act II, Scene 1, when the candidature of Tamino is under discussion, a priest says, 'Yet will Tamino have strength to endure the ordeals that await him? Remember, he is of royal blood.' Sarastro replies: 'He is a man; that is enough.' In the next scene the Ladies allude clearly to the Catholic condemnation of Freemasonry, which Tamino treats with just contempt. Sarastro's air, *In diesen heiligen Hallen,* and the song of the Genii with which the finale begins, recall in their sentiments and phraseology many of the Masonic songs of the day, some of which were set to music by Mozart himself.[1] The attempt of the Queen to destroy the 'impious band' with fire and sword is obviously based on the events of 1743, when Maria Theresa, instigated by the Jesuits, ordered a raid to be made by soldiers on the lodge of which her own husband was a member.

The sources of the remodelled plot have only comparatively recently been investigated. Jahn suggested that the story was merely inverted, and a handful of Masonic allusions thrown in. A later biographer of Schikaneder[2] has shown that even the first plot was not taken exclusively from *Lulu*; the starry Queen of Night and her ladies, the vicious blackamoor, the portrait of the heroine and the three wise Genii, are all additions drawn from other stories in the same collection. An old opera by Hafner, *Megära die förchterliche Hexe,* dating back to 1761, but often given by Marinelli, provided a precedent for female villains and noble-minded sorcerers. Another opera given by Marinelli in 1790, *Das Sonnenfest der Brahminen,* words by K. F. Hensler, music by Wenzel Müller, with a plot rather similar to those of Meyerbeer's *L'Africaine* and Delibes' *Lakmé,* showed Schikaneder what effects could be obtained from scenes of religious ceremony. Schikaneder himself had written the libretto of *Der Stein der Weisen* (September 1790), music by Benedict Schack, who sang the part of Tamino in the first production of *Die Zauberflöte*; this story, taken also from Wieland, contained a magician who related how he has been initiated into the Egyptian mysteries.

We must proceed, however, to the original source of the author's Egyptian inspiration. In 1731 a certain Abbé Jean Terrasson (1670–1750), who in 1721 had become professor of Greek and Latin philosophy at the Collège de France, published anonymously a romance entitled *Sethos, histoire ou vie tirée des monumens anecdotes de l'ancienne Egypte. Traduite d'un manuscrit grec.* Terrasson was a somewhat eccentric scholar,[3] who made a French

[1] Others are quoted by Ludwig Lewis, *Geschichte der Freimaurerei in Oesterreich und Ungarn,* Leipzig, 1872.

[2] Egon von Komorzynski, *Emanuel Schikaneder, ein Beitrag zur Geschichte des deutschen Theaters,* Berlin, 1901.

[3] 'On a dit qu'il n'était homme d'esprit que de profil, et Mme de Lassay ajoutait qu'il n'y avait qu'un homme de beaucoup d'esprit qui pût être d'une pareille imbécillité' (*Biographie Universelle*). His criticism on Molière's *Le Festin de Pierre* has been quoted in an earlier chapter.

translation of Diodorus Siculus, with the object, it is said, of showing the admirers of the classics how dull a classical author could be. Sethos is an Egyptian prince, born in the century before the Trojan War. The first part of the book deals with his education and his initiation into the mysteries; the second part describes his travels in Africa as a universal lawgiver for savage tribes; finally, he returns to Egypt and retires into a college of initiates for the rest of his life. A second French edition of the book appeared in 1732 at Antwerp; in the same year it was translated into English by Thomas Lediard the elder, and into German by C. G. Wend; an Italian translation came out at Venice in 1734. Another German translation was published at Breslau in 1777–8 and the fourth French edition was printed as late as 1813. The book appears to have been much read in Masonic circles, and it is cited by French Masonic historians of a century ago as if it were a standard authority on the Egyptian mysteries. Wieland knew it, and so evidently did Gebler, the author of the Egyptian play, *König Thamos*, for which Mozart had composed incidental music in 1773. The author of *Die Zauberflöte* must have known it intimately, for there are innumerable allusions to it in the opera, and at least two places where passages are borrowed practically word for word.[1]

The very first scene is a reminiscence of *Sethos*, although Tamino falls rather short of the original in both heroism and ingenuity. Sethos himself set out to kill a monstrous serpent, but was clever enough to catch it in a trap and bring it back to Memphis alive, after having first estimated its size exactly by means of trigonometrical observations. This, however, was perhaps ill-adapted to musical treatment, although it might have appealed to Mozart's youthful taste for mathematics. The Queen of Night is modelled on Daluca, the stepmother of Sethos, and the three Ladies also belong to her circle. She was a rather disreputable lady herself, and being desirous of becoming omnipotent at court, did her best

[1] The connection of *Sethos* with *Die Zauberflöte* seems to have been first pointed out by Thomas Love Peacock in a review of Thomas Moore's tale, *The Epicurean* (1827); in Germany it was first noticed by Carl Gollmick in 1842. Julien Tiersot mentions it, but does not pursue the problem, in a series of articles in *Le Menestrel* (1893). It was thoroughly worked out for the first time by Viktor Junk (*Goethes Fortsetzung der Mozartschen Zauberflöte*, Berlin, 1900), who apparently was not acquainted with Tiersot's essay. I had myself arrived independently at the same conclusion before meeting with either of these works, and have added a few details not given by Junk. See note at the end of this chapter.

to get rid of the wise philosophers who had frequented it in the days of the late queen.

'The method she pitched on, as most expedient for her design, was to give the sole empire of conversation to such ladies of the court as she had observed the most vain, and who had the faculty of talking loud and long upon nothing. These ladies, like the queen, had all pass'd their meridian, and having made no provision to supply the loss of exterior beauties by the more valuable qualities of the mind, were extremely subservient to her design, without so much as knowing it. They were always ready to interrupt any discourse that might savour of learning or ingenuity; but they were not often put to the trouble: for their own perpetual talk was so vain, and so little approved, that no man of sense could find room, or thought it worth while, to put in a word.'[1]

The author also gives us to understand that these ladies were more energetic than discreet in securing the affections of handsome young men. Under these circumstances the education of Sethos is carried on by a faithful tutor, Amedes, who in the course of the story takes his pupil to see the Pyramids. Like Tamino, Sethos is much struck with the architectural grandeur of the temples. They explore the interior of a pyramid, using lamps which can be worn on the head like helmets; the Armed Men in Act II of the opera wear similar headgear.[2] At a certain stage of the journey Sethos expresses a wish to be initiated into the mysteries; the reply of Amedes bears a strong resemblance to the speeches of the Genii and the Orator in Act I and to those of Sarastro in Act II:

'From this moment I suppose your youth at an end, and that from the desire you have just testify'd for the initiation, you this day begin to be a perfect man. The initiation, to which we are not allowed to invite anyone whomsoever in direct terms, is the enterprise of which I spoke ambiguously to you, and for which I required particular proofs of your prudence and valour.'

We note that Amedes and Sethos enter the sacred precincts by the northern gate, as does Tamino; while discoursing together on morality they are secretly watched by the priests, who thus prepare themselves for their reception. As in the opera, an initiate

---

[1] The quotations are from Lediard's English translation.

[2] In Victorian days chimney-sweeps and stonemasons who had to work in cellars or other dark places often wore lighted candles stuck in their hats.

is specially appointed as guide to the neophyte. Sarastro's air at the beginning of Act II is taken practically word for word from the prayer offered up to Isis after Sethos has passed through the final tests:

'Isis, ô grande déesse des Egyptiens, donnez votre esprit au nouveau serviteur qui a surmonté tant de périls et de travaux pour se présenter à vous. Rendez-le victorieux de même dans les épreuves de son âme en le rendant docile à vos loix, afin qu'il mérite d'être admis à vos mystères.'

Up to this point the neophyte might, if he wished, return to ordinary life. He stood before a closed door guarded by armed priests, surmounted by an inscription which we find translated almost word for word in the duet for the Armed Men in the opera:

'Quiconque fera cette route seul, et sans regarder derrière lui, sera purifié par le feu, par l'eau et par l'air; et s'il peut vaincre la frayeur de la mort, il sortira du sein de la terre, il reverra la lumière, et il aura droit de préparer son âme à la révélation des mystères de la grande Déesse Isis.'

The door is opened, and Sethos passes through the tests of fire and water; after that, by a curious mechanical device, into the temple, where he is received and congratulated by the priests. The descriptions of the tests and their elaborate machinery are too complicated for quotation here. It will be remembered that in the opera Papageno is unable to keep silence, and therefore does not proceed to the tests of fire and water. He is threatened with lifelong imprisonment, but is at least offered the consolation of a wife. We find in *Sethos* the authority for most of these events:

'For as soon as any candidate had pass'd the little door that was shut, and got a sight of the flames, if he offer'd to return, the three men, who were officers of the second rank, seized him, and made him enter through the door into the subterranean temples, where he was for ever confined, that he might not divulge the nature of the trials. . . . Their imprisonment was not, however, very rigid. They were made, if they desir'd it, officers of the second order in these subterraneous temples, and were allowed to marry the daughters of such officers.'

Even the noise of thunder which occurs so frequently in the opera is here accounted for; Sethos is told afterwards that what he took to be thunder was merely the reverberation through the subterranean passages of the noise of closing doors, which served the double purpose of terrifying the neophyte and of warning the priests of his approach.

Yet one more quotation must be given, to illustrate the position of the female sex in the Egyptian mysteries. The priests were allowed to marry, and—

'their wives, who in compliment were call'd priestesses, tho' in Egypt they had no sacerdotal functions, dwelt with them under the same roof. . . . But that which will appear, without doubt, mortifying to well-bred gentlemen, these ladies, who were mostly of singular beauty, never pass'd by him [the candidate] without paying him their respect, and he was not suffer'd to make the least show of a return. By this he was put to a trial of that fortitude with which every virtuous man ought to resist the charms of the sex when they appear in competition with his duty.'

How far the Abbé Terrasson's ideas of Egyptian mysteries correspond with the mysteries of Freemasonry it is, of course, not for an uninitiated writer to conjecture. It is, however, noteworthy that a German writer on Freemasonry in a book published in 1836 and based on an anonymous French original[1] quotes the passage given above ('Quiconque fera cette route seul', etc.) as being not only a part of the ancient Egyptian ritual (citing *Sethos* as his authority), but also the inscription on the tomb of Hiram, which was read aloud at certain Masonic ceremonies. The passage as given by him in German corresponds closely with the original German words of the duet sung by the Armed Men. I must leave it to more learned investigators to decide whether these words, with many other details of Masonic ritual, were handed down simultaneously and independently through Diodorus and other classical writers on the one hand to the author of *Sethos*, as well as by unbroken and secret tradition on the other hand to the Freemasons of the later eighteenth century, or whether possibly some branches of these latter merely found it convenient to draw upon the learned Abbé's popular romance for a portion of their mysterious liturgy.

The Masonic symbolism of *Die Zauberflöte* is quite definitely accepted by Freemasons in this country and elsewhere who are

[1] R. S. Acerellos, *Die Freimaurerei in ihrem Zusammenhang mit den Religionen der alten Aegypter, der Juden und der Christen*, Leipzig, 1836.

learned both in the history of their own craft and in that of music. Mozart's connexion with Freemasonry has been thoroughly investigated by competent Masonic researchers, and his Masonic music is not infrequently performed, at any rate in England, in its proper framework of Masonic ceremony. None the less, there are three classes of persons who do their best either to deny altogether, or at any rate to minimize, the Masonic significance of *Die Zauberflöte*. The first group is that of the Catholics, Freemasonry being officially condemned by the Catholic Church. A typical example of their attitude is the following extract from *The Universe*, London, 29 May 1942:

'Mozart was "liberally" inclined as a Catholic and was undoubtedly mixed up with Freemasonry, but this had not yet been formally banned by the Church, which may be held as an excuse for him so far as it goes. . . . Suffice it that *The Magic Flute* contains some of the most beautiful music ever written to a nonsensical libretto.'

Another group is that of Freemasons imperfectly instructed in their own doctrines who find it safer to deny any Masonic significance in the opera rather than run the risk of giving away secrets to the uninitiated. This group may be left to the teaching of their own brethren. The third group is that of non-Masons who, without any doctrinal hostility to Freemasonry, merely resent its supposed mystery and generally imagine that it is a foolish if well-meaning masquerade. With Freemasonry after the time of Mozart this book really has no concern, but a rough outline of its origins and activities may be useful to readers who are not Freemasons.

The early history of Freemasonry is very obscure; as far as can be conjectured, there existed in the Middle Ages a considerable guild of skilled stonemasons who travelled from place to place and were employed in the building of the great cathedrals. They appear to have formed a sort of trade union for their own protection; they further protected themselves by secret signs and they also maintained the secrets of their professional methods. In the seventeenth century these guilds still existed, but had begun to admit what we might call 'honorary members', gentlemen of wealth and social position. At what period and in what manner Freemasonry began to develop its peculiar religious and ethical teaching has not been made clear; but a distinction came to be

made between 'operative' Masons, who practised the stone-
mason's or carpenter's trade with their own hands, and 'specula-
tive' Masons, who were interested primarily in the social and moral
aspect of the craft. Similar guilds of Masons certainly existed in
Continental countries, but English Masonic historians maintain
that the English guilds had no contact with them. It is certainly
acknowledged by all Masonic historians, foreign as well as English,
that what is now called Freemasonry, in all countries, arose from
the historic meeting of the four London lodges in 1717 at which
the Grand Lodge of England was established. From this Lodge
colonies were founded by Englishmen, sometimes by ambassadors,
in Paris, The Hague, Rome, Madrid, Gibraltar, and other places,
and the association developed rapidly all over the Continent,
especially in the Germanic countries. According to Sir Alfred
Robbins:[1]

'Freemasonry can be described as an organized system of morality, derived from divine wisdom and age-long experience, which,
for preservation from outer assault and inner decay, is veiled in
allegory and illustrated by symbol.'

It is open to all races and creeds. 'Let a man's religion or mode
of worship be what it may, he is not excluded from the Order,
provided he believe in the glorious Architect of heaven and earth,
and practise the sacred duties of morality.' From this first constitution in 1717 Freemasonry definitely refused to allow religion
or politics to be discussed within its walls, and British Freemasonry accepts Moslems, Buddhists, and Parsees among its
members, as well as Christians of all denominations. The official
German definition of Freemasonry is more explicit:

'Freemasonry is the activity of closely-united men who, employing symbolical forms borrowed principally from the mason's trade
and from architecture, work for the welfare of mankind, striving
morally to ennoble themselves and others, and thereby to bring
about a universal league of mankind, which they aspire to exhibit
even now on a small scale.'[2]

Its main purpose was philosophical and philanthropic, but since
its base was broad enough to include men of all creeds and

---

[1] *English-Speaking Freemasonry*, London, 1930
[2] *Allgemeines Handbuch der Freimaurerei.*

tendencies, it naturally attracted many persons, especially on the Continent, who made use of it to gain political ends.

'This rapid propagation was chiefly due to the spirit of the age, which, tiring of religious quarrels, restive under ecclesiastical authority, and discontented with existing social conditions, turned for enlightenment to the ancient mysteries, and sought, by uniting men of kindred tendencies, to reconstruct society on a purely human basis.'[1]

It was only natural that a secret society which taught ethical doctrines on the basis of pagan symbolism and admitted all creeds to equality should incur the hostility of the Catholic Church. The Freemasons had been persecuted by the civil authorities in Holland in 1735 and in France and Italy in 1737; in 1738 Pope Clement VIII condemned Freemasonry and excommunicated all Catholics who took further part in Masonic proceedings. He regarded it as a rival religion to Catholic Christianity; 'the situation which the Pope envisaged seems to have been not unlike that which we have recently seen created for the ministrations of the Church of England by the superior popularity of the Y.M.C.A. But Clement at any rate perceived the danger in time.'[2]

Yet in spite of persecution (there were further persecutions at Vienna in 1743 and in Switzerland in 1745) the society prospered, and increased even more than was beneficial to itself. Innumerable heretical sects sprang up, led by political intriguers, revolutionaries, spiritualists, alchemists, and charlatans of all kinds; Jesuits joined the order with the object of denouncing its members to the Inquisition. Casanova was initiated at Lyon in 1750; he tells us that every young man of the world ought to become a Freemason, if only for social reasons, and thinks it ridiculous of the Popes to proscribe so harmless an order. But the confusion of sects was so great that a congress was held in 1782 at Wilhelmsbad to reduce matters to order; the choice of the locality shows how strong a hold the originally English ideals of Freemasonry had taken in Germany.

The movement was at its height during the reign of Joseph II (1780–90). Joseph himself was not a Mason, but his father, Francis I, had been initiated at The Hague in 1731 by the British

[1] *Catholic Encyclopedia.*
[2] Rev. Herbert Thurston, S.J., *Freemasonry*, London, 1939.

Ambassador, Lord Chesterfield. Maria Theresa was too devout
a Catholic to regard the craft with favour, but Masonic influence
was strong enough to prevent the Papal Bull of 1738 from being
published in Vienna. She did, however, suppress the order in
1764, but it continued to exist in secret, and was openly protected
by Joseph after his mother's death. The object of Joseph's
youthful admiration, Frederick the Great, had been an ardent
Freemason; so was his successor, Frederick William II, and during
Joseph's own reign all the most distinguished and learned men of
Vienna belonged to the society. Voltaire is said to have been
initiated during his residence in London; Goethe, Herder, Lessing,
and Wieland were all Freemasons. So was Haydn; whether
Beethoven was actually a Freemason is doubtful, but he was
closely associated with Freemasons. Mozart joined the order
early in 1785, and it is clear from his letters and from his compositions that his connexion with it exercised a very deep and
lasting moral influence upon him.[1]

The subsequent history of Freemasonry is outside the scope of
this book; but it is generally acknowledged that most of the great
revolutions from the American and French down to the end of the
last century were to a large extent brought about by Masonic
influence.[2] How far this is strictly true is a matter for scientific
historical research; but in any case most educated Englishmen
would probably agree that these events were ultimately beneficial,
not only to the countries concerned, but to the whole of humanity.
There was always an obvious cleavage between Freemasonry in
the north and in the south; in northern and Protestant countries
it has always been a strong supporter of the constitution, and a
valuable force for law and order, but in Catholic countries it has
been persistently anti-monarchical and anti-clerical. Considering
the history of France and Italy it can hardly be wondered that
Freemasonry in those countries became definitely anti-religious,
so much so that in 1877 the English-speaking Freemasons broke
off all relations with those of the Latin countries. At the present
day it is perhaps less difficult than it was fifty years ago for the
English reader to realize the oppressive conditions under which
Mozart and his fellow Freemasons were forced to live; the political

---

[1] Mr. Herbert J. Ellingford, F.R.C.O., informs me that the last movement of
the 'Jupiter' Symphony is 'incontestably Masonic'.

[2] George Washington, Jefferson, and Franklin were Freemasons; so were
Mazzini and Garibaldi, as well as the South American liberator Bolívar.

and ethical ideals at which they were then aiming were in fact hardly
different from those ideals of religious toleration and social justice
which most Englishmen and all Americans would take for granted
as the normal and indispensable conditions of life.


## NOTE TO CHAPTER 13

*The Epicurean*, a prose romance by Thomas Moore, describes
how Alciphron, a Greek Epicurean philosopher, goes to Egypt in
A.D. 247 to learn the secret of eternal life. A young Egyptian
priestess converts him to Christianity, after which she suffers
martyrdom. Peacock not only points out that this book is based
largely on *Sethos*, but that it is an absurd misunderstanding of the
philosophy of Epicurus, which he sums up as follows:

'Death, says Epicurus, is nothing to us. All good and evil are
in sensation. The right knowledge of this truth, that death is
nothing to us, makes the mortality of life a source of enjoyment;
not adding an uncertain time, but taking away the desire of
immortality. . . . Therefore, the most fearful of evils, death, is
nothing to us, since while we are, death is not present, and when
death is present, we are not. . . . It is vain to fear the privation
of life, when in that privation there is no life to judge if there be
any evil in the privation.'

This bears a remarkable resemblance to Mozart's own words in
an often-quoted letter to his father (1787): 'Since death is the
true end and object of our life, I have in the last couple of years
[i.e. since his initiation into Freemasonry] made myself so well
acquainted with this true and best friend of mankind, that the
idea of it not only has no more terror for me, but much that is
tranquillizing and comforting.'

Can we safely infer from this that Mozart, although definitely
believing in God, did not believe in personal immortality? Sir
Alfred Robbins, in his book, *English-Speaking Freemasonry*,
insists very firmly that Freemasonry requires belief in the Supreme
Being as indispensable, but he says nothing which suggests that
a belief in immortality forms part of the essential Masonic creed.

I am indebted to Mr. Lawrence Haward for drawing my
attention to this essay of Peacock.

## 14

## DIE ZAUBERFLÖTE—III

THE libretto of *Die Zauberflöte* was for a long time credited, and is still pretty generally credited, to Schikaneder himself, since he gave himself out on the original playbill and libretto as the sole author of it. In 1849 Julius Cornet, a tenor singer and opera director of considerable repute (1793–1860), brought out a book on opera in Germany,[1] in which he made the startling announcement that the libretto was mainly the work of C. L. Giesecke, who had eked out a humble existence as a chorus-singer and actor of small parts at Schikaneder's theatre. He had acquired his information in a most curious way, and the story must be told in his own words:

'One day in the summer of 1818, at Vienna, a distinguished-looking old gentleman in a blue coat and white neckcloth, wearing an order, sat down with us at the restaurant table at which Ignaz von Seyfried, Korntheuer, Julius Laroche, Küstner, Gned, and I met every day at noon. His venerable snow-white head, his choice manner of speaking, his entire deportment, made a pleasant impression upon us all. It was the former chorus-singer Giesecke, who was now a professor at the University of Dublin, and had come straight from Ireland and Lapland to Vienna with a natural history collection of specimens from the vegetable, mineral, and animal kingdoms in order to incorporate it in the Imperial Museum. Seyfried was the only one who recognized him. The joy of the old gentleman at the sight of Vienna and at his recognition by the Emperor Francis (who had presented him with a really magnificent gold snuff-box blazing with diamonds and full of newly-minted ducats) was his reward for many years of privation and suffering. On this occasion we learned much about old times; among other things we learned that he (who belonged to the order of Freemasons, at that time forbidden on pain of severe punishment) was the real author of *Die Zauberflöte*, which as a matter of fact Seyfried had himself suspected. I tell this story according to his own statement, which we had no reason for doubting. He made this declaration to us *à propos* of my singing the *cavatina*

[1] *Die Opern in Deutschland*, Hamburg, 1849.

that was added to *Der Spiegel von Arcadien*.[1] Many people
thought that Helmböck the prompter had been Schikaneder's
collaborator. But Giesecke undeceived us on this point too; he
assigned to Schikaneder only the figures of Papageno and his wife.'

Cornet's statement was known to Jahn, and accepted by him;
but Viennese writers on Mozart have flatly refused to believe it.
Deiters, who prepared the third edition of Jahn after Jahn's
death, adopted Komorzynski's view (that Giesecke had no share
in the work), but obviously misunderstood a statement of Jahn
which he reprints *verbatim* in the same footnote. Abert in the
fourth edition of Jahn quotes my Cambridge booklet of 1911[2]
(most of which is incorporated in this book) and seems to leave
the matter as an open question. The whole thing obviously rests
on whether Cornet or Giesecke, or both, told the truth or not.
Jahn not only accepted their statements, but adds that Giesecke's
authorship was confirmed to him personally by Neukomm, who
had known Giesecke himself. Deiters seems to have completely
misunderstood this sentence and infers that Neukomm had
known Cornet and confirmed that Cornet made his statement;
this is simply senseless, whereas Jahn's words can only be logically
understood in the sense that I have given.

In any case it seems clear from Cornet's own words that he gave
a substantially accurate account of the meeting. He made two
mistakes, excusable in writing thirty years after the event.
Giesecke did not revisit Vienna in 1818, but in 1819, as I shall
show later. Further, it was not punishable with death to be a
Freemason at Vienna in 1791; on 17 December 1785, Joseph II
issued a decree that not more than three lodges were to be allowed
to exist in Vienna, and no persecution of the Freemasons took
place until 1794, when they were suppressed by Francis II. These
errors are not in themselves important, and are quite irrelevant
to the truth or falsity of the main statement that Giesecke wrote
most of the opera libretto. Cornet's detailed description of Giesecke's appearance and manners show that the encounter left an
indelible impression on his memory; and we shall see later that
Cornet's description tallies exactly with that given of him by
those who knew him in Dublin.

---

[1] *Der Spiegel von Arcadien*, words by Schikaneder, music by Süssmayr, produced at Vienna in 1794. Loewenberg says it was given 113 times in Vienna until
1804, and last revived there in 1826.

[2] *The Magic Flute, its History and Interpretation*, Cambridge, 1911.

The other persons mentioned can all be identified. Seyfried was naturally the only one of the party to recognize Giesecke, since he was the only one old enough to have known him in his theatrical days. He had been a pupil of Mozart, and was fifteen years old when *Die Zauberflöte* appeared. He eventually became conductor at Schikaneder's theatre and died in 1841. Cornet himself was twenty-five, studying singing under Salieri; Korntheuer was manager of a theatre at Budapest, but came over to Vienna for occasional performances; Küstner, a well-educated man who had been influential as an amateur in theatrical matters, was then director of the Leipzig theatre. Julius Laroche was probably the son of Julius Laroche (*d.* 1807) who had created the part of Käsperle at Marinelli's theatre. Gned was a bass singer who sang at Prague, Dresden, and Vienna.[1]

Later writers on Mozart have come gradually to suggest vaguely that Giesecke was not what he gave himself out to be, and it is perhaps a general tendency of Viennese journalism to regard Great Britain and even Eire in much the same way as we regard Ruritania. It is, however, beyond all doubt that Giesecke's statements about his travels and his Dublin professorship were substantially true, and, curiously enough, the years which he spent as an actor in Vienna form just that period of his life about which we now know least.

His real name was not Giesecke, but Johann Georg Metzler. He was born at Augsburg in 1761, the son of a tailor, and studied law at the University of Göttingen from Michaelmas, 1781, to Michaelmas, 1783.[2] (Cornet states erroneously that he was a native of Brunswick and was expelled from the University of Halle.) How he came to change his name is not clear. The writer of a memoir in the *Dublin University Magazine* (February 1834) suggested that he adopted his mother's maiden name on leaving the stage later on; but although he was entered as 'Johannes Georgius Metzlerus' on the books of the University of Göttingen, he himself writes his name in his own album (now in the National Museum, Dublin) as 'Carolus Ludovicus Metzler cognomine Giesecke'. His mother's name was not Giesecke, but Götz. The album, which is an important document for his biography, was

[1] Information kindly supplied by Dr. Robert Fellinger from the *Allgemeine Musikalische Zeitung*; Gned is not mentioned in any musical dictionary.

[2] K. J. V. Steenstrup, *Karl Ludwig Gieseckes mineralogisches Reisejournal über Grönland*, Copenhagen, 1910.

evidently begun on his departure from Augsburg for Göttingen;
it contains a number of signatures, mostly of schoolmasters and
officials, with quotations in Latin, French, English, and even
Hebrew. He is supposed to have gone to Vienna on leaving
Göttingen in 1783, but the first definite date we have is a statement that he was editing an actors' newspaper in Regensburg in
1786.[1] Koch, who appears to be responsible for this statement,
further says that Giesecke's name occurs in a list of members
present at the Lodge 'Zur Neugekrönten Hoffnung' in Vienna on
St. John's Day, 1788. On the other hand, his Masonic certificate,
now in the possession of a Lodge in Dublin, is dated from '*L'Espér-
ance Couronnée*', 1793.

His earliest known literary work is the German translation of
Anfossi's opera *I Viaggiatori Felici*, performed at Graz in 1788;
the next is *Oberon*, set to music by Wranitzky (November 1789)
for Schikaneder. He stated himself that he began travelling for
scientific purposes in 1794, and his Dublin biographer gives this
as the year in which he went to study mineralogy at Freiburg.
But he continued writing original librettos and making translations from Italian and French operas until 1801, and there are
entries in the album which show that he was in Vienna as late as
November 1800. It is extremely probable that he went to Vienna
mainly for purposes of scientific study, and that his theatrical
activities were partly an amusement and partly the means of
earning a living. Ignaz von Born, the eminent scientist who is
supposed to be represented in Sarastro, founded the Masonic
lodge 'Zur Wahren Eintracht' at Vienna, in 1781; its primary
objects were scientific research and religious enlightenment. In
1783 he began the publication of its scientific papers, and in the
same year he brought out his famous satire on the monastic orders,
*Joannis Physiophili Specimen Monachologiae methodo Linnaeano*,
of which two editions were printed at Augsburg.

If Born had some connexion with Augsburg, Giesecke may
perhaps have made his acquaintance there. Giesecke seems to
have travelled about a good deal in Germany during these years.
Under the date of 13 November 1800, Nannette Schikaneder,

[1] R.W. Bro. Herbert Bradley, 'Bro. Mozart and Some of His Masonic Friends',
in *Ars Quatuor Coronatorum*, xxvi, 3 (p. 241). Mr. Bradley derived most of his
information from Richard Koch, *Br. Mozart, Freimaurer und Illuminaten*, Bad
Reichenhall, 1911. Koch gives as authority for this statement 'papers left by
the late Br. Kupferschmidt'. But Mr. H. W. Hunt informs me that Koch is not
trustworthy.

niece of the manager, who had sung the part of First Genius in
*Die Zauberflöte*, writes:

> 'der Augenblick des wiedersehens
> Lont der trennung banger stunden.'

This may mean that Giesecke had returned after a long absence,
or that he was on the point of departure. To about the same date
probably belongs an entry by Joseph Graf von Salm (1773–1861),
a distinguished botanist, who quotes four lines from the opera:

> 'Nur der Freundschaft Harmonie
> mildert die Beschwerden
> ohne diese Simpathie
> giebts kein Glück auf Erden.'

Other entries about this date suggest that he was constantly in
the society of actors and singers, but in 1801 he was hearing the
lectures of Karstens in Berlin, and Karstens himself signs the
album. He was in various north German towns in 1802–3, as
well as in Denmark and Sweden. In 1804 he seems to have settled
at Copenhagen. The Dublin biographer says that he entered the
Austrian diplomatic service and was sent to Constantinople and
Naples, but there is no evidence in the album or anywhere else of
such travels.

At Copenhagen he opened a school of mineralogy, and was also
a dealer in minerals; in 1806 Christian VII sent him on a scientific
expedition to Greenland, where he remained seven and a half
years. In August 1813 he landed at Hull, looking probably rather
like Papageno, for his European clothes had worn out and he was
dressed like an Eskimo in fur and feathers.

He was given a hearty welcome at Edinburgh, where Sir George
Mackenzie, Provincial Grand Master of the Northern Counties,
introduced him to the Grand Lodge of Scotland on 30 November.
In December he was elected to the Royal Dublin Society's newly
founded professorship of mineralogy, although his knowledge of
English was not then sufficient for lecturing purposes. The following year he visited Denmark and received the order of the Danne-
brog from Frederick VI; henceforth he was known in Dublin as
Sir Charles Lewis Giesecke, although he does not appear to have
been knighted by George III. He may, however, have been

knighted by the Lord-Lieutenant of Ireland.[1] In 1816 he was
elected a member of the Royal Irish Academy; in 1817 his portrait
was painted by Raeburn and presented by Sir George Mackenzie
to the Royal Dublin Society.

Giesecke went to Copenhagen again in 1818 and thence to
Vienna, where he spent the winter, lecturing before the court on
his discoveries in Greenland, and depositing in the Imperial
Museum a fine collection of objects from that country. He also
took with him a second album, the entries in which are sometimes
illuminating. In the early months of 1819 we find the signatures
of men of science: Joseph von Hammer-Purgstall the orientalist,
Chladni the acoustician, Franz von Jacquin the botanist, whose
son was Mozart's dearest friend. It must have been in May 1819
that the meeting with Cornet and Ignaz von Seyfried took place;
during May the album was signed by various people in musical
circles. We find the Streicher family, headed by Andreas the
pianoforte-maker and his wife Nannette, *née* Stein of Augsburg.
She was a devoted friend of Beethoven. On 20 May we find the
name of Giesecke's cousin Friedrich Metzler; he must have left
Vienna on 24 May, judging by an entry made at Purkersdorf,
a village seven and a half miles west of Vienna, with the signature
of Joseph von Seyfried, brother of Ignaz, who was perhaps
travelling with him to Munich, or setting him part of the way.
He was at Munich in June, and in September at Augsburg, where
he was received with great ceremony; the album gives pictures of
the illuminations and Masonic devices. There is also a very
mysterious inscription—not Masonic, since the writer was a lady
—signed 'Ihre Freundin A. R. E.', with a sort of pictorial rebus.
The tone of the inscription is devoted, but respectful rather than
affectionate. But there is also a little green slip in the book with
the words 'auf der Reise macht man verdammte Streiche' in the
same lady's handwriting, and she has added the words 'in meiner
Gegenwart' to a much earlier inscription of Hamburg, 1802, which
says 'Geniesse das Leben!'

[1] In 1822 J. W. Croker, out of pure malignant desire to injure Lady Morgan,
obtained an opinion from the Attorney-General and the Solicitor-General that,
since the Union, the Lord-Lieutenant of Ireland had not possessed the right of
conferring knighthoods, and that accordingly the titles of thirteen Irish knights
were null and void. The case dragged on for eighteen months, until the Privy
Council ruled that the charge was baseless and the knighthoods perfectly valid.
Was Giesecke one of the thirteen?

For this and for the reference to *Harry Lorrequer* which follows, I am indebted
to Mr. Lionel Stevenson's book, *The Wild Irish Girl. The Life of Sydney Owenson,
Lady Morgan*, London, 1936.

After his return to Dublin he seems to have settled down to regular scientific work. He continued to lecture, and travelled over the greater part of Ireland in search of minerals. He seems to have been regarded with great affection in Dublin. A testimonial recommending him for the professorship in 1813 says that 'his manners are peculiarly prepossessing and gentlemanlike'—a rather unusual compliment in these islands to a foreigner who could hardly speak English and had just come back from seven years' solitude in Greenland. But he had an extraordinary adaptability to circumstances; he writes in 1807 to a friend in Copenhagen:

'I have now lived through a whole winter on this great stony frozen scene. You know I make myself at home at once everywhere, and act a play one day or go to sea the next with the same gusto! And so I can never say, "That was not what I expected!"'

He was evidently a man with a genius for friendship; this is shown by the albums, and by the fact that he must have taken them (as well as his Masonic certificate) to Greenland with him, since all his other books were destroyed in the bombardment of Copenhagen in 1807. He remained a bachelor to the end of his days. The Irish novelist Charles Lever paints an odd portrait of him in *Harry Lorrequer* (1837):

'Poor old Sir Charles, one of the most modest and retiring men in existence, was standing the other night among the mob, in one of the drawing-rooms [at Lady Morgan's], while a waltzing-party was figuring away . . . when my Lady came tripping up, and the following short dialogue ensued within my earshot:
'"Ah, mon cher Sir Charles, ravie de vous voir. But why are you not dancing?"
'"Ah, mi ladi, je ne puis pas, c'est à dire, ich kann es nicht; I am too old, ich bin——"
'"Oh, you horrid man, I understand you perfectly. You hate ladies, that is the real reason. You do—you know you do."
'"Ah, mi ladi, gnädige Frau; glauben Sie mir; I do loave the ladies, I do adore de sex. Do you know, mi ladi, when I was in Greenland I did keep four womans."
'"Oh, shocking, horrid, vile Sir Charles, how could you tell *me* such a story? I shall die of it."
'"Ah, mine Gott, mi ladi; Sie irren sich, vous vous trompez. You are quite in mistake; it was only to *row my boat*."'

'I leave you to guess how my lady's taste for the broadside of the story, and poor Sir Charles's vindication of himself, amused all who heard it.'

On 5 March 1833, though in failing health (he was not quite seventy-two), he went out to dine with a friend in Dublin; after dinner, as they were sitting over their wine, he fell back in his chair and died.

It has been necessary to trace the course of Giesecke's strange career in detail, because the case for his authorship, or part-authorship, of *Die Zauberflöte* rests almost entirely on the statement which he made to Cornet. Neukomm's confirmation of it to Otto Jahn is to be respected, as Neukomm (1778–1858) had known Giesecke in Vienna, although he did not go to Vienna until 1798. Cornet says expressly that he and his friends had no reason for doubting Giesecke's word, and Professor Steenstrup remarks that the reader of the diary in Greenland always has a sure conviction that he can rely absolutely on every one of his statements.

It will naturally be asked why Giesecke did not claim the authorship of the libretto while he was living in Vienna. Mr. Bradley, basing his statement on Koch, as I have already noted, says that he did; the Preface to *Der Spiegel von Arcadien* (1794, words by Schikaneder) said that a theatrical journalist had been impertinent enough to claim co-authorship in *Die Zauberflöte*. We may note that Giesecke's remark to Cornet was made *à propos* of this very opera. It is possible that there were Masonic reasons, so to speak, for Giesecke's silence. If Schikaneder was continuing to make large profits from this 'Masonic' opera long after Freemasonry was definitely forbidden in Vienna, Giesecke could have had no fears for himself either before 1794 or after; but it was no doubt thought advisable by Schikaneder and others too that the opera should contain no word that could offend the police, whatever its hidden meanings might be for the initiated. But Freemasonry insists, like the Christian Church, that its members should give up all feelings of animosity against others before partaking of its most intimate rites, and it is conceivable that some motive of this kind closed Giesecke's mouth. That Giesecke in the later years of his life was very reticent about his connexion with the stage is easily explained by the general state of British public opinion on the theatre in those days. To have been an actor or even a dramatic author could hardly be considered a favourable qualification for a man of science and a university professor.

Evidence based on literary style and evidence of actual plagiary are both of them valueless in a case of this kind; plagiary was common practice in those days as regards opera librettos in any language, and few of them, apart from those of Goldoni and Da Ponte, show any qualities that can be dignified by the name of style. Nettl[1] draws attention to a much older 'Egyptian' opera, *Osiride*, Italian words by Mazzolà, music by J. G. Naumann (1741–1801), composed for a princely wedding at Dresden in 1781. Naumann was an enthusiastic Freemason, and the opera shows certain resemblances to the outline of *Die Zauberflöte*. Nettl suggests that, as Da Ponte was in Dresden at that time helping Mazzolà with his literary work, he may have been the first to give Mozart the idea of a Masonic opera.

Cornet, after apologizing for his digression on the subject of Giesecke and his reappearance at Vienna, goes on to say, with an insight that was probably in advance of his time: '*Die Zauberflöte* is the central starting-point of German opera, and it will have to be taken into account centuries hence, if anyone wishes to study the fundamental principles of the German operatic style; it is therefore not without interest to know who was the real author of the libretto, which was afterwards altered by various arrangers, to the detriment of its original German simplicity.' The literary style of the libretto certainly does not reflect much credit on its author, whoever he was; but it would be unreasonable to expect him to have aimed at anything different from the current style of fairy opera at that time fashionable. It was no doubt begun simply as a piece of hack work; the remarkable thing about it is the creation of the whole personality of Sarastro, who is not merely the central figure of the whole drama, but one of the most striking and individual personalities of all operatic history. Sarastro, as has been said, is supposed to be a portrait of Ignaz von Born; and even though Schikaneder, the clever comedian and astute manager, may have felt a sincere admiration for him, he is hardly likely to have been so well able to appreciate his inmost character and realize it in the person of the high priest of Isis as Giesecke, the young man fresh from the enthusiasms of university life and himself an ardent devotee of those same scientific studies which

---

[1] Paul Nettl, *Mozart und die königliche Kunst*, Berlin, 1932.

had given Born his claim to eminence and were eventually destined
to bear similar fruit in his own case.

Mozart, as we have seen, was not a practised hand at writing
the kind of opera that Schikaneder wanted. 'If we make a *fiasco*',
he said, 'I cannot help it, for I never wrote a magic opera in my
life.' We may therefore well imagine that his first step, as indeed
always in his operatic compositions, was to cast about for a model;
and the obvious model to take was Wranitzky's *Oberon*. The most
conspicuous feature of that would naturally have been the part
of Oberon himself, sung by his own sister-in-law, Madame Hofer;
Wranitzky had evidently composed it to suit her peculiar abilities.
She was a soprano of exceptional compass and agility; in the first
act she had an aria in B flat, common time, and marked *allegro
maestoso*, in which she went up to the high D. Mozart gave her
an aria in the same key, time and *tempo*, but took her up to the
F above. Titania and her two-part chorus of nymphs gave him
the idea how to treat the three Ladies; Huon and Scherasmin,
hero and comic servant, suggested the style of Tamino and Papageno. Scherasmin was Schikaneder's own part, well stocked with
tunes of a popular cast; and if the story is true that Schikaneder
made Mozart write and re-write the songs of Papageno until he
was satisfied with them, and even suggested the tunes himself,
we may well suppose that he held up Wranitzky's trivial jingles as
an example of what true German melody ought to be. Even in
the more solemn parts there was something to be learned from
Wranitzky; the chorus at the end of Act I begins with a *Larghetto*
in E flat (3/4 time) that gives a foretaste of Pamina's ensemble
with the Genii, as well as of the quartet sung by Pamina, Tamino,
and the Men in Armour, and it is followed by a brisk movement,
*allegro assai* in C major (common time) that corresponds to the
chorus at the end of Mozart's Act I. In all these cases the corresponding movements of Mozart's opera are in the same keys. Yet
one more movement was suggested by *Oberon*, and that a most
important one, the March of the Priests at the beginning of Act II,
though this was not composed until after Mozart's return from
Prague. The story goes that Mozart was accused of stealing it
from Gluck's *Alceste*; but the resemblance between Mozart's
march and Gluck's is of the faintest, whereas Wranitzky's is the
most open and shameless imitation. (See Ex. 32, p. 244).

At the first rise of the curtain we notice Mozart's genius.
Tamino rushes on, pursued by a huge serpent. There must be time

perhaps to let a few slaves hurry across in flight, certainly time
for us to get a good view of Tamino and realize that he has no
arrows left, time too to take due note of the serpent, which
Schikaneder has no doubt had made at great expense, with the
latest ingenious methods of rolling its eyes and breathing flame
from its nostrils, for Schikaneder was not the kind of manager to
let any effect be suggested imaginatively rather than concretely
materialized. Mozart therefore gives us an introduction of
seventeen bars for orchestra alone. There is no parallel to this in
any of his previous operas; the storm in *Idomeneo* is a small affair

Ex. 32.

compared with this intense and vivid piece of musical description,
But we feel that he grasps the situation firmly at once; he sees all
its possibilities, he knows exactly what effect he wants to get and
makes straight for it, with perfect success, owing to his absolute
mastery of the orchestra, of poignant expression—giving us the
accent of terror in the very first phrase—and of the symphonic
style, which enables him to take a small rhythmic figure and work
it up in a gradual *crescendo* to the utmost agony of despair. With
Mozart the opera is going on the whole time; if the singers are
resting, the orchestra is acting, the dramatic imagination is never
relaxed for an instant until the movement comes, often reluct-
antly, to an end. This was new to his audiences. Gluck would
have done it, if he could, but his technique of composition was not
sufficiently accomplished.

Mozart, as invariably, is inclined to let his musical ideas run
away with him at the beginning of an opera. The first trio of the
three Ladies is disproportionately long, though few listeners
would wish it to be shortened. There exists the manuscript of a
cadenza for the Ladies which Mozart cut out because his ladies

could not sing it; it might well be restored. It is interesting to compare *Die Zauberflöte* with the earlier operas as regards the introductions to the musical numbers. In *Don Giovanni*, as we saw, they are cut down to almost nothing, except for the serenade, and the same is the case in *Così fan Tutte*, except for those numbers which open a new scene. The pace of *Così fan Tutte* is much more leisurely than that of *Don Giovanni*; the one is a drama of action, the other mainly a drama of conversation, and at the beginning of a scene we need a little time to look at the characters before they begin to talk. It is obvious that Schikaneder would have insisted on introductions to the songs of Papageno; he certainly wanted to be looked at, especially on his first entrance, and no doubt he had plenty of comic 'business' with which to fill up the long introduction. In his other songs the introduction is needed to show off the bells, and we can see that Mozart was obviously as much delighted with this toy as Handel was with his 'Tubal-Cain' that he employed in *Saul*. He tells us himself in a letter to his wife how he once went behind the scenes and played the instrument himself, putting in a *cadenza* which took Schikaneder completely by surprise.

Action and talk are pretty evenly balanced in *Die Zauberflöte*. Most interesting in this respect are the various ensembles, from both the dramatic and the musical point of view. As far back as *Idomeneo* Mozart had seen the obvious advantage of contrasting conversational or contrapuntal passages with episodes of block harmony. The quartet in *Idomeneo* is an expression of feelings only; no action takes place in it. The introductory scene of *Die Zauberflöte*, like that of *Don Giovanni*, contains a good deal of action, and the quintet which follows the vision of the Queen has still more. The trio of the Ladies is much prolonged by the conventional repetitions that form the *coda*; an expert producer can utilize this for amusing stage effects, but Mozart was certainly wiser to be more concise in the quintet. The block harmony passages of the quintet have not only a musical value; they are the expression of moral sentiments which it is fundamentally important to impress clearly on the audience:

> 'If lying lips could all be fetter'd
> And made secure with lock and key,
> Then falsehood's hateful might were shattered.
> And man with man at peace might be.'

The Queen obviously needs an impressive introduction to accompany her mysterious entrance in Act I, where she descends from the skies; when she comes up suddenly from below in Act II she starts off singing at once—she is in fact in a frantic hurry and has no time to lose. The introduction (for wind instruments) to the trio of the Genii which opens the second finale may be compared with the serenade for wind instruments in the second act of *Così fan Tutte*; no action is needed, and we are happy to contemplate a tableau to the sound of exquisitely beautiful music.

Another point that must be considered is the relation of music and words. Classical operas in general often annoy the modern listener by the interminable repetition of words. The Italians, it may be thought, set a bad example, and Handel is usually considered to be the worst of sinners in this respect. He may be guilty of 'vain repetitions' in his English oratorios, but when he repeats words in his Italian operas it is generally done on a systematic principle common to all the Italian opera composers of Metastasio's time and obviously sanctioned by Metastasio himself. The stanza divides into two sentences, which form the first and second subjects of the binary form; when the music returns from the dominant to the tonic in the second half of the aria these are obviously and necessarily repeated. The annoying repetitions of the later classical composers are generally to be found in the coda, especially if there is a series of codas. The first trio of the Ladies is an obvious example; but in the rest of the opera there is very little repetition to make a coda, except in songs of a very simple structural form, like those of Papageno and Sarastro. When Handel or Mozart writes a grand Italian aria in the tragic manner, as in *Idomeneo*, there is no need for an extended coda; the aria has its own properly balanced shape. But trivial tunes of a 'folksong' type are too slight to make much effect on the stage by themselves; so they have to be helped out by some sort of extension or reiteration. From early times they were given what the French called a *petite reprise*, the repetition of the last two or four bars. We see the procedure more elaborated by Cherubini and his French contemporaries, by whom Beethoven was strongly influenced. In pure instrumental music it has more justification, and Beethoven's treatment of the instrumental coda was a new contribution to music; but that is quite outside the type of vocal coda that we are discussing. We see it used in desperation by Rossini, Weber, and the early Verdi—not one coda, but sometimes (especially in

Verdi) a whole string of codas to whip up the audience into the
sort of excitement that will 'bring down the house'. Mozart
never 'brought down the house', except perhaps at the very end
of an act; it was the complaint of his Italian audiences that his
musical numbers ended so unobtrusively that they never knew
when to applaud. In *Die Zauberflöte* the only characters who are
provided with an instrumental *claque* are, as one might expect,
the Queen of Night and the actor-manager. But even in their
cases there is hardly any verbal repetition; that is more noticeable
in the ensembles of the Ladies and in that of Pamina and the
Genii. It is really the instrumental treatment of a vocal ensemble.
Mozart tends to write for his vocal ensemble as if it was a symphony orchestra of his own time, Verdi (in the early operas)
regularly treats his like a brass band. The weakness of Weber is
that whenever he wants to work up an excitement at the end of an
aria he makes the orchestra dominate the situation and eclipse the
singer completely; Mozart never does this—his voices always
reign supreme. That is one of the reasons why his operas are
still acknowledged masterpieces in spite of their antiquated
technique.

Another aspect of music and words is the relation of the musical
numbers to the dialogue. The standard conception of German
opera or *Singspiel* was a spoken play with musical numbers, like
the French *opéra comique*. The dialogue told the story, the songs
expressed the emotions; accepting the Italian system of *recitativo
secco*, that is the principle of Metastasian *opera seria* too. The
whole subsequent history of opera has been the history of the
attempt to make an opera a continuous unbroken piece of music
(as in Wagner) and to solve the very difficult problem of conveying
the necessary 'business information' without breaking the musical
continuity. This problem has been very adroitly solved by Puccini,
whose technical ingenuity must command our admiration,
however detestable we may find his subjects and the music with
which he dressed (or undressed?) them. *Die Zauberflöte* inevitably
has a good deal of dialogue in the first scenes, because so much has
to be explained. But the first temple scene is all continuous music,
and the second act has much less dialogue, apart from the Papageno episodes, in which Schikaneder obviously wanted a free
hand, and the priestly formalities which needed spoken dialogue
to make them clear. There remains only the scene in the garden
for Pamina, Monostatos, the Queen and Sarastro, which Mozart

may well have been content to leave as it stood, since it is theatrically the most effective scene in the opera.

The entrance of the Genii in the temple scene of Act I presents us with a musical style that is new to Mozart and new to opera in general; it is in fact what we can only call the *Zauberflöte* style, a style easy to recognize, but difficult to describe in words. Some writers on Mozart have called it his 'Masonic' style; as a non-Mason, I have no authority to make use of such an epithet. But what may come as an unexpected shock to the reader is that this is almost the first occasion in his life when Mozart has had to set to music solemn and serious words in his native language. His sacred music (apart from the German oratorio which he composed at the age of ten) is all in Latin, his serious dramatic music in Italian; *Die Entführung* and *Zaide* contain a few sentences that one can call serious, but no more; among the songs, *Abendempfindung* is the only one which touches deeper emotions. The only works which anticipate the *Zauberflöte* style are the choruses in *König Thamos*, also Egyptian and possibly with a Masonic background, the cantata *Dir, Seele des Weltalls* (1783—Masonic, but before Mozart's own entrance into Freemasonry), and the Lodge music of 1785. The atmosphere of all these works is the same, because the literary background is in all these cases Egyptian and Masonic; there are no other examples of serious music to German words among Mozart's works.

The only models that Mozart can have had before him were the oratorios of Handel performed in German under the direction of Baron von Swieten, and such works of J. S. Bach as he was able to study during his visit to Leipzig in 1789. The remembrance of Bach is apparent in the duet of the Men in Armour; the melody which they sing is a Protestant chorale—*Ach Gott von Himmel sieh darein*. It is natural to wonder why Mozart should have chosen a Protestant chorale for this scene. A German critic writing from the Catholic point of view has suggested that he did so because to have used a Catholic melody might have offended a Viennese audience. It seems more natural to imagine that the solemnity of the scene, and especially its preoccupation with the idea of death, naturally recalled Bach to Mozart's imagination, and the thought of Bach would naturally suggest a Lutheran chorale; moreover, the metrical chorale could easily be adapted to the metrical words.[1] It is difficult to think of any Catholic

---

[1] Busoni, the most devoted student of Bach in some aspects, was positively

melody that could possibly have been utilized in such a situation, except perhaps the *Dies Irae*, and as we shall see later, that, for Mozart, and especially at this moment, would have had completely opposite metaphysical implications. But there is more of Bach in the opera; we may say that the whole dialogue between the Orator and Tamino is like a dialogue between Bach and Weber. Tamino is youthful and chivalrous, or hot-headed and unreflecting, according as we regard him from the Queen's point of view or Sarastro's; the Orator has learned in years of experience, not only wisdom, but a sympathy with Tamino himself far deeper than Tamino can realize.

It is at the moment when Pamina throws herself at Sarastro's feet with the words, '*Herr, ich bin zwar Verbrecherin*', that Mozart's new treatment of dramatic speech is seen at its best. We feel here, as we feel so often in listening to Purcell or Scarlatti, that the absolutely natural musical expression of words has produced of itself a melody that is beautiful and individual. Throughout that scene Pamina and Sarastro are vivid and real without ever breaking the continuous flow of the music; indeed the whole opera bears witness to the fact that Mozart is most dramatic when he is most essentially musical. The trio for Pamina, Tamino, and Sarastro in Act II is perhaps the most deeply moving moment in the opera, and a complete illustration of this point. Dramatically, the supreme moment of the opera is, of course, the march through the elements, and the whole construction of this scene is masterly. It begins with the three Masonic knocks; then comes the duet of the Men in Armour, reading the mysterious inscription to the elaborate contrapuntal accompaniment. The *fugato* stops abruptly, and we feel at once that we have come through an experience of strain and effort into a new world. The *terzetto* of Tamino and the Men in Armour is difficult to make convincing on the stage; it needs an intense expression of rapture on the part of Tamino to dominate the rather conventional accompaniment of the other two voices. Pamina enters, and for the first time in the opera she takes the leadership. Hitherto she has been almost a child, terrified by Monostatos and her mother, dominated, even if with all tenderness, by Sarastro; her first experiences of trial have driven her to utter despair. She now reappears, not merely serene and self-possessed, but with complete knowledge of what

repelled by Bach's German 'pre-occupation with death' in some of the Church Cantatas.

has to be done. She knows all about the magic flute and the function of it; she herself is now Tamino's guide. The gradual unfold-
ing of Pamina's personality is a most extraordinary conception;
we cannot ascribe it to Mozart alone, and it is difficult to think of
Schikaneder as so sensitive a psychologist. The obvious parallel
is the mental development of Iphis in Handel's *Jephtha*.[1] The
music in which she tells Tamino about the origin of the magic
flute is most remarkable; it almost sounds like Wagner, and the
hint of Nordic saga at the back of it naturally suggests
*The Ring*. But when the gates of terror are opened and we are
confronted with the fire and the water there is no anticipation of
Wagner at all. Wagner obviously would have provided descriptive
music in the orchestra, a *Feuerzauber* or a *Rheintiefe*; Mozart
makes no attempt to be pictorial—that was Schikaneder's
department. For Mozart the first idea is the Flute itself. We have
heard it only once before, in Act I; we ought, I think, to have
heard it a second time, after it is restored to Tamino by the Genii
in Act II. Tamino does in fact play it, according to the stage
directions, and what happens in performance is that Tamino
appears to be practising his former *obbligato* and to be rather
annoyed at Pamina's interruption of his studies. There is no
special music written for the flute in this scene; but in view of the
perpetual insistence on the mystic number three throughout the
opera, we may wonder whether there should not have been three
definite presentations of the flute, as there are of the bells. The
march has something of the solemnity of the Dead March in *Saul*.
The solitary melody of the flute stands out strangely above the
mysterious chords of soft trombones and the pulsation of the
drums; the oddity of the orchestral combination[2] forces upon the
listener a tense feeling of self-concentration, and gives us exactly
the sensation of going through some difficult and dangerous
experience. One cannot describe it in words; one can only suggest
musical commentaries on it—the march in *Saul*, the flute solo in
the Elysian Fields of Gluck's *Orpheus*, and, for its deepest significance, the last movement of Beethoven's C minor symphony.
It is this extraordinary simplicity that gives the characteristic
colour to all the solemn scenes of this second act. Yet this
simplicity is deceptive; it is only after we have been through the

[1] See R. A. Streatfeild, *Handel*, London, 1909.

[2] It was very skilfully and effectively imitated by Humperdinck in his incidental music to *The Tempest*.

complexities of the earlier works, perhaps only after we have grasped the complexities of Beethoven, that we can understand its innermost significance. The story of the opera is itself a lesson to those who would understand its music; we must prepare ourselves by silence and meditation, we must pass through the fire and water, before we can enter the temple of wisdom.

## 15

## DIE ZAUBERFLÖTE—IV

MOZART during the last year of his life seems to have become gradually more and more obsessed with the consciousness of his approaching end. It is important to realize the psychological conditions of these tragic months: the anxiety which his wife's health caused him, the mysterious commission of the Requiem, his own conviction that he had been poisoned. The idea of death is the ever-recurring motive of the second act of *Die Zauberflöte*: Sarastro's first air, the dialogue between Tamino and the Orator, the duet for the Priests, Sarastro's second air—all allude to it, and the climax is reached in the scene of the Men in Armour. It was a time when Mozart was thrown more than ever into the society of his Masonic friends, and the death of Ignaz von Born on 24 July must have deeply affected all those who were members of his circle. Indeed, one might almost be tempted to think that it was Born's death which induced Mozart and Schikaneder to introduce the Masonic element into their opera, if we did not know from a letter of Mozart to his wife that the change had already been decided on at the beginning of June, since he quotes to her the line, 'Tod und Verzweiflung war sein Lohn'.

There was, however, another and an opposing force at work on Mozart's mind—the composition of the Requiem. He had written no Church music at all since he left Salzburg and its Archbishop for good, except the unfinished Mass in C minor, begun in 1782, and the little motet, *Ave verum corpus*, composed at Baden on 17 June 1791 for his friend the choirmaster Stoll, who sometimes performed his early Salzburg Masses. Mozart always prided himself on his organ-playing and on his knowledge of the ecclesiastical style; but we may suspect that it was more a just pride in his mastery of counterpoint and fugue than a sense of vocation to the music of the Church. It is therefore interesting to compare the Requiem with *Die Zauberflöte*, the Catholic with the Masonic idea of death, and see what light they throw upon each other.

The difference is at once apparent; the words of the Requiem insist constantly upon just that fear of death which Freemasonry had taught Mozart to overcome. To compare the two works in detail would require a profusion of musical examples and an elaboration of technical analysis for which there is no space here. I can only invite the reader to study the two compositions together; their similarity of style will strike him immediately. One very conspicuous point of resemblance is the employment in both of trombones and basset-horns, neither of which instruments were in common orchestral use at that date. Here they are not merely normal constituents of the orchestra; they stand out prominently, so that both Requiem and opera are dominated by the sound of them. There is, of course, nothing strange about the employment of trombones in the Requiem; Florian Gassmann's Requiem, which must undoubtedly have served Mozart as a model, makes almost continuous use of them in certain movements.[1] It is therefore all the more remarkable that we should find them employed in a similar way in *Die Zauberflöte*. Their dramatic value has already been discussed in the chapters on *Idomeneo* and *Don Giovanni*; but in those operas their effect is scenic rather than orchestral, and they appear only for exceptional moments. In *Die Zauberflöte*, apart from the occasions when the priests blow their trumpets on the stage, they form the main background of the opera, and Mozart wishes by this means to make us understand that we are not to look upon mystical experience as a thing revealed to us by miraculous agencies, on occasions so rare as to be recorded only in legend, but as an essential part of our own lives, if we are willing to open the eyes of our souls to the contemplation of it. That 'unknown region' of which only a glimpse is shown us in *Idomeneo* and *Don Giovanni* here becomes the actual scene of the whole opera. Just as it requires a conscious volition to transfer our minds from the world of every day to the world of musical drama in which we feel that music is our real and normal mode of expression and speech a foreign language, so, if we have accomplished this first step, the new sound of Mozart's orchestra in *Die Zauberflöte* transfers us from the world of heroes to yet another world where ordinary human passions, even in their musical form, hold sway only over those upon whom the new light has not yet arisen. And if we compare the opera with the Requiem, we shall find not merely a common background but a common back-

---

[1] See two papers by me on 'The Predecessors of Mozart's Requiem' in the *Monthly Musical Record*, June and July 1907.

ground seen from two different points of view, like one of those
silks which show a bright pattern against a dark fabric, or a dark
pattern against a bright fabric, according to the angle at which the
light strikes them. In the *Tuba mirum* we shall recognize certain
phrases of Tamino and Pamina while still undergoing the agony
of their ordeals; in the *Dies Irae* and *Confutatis* we see even more
clearly the baffled rage of Monostatos and the Queen of Night.

The Requiem, despite its beauty, can hardly be contemplated
without pain; it is the product of a morbid and diseased imagination, fascinating indeed, like some of Schumann's late works
(and notably Schumann's Requiem), from a pathological standpoint, but only distressing to those who have yielded to the
natural temptation to regard the personality of Mozart with
affectionate interest.[1] It is to *Die Zauberflöte* that we must turn
to know Mozart's religious feelings at their sanest and most
exalted degree. That quality which we can only call 'the sublime'
is peculiar almost exclusively to Handel and Haydn; it is
definitely not a characteristic of Mozart, but if he ever approached
the vision of it, it was in this opera, and nowhere else. Jahn
observes of the choruses in *König Thamos*:

'There is no question that their whole conception is grander,
freer and more imposing than that of any of his Masses belonging
to that period; but this is because he felt himself unfettered by
conventional restrictions. A solemn act of worship was represented on the stage, the expression of reverence to the Supreme
Being was heightened in effect by the Egyptian surroundings,
and Mozart's endeavour was to render the consequent emotions
with all possible truth and force.'

There are clear reminiscences of these choruses in *Die Zauberflöte*, notably on the entrance of Sarastro. It is just this sense of
freedom and grandeur that is often wanting in Mozart's church
music; we see even in the Requiem that he is at times not expressing primary and elemental religious emotions, but seeking rather

---

[1] We may note in this connexion that when Mozart was dying his sister-in-law
went at his wife's request to the priests of the Peterskirche and begged that one
might be sent to Mozart 'as if by chance'; they refused for a long time, and it was
with difficulty that she persuaded 'these clerical barbarians' to grant her request
(Jahn). This looks as if Mozart was unwilling to receive sacerdotal ministrations,
and the priests equally unwilling to visit him, owing to his unorthodox views.
Jahn's very detailed account makes no mention of a priest ever arriving at the
house.

to reproduce the correct and conventional ecclesiastical atmosphere.[1]

Schikaneder was one of those rare managers who knew the value of perseverance. *Die Zauberflöte* was not at first so successful as he had expected, but he had the courage to go on performing it until it became thoroughly popular. He was also astute enough to exaggerate its popularity by unscrupulous publicity; he advertised the eighty-third night (29 November 1792) as the hundredth, and the hundred-and-thirty-fifth (22 October 1795) as the two hundredth performance, with a three-hundredth on 1 January 1798. Actually there were 223 performances at Schikaneder's theatre by May 1801. Accusations have been made against him that he kept all the profits for himself and handed over nothing to Mozart or even to his widow and children; whether this is true or not seems still uncertain. The opera was given at Prague on 25 October 1792; in 1794 it was performed there both in Italian and in Czech. It made its way over Germany in the course of 1793, though it did not reach Berlin till May 1794.[2] Goethe had a great admiration for it, and it was performed at Weimar in 1794, but with the words re-written by his brother-in-law, C. A. Vulpius. German critics are in general agreement that this version was no improvement on the original, and it never held the stage. Goethe's appreciation of the opera is a high tribute to its inner significance. In speaking to Eckermann of his own second part of *Faust*, he remarked: 'I am content if the general public enjoys what it sees; at the same time the higher meaning will not escape the initiated, just as is the case with *Die Zauberflöte* and other things.' His most remarkable homage to its merits is the fact that he began to write a sequel to it, which was printed as a fragment in 1802.[3]

He appears (from a letter to Schiller) to have conceived this idea in 1795, and in January 1798 he wrote to Wranitzky suggesting that the Imperial Opera should take it up. His reason for selecting Wranitzky was probably twofold. Wranitzky had not only made a success with *Oberon*, which was often given at Weimar, but he was also a Freemason. Wranitzky, however, replied that

---

[1] See my introduction to the vocal score of Mozart's Requiem published by the Oxford University Press.

[2] See A. Loewenberg, *Annals of Opera*. Most of the dates given in the first edition of my own book are wrong.

[3] An English translation by Mr. Eric Blom was printed in *Music and Letters*.

the management of the Imperial Opera would not entertain the
project, since the original *Zauberflöte* was being performed by a
private manager at a suburban theatre. Most probably the real
reason behind this excuse was that the original opera was Masonic,
and that, although a supposedly Masonic opera might be performed at a suburban theatre, it could not be given the official
sanction of the Imperial Opera House. Mozart's opera, in fact,
was not performed there until February 1801. Goethe let the
matter drop, and only took it up again in 1798 at the suggestion
of Iffland, who wished to bring out the work at Berlin. Schiller
warned him that the success of the opera would depend entirely
on the choice of the composer. Wranitzky had at any rate had
the modesty to suggest that the contrast between Goethe's play
and Schikaneder's would be as unfortunate as that between
Mozart's music and his own. Zelter seems to have had some idea
of setting Goethe's play, but cannot have taken it very seriously,
for when Goethe asked him in 1803 'how the music to the second
part of *Die Zauberflöte* was going', he entirely misunderstood the
question and replied with a long account of the Berlin performances of quite another 'second part of *Die Zauberflöte*'—namely
Schikaneder's own sequel, *Das Labyrinth*, set to music by Peter
von Winter, and produced at Schikaneder's own theatre in 1798.
Whether Goethe was directly influenced by the libretto of this
opera has been much disputed by German critics, and it seems
equally uncertain whether it was definitely Masonic or not. The
rhythm of the 'three chords' which is so conspicuous in Mozart's
work certainly reappears in *Das Labyrinth*, but in a rather different form and with quite different associations. According to
Dr. Paul Nettl, not only was Freemasonry at that time in bad
odour, but Schikaneder himself had been expelled *cum infamia*
from his lodge, and Winter was never a Freemason at all.

Goethe's sequel remained a fragment and was never set to
music by anyone. Yet it has a strange interest for us of to-day,
for it contains the germs, not only of the Second Part of *Faust*,
but even of Wagner's *Ring*. A child is born to Tamino and Pamina
but is mysteriously imprisoned by the spells of the Queen, until
finally, like Euphorion, the son of Faust and Helen, he bursts his
earthly fetters and disappears into the viewless heights. We find
*The Ring* foreshadowed in the scene where the Queen of Night
sits brooding, solitary and inactive, like Erda, while Sarastro, like
Wotan, leaves the community of the priests and goes forth as an

unknown 'wanderer' over the face of the earth. We have already noted the curiously Wagnerian touch in Mozart's music at the moment when Pamina tells Tamino how her father made the magic flute; and Nohl tells us that Liszt once said that *The Ring* would eventually become the 'the *Zauberflöte* of our time'.[1]

It could only be Mozart of whom Goethe was thinking when he said to Eckermann in 1827 that his ideal composer for the Second Part of *Faust* must be a man who had lived long in Italy, so as to unite a German temperament with an Italian style. Unfortunately, the only composer who seemed to him to fulfil these conditions was—Meyerbeer. To us the ideal composer for the Second Part of *Faust* would undoubtedly have been Beethoven; but Beethoven was probably not Italian enough for Goethe, and there can be little doubt that each would have found the style of the other's 'third period' completely unintelligible.

Beethoven, like Goethe, was profoundly influenced by *Die Zauberflöte*, and his unconscious commentaries on it are often illuminating. How intensely real its characters were to him may be seen in his letters, with their constant reference to Schindler as Papageno and to his sister-in-law as the Queen of Night. His brother Carl died in 1815, leaving him guardian of his son; the widow and Beethoven were bitter enemies, as he would never allow her to see her son if he could help it, believing her to be a woman of thoroughly bad character. On 28 July 1816, he writes to his nephew's schoolmaster:

'With regard to the Queen of Night, things will go on as before, and even if Carl should undergo his operation at your house, seeing that he will be poorly for a time, hence more sensitive and excitable, she must not be allowed to see him; all the less, seeing Carl might easily recall former impressions, a thing we can't allow. . . . Meanwhile, I have not treated her this time like a Sarastro, but answered her like a Sultan.'

She was perpetually making attempts to visit her son, or to correspond with him secretly. Another letter of 1816 mentions 'The Queen of Night, who never ceases to direct the full force of her vindictive disposition against me'.[2]

[1] L. Nohl, *Mosaik*, 1882.

[2] *The Letters of Ludwig van Beethoven*, translated by J. S. Shedlock, London, 1909.

The purely musical influence of *Die Zauberflöte* on Beethoven is to be seen in such early works as *The Mount of Olives* and *Prometheus*, both composed about 1800. The first aria sung by Jesus in the oratorio is unmistakably developed out of Tamino's first entrance, and the Seraph seems obviously modelled on the Queen of Night. The final chorus of the opera may well have suggested the theme in *Prometheus*, which afterwards became famous through its employment for a great set of pianoforte variations and for the last movement of the *Eroica* Symphony.

The influence of Mozart on *Fidelio* is not so obvious as one might expect. We must remember that Beethoven had been thoroughly saturated with French opera (Grétry, Monsigny, Dalayrac, etc.) during the years when he played in the theatre band at Bonn; the repertory has been preserved.[1] By the time he came to compose his own opera in 1805 his style was already matured, and a new influence had come into his life—the music of Cherubini, for which, as is well known, he had an enormous admiration. Further, *Fidelio* is itself based on a French libretto already used by Gaveaux (Paris, 1798). A sketch-book of Beethoven's is in existence in which sketches for *Fidelio* are mixed up with extracts from Cherubini's *Les Deux Journées* and from *Die Zauberflöte* as well. Pizarro, as a singing character, is the creation of Beethoven; in Gaveaux's opera he does not sing at all. Beethoven makes one think he might be the son of the Queen of Night by Monostatos. In the duet between Pizarro and Rocco we are often reminded of Monostatos and Papageno; the most curious reminiscence of Mozart is the resemblance between the duet for Florestan and Leonora (after she has rescued him) and that for Papageno and Papagena. More important is the derivation of the final chorus from those in Mozart's opera, especially the chorus at the end of the first act; here we can see the germ of all Beethoven's characteristically merciless writing for chorus—it foreshadows, not merely *Fidelio*, but the Choral Fantasia, the Choral Symphony, and even the Mass in D. Both composers—Mozart here, Beethoven almost always—seem to conceive the chorus, not as a crowd of actual human beings, but as a host of disembodied voices, ideal and infinite. What the trumpets had been to Purcell and Handel, what the trombones had been to Mozart and Beethoven themselves, this the voice of the chorus was to be, vaster than any instruments, not merely in physical strength, but still

---

[1] J.-G. Prod'homme, *La Jeunesse de Beethoven*, Paris, 1920.

more essentially in the moral grandeur of its utterance—the voice of humanity itself.

We are at the turn of the century. Tamino and Pamino have grown up into real man and woman, Florestan and Leonora—a change such as takes place in Siegfried and Brünnhilde when they leave their mountain summit and descend to earth, except that Mozart's figures seem to be more ideal and Beethoven's more real than those of Wagner. There is a strange sense of connexion between the two operas; we feel that *Die Zauberflöte* stands much closer to *Fidelio* than it does to *Don Giovanni* or *Così fan Tutte*, and that *Fidelio* stands closer to *Die Zauberflöte* than to *Der Freischütz* or *Euryanthe*. It was the Mozart of *Die Zauberflöte* who struck the deathblow to the music of the eighteenth century. A later age thought him the typical exponent of the *rococo* period; his contemporary Naumann knew better when he called him a musical *sans-culotte*. Yet neither he nor even Beethoven can be classed as romantics. Mozart is a child of the *Encyclopédie*, Beethoven of the Revolution; their very greatness lay in the fact that they expressed the humanity of their own time, not the sentimental hankering after the emotions of the past. Tamino and Pamina are in music what Faust and Helen are in poetry, though in the opera it is Tamino who is Italian and classical, Pamina who is German and almost romantic.

It is by working backwards from Florestan and Leonora that we shall arrive at understanding the hero and heroine of *Die Zauberflöte*. Florestan and Leonora are real people, existing in a real place, moving in actual time.[1] Tamino and Pamina are ideal figures, living only in imagination, and passing through the experience of a lifetime in the course of a few bars of music. Tamino, like Euphorion, may be regarded as Mozart himself; it is certainly just as reasonable to say this as to say with many writers that Mozart painted himself as Don Giovanni—reasonable, because Tamino is not only Mozart, but Everyman.

We see him fly in terror from a monster of his dreams, terrified, because for the first time in his life he has felt himself to be alone. The Three Ladies, equal to all ordinary emergencies, take possession of his inexperience. They have no imagination; they live only in the practical daily round of the social world, ruled by the

---

[1] Bouilly, the original author of *Léonore, ou l'Amour conjugal*, which was translated and adapted for Beethoven's libretto, tells us that his story was taken from actual events within his own personal knowledge which took place at Tours during the Reign of Terror.

Queen and content to obey her conventions without question. Tamino is young and romantic; he has not been allowed to think, but only to feel. Any woman is a goddess to him; the mere portrait of Pamina and the story of her captivity are enough to set his heart on fire, and we cannot blame him for being imposed upon by the flashing and mysterious magnificence of the Queen. Moreover, he has learned something even from the Ladies, something of which they themselves have not realized the full potentialities. They have provided him with a slave, Papageno; they have taught him an accomplishment, music, symbolized by the magic flute; they have even awakened him to the dawning consciousness of a new but elusive power within himself which is made visible to us in the figures of the Three Genii. Silence, patience, perseverance—even in the realms of the Queen and her Ladies those words meant wisdom, even though it were only *savoir faire*.

He arrives at the temple. He is a prince, with all those privileges, hereditary and acquired, which his rank confers; and shall anyone dare to say to him, 'Stand back'? But he has forgotten Nature, he has not been allowed to know Reason, and he must wait before he can acquire Wisdom. The priest who meets him on the threshold is not what he expected to see; he had meant to force an entrance and proceed like a brave knight to deeds of chivalry. Yet he finds neither fair lady nor dragon—only a philosopher, who neither admits him nor refuses him admittance. He turns away despondent; his old ideals have suddenly been shattered. But he has begun to think for himself instead of accepting the ideas of the world. Meanwhile, the slave, whom as a prince he very properly despised, has been cleverer than his master. He has found the fair lady, and found her to be just a simple child, ready enough to make friends, and almost as free from artificial ideas as himself. She is guarded by a brute under the name of Authority; but Papageno is a child of nature[1] and the word authority means nothing to him, just as the word 'nature' means nothing to Monostatos. Yet it is not easy to escape from authority when authority has no basis of reason; Papageno and Pamina run away, but are soon caught again. However, even Papageno has learned something from the Ladies, for it is of incongruity that laughter is born. The magic bells have the gift of setting all who hear them laughing, and it is by this means that Papageno and

---

[1] Tiersot very happily calls Papageno *'une sorte de Parsifal comique'*.

Pamina get rid of their tormentors. Tamino, on the other hand, is captured and brought before Sarastro. At the moment, indeed, he has no eyes for anyone but the fair object of his dreams, who hastens in all simplicity to meet him. Here again it is brute authority that intervenes; the philosopher looks on unconcerned. He has foreseen it from the beginning; but the young lovers must undergo a period of preparation if they are to be worthy of each other as full-grown man and woman.

Now begins the ordeal. Music and laughter have been taken away; prince and slave are left to meditate in darkness. Prince and slave they are no more, they have become merely friends, each realizing that he has something to receive from the other and something to give him. The Ladies reappear, seeking to distract them from their new course; but Tamino remains firm, resisting threats and blandishments alike. He knows now that wisdom and independence are better than submission to the Queen's gracious approval, and that love can be a nobler if a more tranquil passion than it had been painted for him outside.

Pamina when we first see her is a child, with a child's simplicity and a child's seriousness. Yet she has learned more under Sarastro's care than she would ever have done from the Queen. She still believes in her mother, until the shock comes which is to make her think for herself, as Tamino has been made to do. It is when the Queen bids her kill Sarastro that she realizes that she must give up her mother altogether if she is to work out her own life. She has, in fact, passed through the same ordeal that Tamino has endured.

The flute is restored to Tamino; he has shown that he will not misuse the gift. The lovers proceed to the second test; it is more severe than the first, for here each suffers in the other's presence, and it is that very presence which causes the suffering. Tamino must not allow even love to distract him from his ideals; Pamina must learn that for him love is only a part of life, while for her it is the whole. Each test brings its reward, first the recovery of the flute, then admission to the presence of the initiated. The man's conviction of his duty deepens; the woman, lacking his intellectual strength, feels that he is lost to her, because he is seeking something that she cannot understand. She gives way to despair, and it is only when she has begun to reason calmly again that she knows that her love is not complete until it has included sacrifice. Not until then can she join her lover, to pass through those ordeals

which under the symbolism of fire and water represent the experiences of a lifetime. It is then that they learn the full power of
the magic flute, dispassionate, equable and gentle:

> 'the Dorian mood
> Of flutes and soft recorders—such as raised
> To height of noblest temper heroes old
> Arming to battle, and instead of rage
> Deliberate valour breathed, firm and unmoved
> With dread of death to flight or foul retreat;
> Nor wanting power to mitigate and swage
> With solemn touches troubled thoughts, and chase
> Anguish and doubt and fear and sorrow and pain
> From mortal or immortal minds. Thus they,
> Breathing united force with fixed thought,
> Moved on in silence to soft pipes that charmed
> Their painful steps o'er the burnt soil.'

It is the wonderful sense of growth and development that makes
*Die Zauberflöte* comparable only to the operas of Wagner. In all
his operas, Mozart is remarkable for his powers of characterization;
but in none of them before this, except to a slight extent in
*Idomeneo*, did he make a single character show a gradual maturing
of personality such as we see in Tamino and Pamina. It was
indeed hardly possible to do so within the limits of conventionl
drama. But *Die Zauberflöte*, although it starts as a conventional
opera, very soon departs from all precedent. Yet its development
is so logical and inevitable that it is only when we look through the
table of contents that we become aware that hero and heroine
have no more than one solo aria apiece! Only when we read
through the libretto carefully do we realize that hero and heroine
have practically no love-scenes. Like Florestan and Leonora,
they have taken love for granted. They are both so essentially
truthful and sincere, so devoid of all self-torture on the one hand
or coquetry on the other, that there is no need to play variations
on the eternal operatic theme. Tamino's ardour sees beyond
passion, and Pamina, even if her intellect cannot grasp his ideals,
is content to follow him. She has well been compared to Miranda,
and Sarastro to Prospero;[1] Tamino is indeed not far removed from

---

[1] This is pointed out by R. A. Streatfeild, *Modern Music and Musicians*,
London, 1906. It is very probable that Giesecke was acquainted with *The Tempest;*
Schikaneder's repertory included several plays of Shakespeare. An opera libretto
on *The Tempest* by F. W. Gotter, *Die Geister-Insel*, was set to music by Reichardt
(Berlin, 1798) and also by Zumsteeg (Stuttgart, 1798).

Ferdinand, and there is a curious similarity between the direct yet reticent understanding of the two pairs of lovers. We might even find something of Ariel in the Genii, and of Caliban in Monostatos, though Caliban is by far the less unpleasant character of the two.[1]

The preceding chapters have been devoted mainly to a study of the seven major dramatic works of Mozart's maturity, and I make no apology for having treated those of his adolescence in very summary fashion; this book has been written for English readers, who may very possibly have the chance of seeing every one of these seven presented on the stage in this country and in our own language. They may even have a chance—but it will be a rare one—of seeing some of the earlier operas, and perhaps too that amusing trifle of Mozart's ripest accomplishment, *The Impresario*. Of these seven, the first, *Idomeneo*, must be considered what I call a museum piece; but I hope that no reader will regard this description as implying any want of respect or admiration. It is obviously not a work for the ordinary practical repertory; a revival of it calls for some special occasion, a festival performance which we shall attend in a spirit of pilgrimage. The director of a national opera house might well ask himself whether the operas of Gluck should or should not be relegated to the same category. If he is a practical man of the theatre, his answer will probably be that the success of *Orpheus* depends on some particular singer, and he might say the same of *Iphigenia in Tauris*. They are traditionally regarded, and especially by all those whose operatic outlook is dominated by tradition, as 'one-woman' operas. There are plenty more of that type, right down to modern times. And it is the 'one-woman' tradition that distorted the conventional outlook on Mozart all through the last century, and is by no means extinct even now. For her sake, the connoisseurs will put up with—and indeed adore—a female Orpheus, while they will condemn the impropriety of a female Idamante. There is no tradition of famous singers in *Idomeneo*, no memory of Pauline Viardot-Garcia or Giulia Ravogli with whom to compare a singer of to-day, and indeed there is no outstanding female part in that work, so that like Gluck's *Armide* it has to be taken purely on its own merits as the work of a composer.

[1] Those who are well acquainted with Mozart's opera may be recommended to read G. Lowes Dickinson's *The Magic Flute, a Fantasia* (London, 1925); it is not a commentary on the opera, nor yet a sequel to it, like Goethe's, though Dickinson was a devoted student of Goethe.

Every opera director must indeed ask himself how far backward in time his audience is prepared to follow him. His own personal taste may lead him to historical revivals, but he cannot enforce that on an unwilling public. The question is of serious importance, for if Gluck belongs to the museum in these days, how long will it be before, not only *Idomeneo*, but the whole of Mozart must follow him thither?

Mozart's next opera, *Die Entführung aus dem Serail*, stands perilously near the museum gate. The votaries of 'one-woman' may do their best to save it, but the plain fact is that despite its many strokes of genius it is, taken as a dramatic whole, a thoroughly unsatisfactory work, and the operatic world, even in Germany, has in practice admitted the truth of this criticism.

We now come to the popular works of Mozart, *Le Nozze di Figaro*, *Don Giovanni*, and *Così fan Tutte*. All three belong to the same operatic category, and one that was new to Mozart's style, apart from his adolescent experiments. They stand close together in date, and their librettos are all by Lorenzo Da Ponte, whose collaboration was again something quite new as a factor in Mozart's development. The popularity of the first two is of very long standing, but it is gratifying to observe that the third has now become assuredly popular, at any rate in England and in English. It is by these three works that Mozart is mainly known in this country; they conventionally represent the normal Mozartian style, the typical Mozart. This means that to the majority of musical people the typical Mozart is the Mozart of comic opera. Some writers have learned that *Don Giovanni* was originally described by both Da Ponte and Mozart as a *dramma giocoso*, and have deduced from this that *dramma giocoso* was an absolutely unique description, peculiar to *Don Giovanni* alone, and therefore implying anything that their romantic fantasy may inspire them to imagine. The historical fact is that *dramma giocoso* is the standard title-page description for all Italian comic operas of Mozart's period and is precisely the same thing as *opera buffa*. *Figaro* and *Così fan Tutte* were given the same designation by both librettist and composer, as well as the innumerable comic operas of Sarti, Anfossi, Cimarosa, and the rest.

*La Clemenza di Tito*, on the other hand, is an old-fashioned *opera seria* which as I have already said was a museum piece when it was written. *Die Zauberflöte* is an entirely different type of opera; it was German, and composed for a much humbler type of audience. It was the first and perhaps the only great masterpiece of music ever created deliberately for 'the masses'. It has certainly become popular with English audiences, but it is less often performed than *Figaro*.

Considering the popularity of Mozart's operas in this country to-day, it is surprising that many of his admirers are quite uncertain as to which were composed to Italian words and which to German. The Victorians generally heard all the operas in Italian; it is only during the present century that large numbers of English people have heard them at Munich and Salzburg, perhaps on other German stages as well. This has no doubt led many to imagine that German was the original language of all of them; those who are not German scholars perhaps hardly realize the fact that the current German translations of the Italian operas are quite as uncouth and absurd as the worst of the various English ones. English is a far more elastic language than German and far more suitable to the rapid rhythms of Italian comedy. The practice of German theatres is no safe guide for the interpretation of Mozart's Italian operas.

For the interpretation of *Die Zauberflöte*, we ought naturally to pay considerable respect to the traditions of the German stage; but we have the authority of many German critics for believing the older 'traditions' to be extremely corrupt, and we have the evidence of our own senses (if we have frequented German theatres) for the vanity and pedantry of modern German producers and conductors whose one aim seems to be to produce the opera in a way that no one has ever seen before, regardless both of tradition and of the original libretto and score.

If we are to understand Mozart rightly in this country, we must insist on seeing all these operas habitually in our own language, because only thus can we distinguish clearly between comedy and tragedy. It is distressing to see one of the comic operas performed in Italian (and probably with various Central European diversities of accent) before an audience which sits in solemn silence and shows not the faintest appreciation of the wit and humour of Da Ponte and Mozart. To such an audience, indeed, it does not matter whether the work is sung in Italian or in a German translation. It is to counteract this misunderstanding—the assumption that Mozart had no operatic style other than that of his comedies— that we ought periodically (and at not too long intervals) to put *Idomeneo* on the stage, in English too—certainly not in the strange and very German modernization made by Richard Strauss—and with all the dignity and spaciousness that can be provided, in order to exhibit to music-lovers in general and to critics in particular a much-needed demonstration of the classical grand tragic manner—of which indeed *Idomeneo* and *La Clemenza di Tito* are the last historical survivors. We need such revivals, to set a standard of style, as we need Michelangelo and Milton in sculpture and poetry. And more than ever now, in these times of turmoil and confusion, do we need the profound and noble sincerity of *Idomeneo* and the serene spirituality of *The Magic Flute*.

# INDEX